T0186282

Management in the
Era of Big Data

Data Analytics Applications

Series Editor
Jay Liebowitz

Big Data in the Arts and Humanities: Theory and Practice
By Giovanni Schiuma and Daniela Carlucci
ISBN: 978-1-4987-6585-5

Data Analytics Applications in Education
By Jan Vanthienen and Kristoff De Witte
ISBN: 978-1-4987-6927-3

Data Analytics Applications in Latin America and Emerging Economies
By Eduardo Rodriguez
ISBN: 978-1-4987-6276-2

Data Analytics for Smart Cities
By Amir Alavi and William G. Buttlar
ISBN: 978-1-138-30877-0

Data-Driven Law: Data Analytics and the New Legal Services
By Edward J. Walters
ISBN: 978-1-4987-6665-4

Intuition, Trust, and Analytics
By Jay Liebowitz, Joanna Paliszkiewicz, and Jerzy Gołuchowski
ISBN: 978-1-138-71912-5

Research Analytics: Boosting University Productivity and Competitiveness
through Scientometrics
By Francisco J. Cantú-Ortiz
ISBN: 978-1-4987-6126-0

Sport Business Analytics: Using Data to Increase Revenue and Improve
Operational Efficiency
By C. Keith Harrison and Scott Bukstein
ISBN: 978-1-4987-8542-6

https://www.crcpress.com/Data-Analytics-Applications/book-series/
CRCDATANAAPP

Management in the Era of Big Data
Issues and Challenges

Edited by
Joanna Paliszkiewicz

CRC Press
Taylor & Francis Group
Boca Raton London New York

CRC Press is an imprint of the
Taylor & Francis Group, an **informa** business
AN AUERBACH BOOK

First edition published 2020
by CRC Press
6000 Broken Sound Parkway NW, Suite 300, Boca Raton, FL 33487-2742

and by CRC Press
2 Park Square, Milton Park, Abingdon, Oxon, OX14 4RN

© 2021 Taylor & Francis Group, LLC

CRC Press is an imprint of Taylor & Francis Group, LLC

ISBN: 978-0-367-89557-0 (hbk)
ISBN: 978-0-367-52276-6 (pbk)
ISBN: 978-1-003-05729-1 (ebk)

Typeset in Garamond
by codeMantra

I dedicate this book to Jay for his scientific inspirations.

Contents

SECTION II BIG DATA IN MANAGEMENT: APPLICATIONS, PROSPECTS, AND CHALLENGES

Foreword by Jay Liebowitz, D.Sc.

With artificial intelligence (AI)-powered analytics, cognitive computing, machine learning, blockchain, and the Internet of Things (IoT) becoming more commonplace, how does this affect management's role in today's and future organizations? Management will have to become more aware of the benefits of applying these technologies, and others, to improve their decision-making at all levels—strategic, operational, and tactical. In addition, managers will need to enhance their "intuitive awareness" to take advantage of their experiential learning for making better decisions.

This book is a wonderful collection of chapters that posits how managers need to cope in the Big Data era. Most of the book is written by contributors from Poland, especially those with the new Institute of Management at the Warsaw University of Life Sciences, led by Professor Joanna Paliszkiewicz. The chapters highlight many of the emerging developments in technologies, applications, and trends related to management's needs in this Big Data era.

"Soft skills" are also important in being successful as a manager or an executive. Companies typically list oral and written communications, ability to work with others, project management, listening, emotional intelligence, and related skills as the top qualities for management and executives. This combination of "hard" and "soft" skills, as mentioned in this book, is a critical part of being a "complete" manager.

With the 5 V's of Big Data (volume, variety, velocity, value, and veracity of data) upon us, managers must learn how to cope with this firehouse of structured and (mostly) unstructured data. Becoming adept at speaking the "Big Data Analytics" language and better understanding how data visualization plays a key role (along with the ethics, privacy, and security of data) will continue to be important areas for the manager to comprehend.

In 2020 and beyond, we are in for a thrill and this book serves as a helpful guide to help managers and executives cope with the journey ahead.

Jay Liebowitz, D.Sc.
Distinguished Chair of Applied Business and Finance
Harrisburg University of Science and Technology

Foreword by Alex Koohang, PhD

I am pleased to write this Foreword for this insightful, informative, and educational book edited by Joanna Paliszkiewicz.

The book includes 15 chapters divided into two sections—theory and application. Section I begins with a thoughtful introduction of the Big Data Analytics in innovation management and value creation following with human resource management as one of the "most critical and sensitive areas, where individual people face new, unknown, and overwhelming solutions", and continues with perspectives on the use of Big Data in knowledge management for improving business processes. Section I ends with two chapters that cover a thorough explanation of the role of IT in processing/analysis of Big Data and the financial management of Big Data to meet the challenges of the rapid development of micro-/macro-financial data.

Section II of this book includes nine chapters that cover some of the most significant applications, prospects, and challenges of Big Data Analytics such as farm management, agribusiness, tourism, customer relationship management (CRM), blockchain, and management and support for real-time quantitative Big Data for understanding everyday innovative businesses.

This book presents some meaningful work on Big Data Analytics and its applications. Each chapter generates some helpful guidance to the readers on Big Data Analytics and its applications, challenges, and prospects that is necessary for organizational strategic direction.

The editor of this book has done a remarkable job of structuring the chapters in a meaningful way for readers to follow and understand. This book is easy-to-read, educational, engaging, realistic, noteworthy, and appealing to both practitioners and academicians.

Alex Koohang, PhD
Eminent Scholar and Endowed Chair in Information Technology
Professor of Information Technology
Middle Georgia State University, USA

Preface

Big Data is an important concept, which has caught the attention of practitioners, academicians, and researchers. The possibility of organizations to manage, collect, analyze, store, and transfer data has increased over the past decade. This has resulted in significant new issues and challenges regarding how data can be used for improving management. Big Data can be understood as a massive amount of data generated by the Internet, mobile phones, tablets, cameras, smart devices, sensors, etc.

The adoption of advanced Big Data Analytics methods has attracted significant interest mostly due to its access through web-based interfaces. In the market, there is a belief that businesses must actively engage with this innovative technology to remain more competitive. Organizations should understand and learn how to transform their business models in the era of Big Data, and how they can ensure compliance with correct practices not only from the perspective of technology but also from the managerial, ethical, and societal viewpoints.

From a management perspective, it is essential to understand how to recognize which business processes can benefit from what kind of Big Data models; how the data can be organized, transferred, stored, and used; and how analytical results can be incorporated into decision-making. Big Data Analytics provides new opportunities for extending the utilization of knowledge management because it can extract information that is more accurate, richer, and therefore, more valuable.

This book presents and discusses the main challenges posed by Big Data in a manner relevant to both practitioners and scholars. It is important to learn how companies should leverage Big Data Analytics to take action and optimize the business.

The purpose of this book is to bring together the theory and practice of management in the era of Big Data. This book offers a look at the current state of Big Data, including a comprehensive overview of both research and practical applications. This book is divided into two parts: the first covering theoretical foundations and the second covering applications, prospects, and challenges. Details of the chapters are summarized below.

The first part contains six chapters. **Chapter 1** discusses the use of Big Data Analytics (BDA) in innovation management and value creation. Based on a literature review, the features and nature of this type of data have been explored, and examples of innovation resulting from BDA methods have been presented. In **Chapter 2**, the authors, based on the literature review and the described practiced solutions, identify the challenges related to the implementation of Big Data into human resource management (HRM). Through the use of the analysis cross-matching technique, by crossing HRM practices with Big Data attributes and further assessing the degree of mutual alignment, the authors indicate the main challenges for researchers and practitioners and future research directions. **Chapter 3** addresses the perspectives on the use of Big Data as evident in the management of the knowledge necessary to improve business processes. The attention is initially focused on the challenges within the area of knowledge management that the organizations face during the era of Big Data and artificial intelligence analytics. It is followed by the presentation of the approach toward knowledge management in the context of Big Data. Within **Chapter 4** entitled "Information Management and the Role of Information Technology in a Big Data Era", the authors attempt to indicate the key fields within the theory of management and to propose chosen information technologies to process Big Data. The basis of the conducted analysis is a review of source literature. Directions of further research within the field of information management and technology and techniques within this scope are indicated. **Chapter 5** includes a systematic review and synthesis of Big Data in financial management related to literature and the conceptual application. Big Data in financial management provides new opportunities in the area of creating the value of firms, better customer segmentation, the formation of personalized marketing, the composition of industry compliance, managing with risk management, or fraud detection. **Chapter 6** presents digital risk and trust issues in the context of Big Data. It begins by discussing the place of Big Data in the concept of digital risk. Next, the problem of trust in Big Data and the process of building it are characterized. This chapter ends with an analysis of the impact of solutions in the field of Big Data ethics on organizational innovation.

The second part contains eight chapters. **Chapter 7** discusses the applicability of Big Data in modern farm management and presents some of its key elements. Based on the literature, the advantages and some disadvantages of applying Big Data in agriculture are listed. It has been confirmed that Big Data has great potential to transform agricultural production methods and management methods. The aim of **Chapter 8** is to determine the relationship between corporate social responsibility (CSR) activities and dialogue with stakeholders and recognizing the level of implementation of CSR solutions. According to research results, the enterprises poorly identify the needs and underestimate the importance of dialogue with stakeholders. The primary purpose of **Chapter 9** is to present the importance of Big Data in tourism. The enormous opportunities for using Big Data to create an effective personalization of the offer for the client were pointed out. Based on the analyses carried out, current trends regarding the use of Big Data in tourism are indicated. **Chapter 10** entitled "Use of Big Data for Assessment of Environmental

Pressures from Agricultural Production" presents the use of data from the Farm Accountancy Data Network (FADN) database to estimate greenhouse gas (GHG) emissions from Polish agriculture. The FADN database possesses key elements of Big Data datasets. By purpose, FADN data is used to shape agricultural policy in the EU and for scientific analyses. The approach used indicates the possibility of extending applications of FADN data for analyzing the impact of agricultural production on the environment. **Chapter 11**, entitled "Big Data as a Key Aspect of Customer Relationship Management: An Example of the Restaurant Industry", is a description of the potential to use digital technologies in the food industry. The research aims to present digitization as an element of creating a personalized offer and the possibility of using it in the process of customer relationship management in the catering industry. The aim of **Chapter 12** is to present the possibilities of using innovative blockchain technology to improve the functioning of the beef production chain. The research has shown that blockchain is a technology that can solve many problems and shortcomings of the current beef production system and contribute to ensuring food safety and quality. **Chapter 13**, entitled "Big Data Analysis for Management from Solow's Paradox Perspective in Polish Industry", presents the results of research related to the relationship between the enterprises using Big Data and the average results obtained by these enterprises. **Chapter 14** shows the application of Big Data on commuting. The multiple-case study method is applied with theoretical sampling allowing for presenting success stories of companies using Big Data on commuting for the development of their products and services. The primary goal of **Chapter 15** is to support the decision-making process in innovation strategy. It proposes a quantitative model for decision-making in the area of innovation strategy keeping in mind sustainable competitive advantage concept. This chapter proposes the innovation strategy index and applies it in two case companies operating in biotechnology and *in vitro* diagnostics industries.

This book provides the theoretical background and practical issues related to management in the era of Big Data. The editor believes that the collection of chapters is relevant and beneficial to the needs of professionals, researchers, and post-doctoral and graduate students. The authors of this book try to unify the extent of research on Big Data in management and to stimulate new research directions, showing issues and challenges. It brings together conceptual thinking and empirical research on the nature, meaning, and development of Big Data in management.

Editor

Joanna Paliszkiewicz works as a full professor at the Warsaw University of Life Sciences (WULS—SGGW). She is the director of the Management Institute. She is also an adjunct professor at the University of Vaasa in Finland. She is well recognized in Poland and abroad for her expertise in management issues: knowledge management and trust management. She has published over 200 papers/manuscripts and is the author/co-author/editor of ten books.

She has been a part of many scholarship endeavors in the United States, Ireland, Slovakia, Taiwan, the United Kingdom, and Hungary. She has actively participated in presenting research results at various international conferences. Currently, she serves as the deputy editor-in-chief of the *Management and Production Engineering Review*. She is an associate editor for the *Journal of Computer Information Systems*. She is the vice president of the Polish Association for Production Engineering. She also serves as chair of the International Cooperation in European Business Club. She serves as the vice president of the International Association for Computer Information Systems in the United States. She is a board member of the Intellectual Capital Accreditation Association. In addition, she serves as a member of the editorial board of several reputable and high-impact international journals such as *Expert System with Application*. She has successfully supervised many PhD students leading them to completion of their degrees. She has also served as an external reviewer for several PhD students in Poland, India, and Finland. She is actively involved in participating in the scientific committees of many international conferences. She was named the 2013 Computer Educator of the Year by IACIS.

Contributors

Nina Drejerska (PhD) is a researcher and an academic teacher at the Institute of Economics and Finance, Warsaw University of Life Sciences (WULS—SGGW) Her main research interests are regional development, labor economics, and business models in bio- and circular economy. She has 15 years of experience in statistical analysis and reporting on economic and business issues. She has been involved in ten international projects and a number of research projects commissioned by Polish government units. As a result, she has published over 80 original papers and book chapters, as well as 2 books. She has been a reviewer and a guest co-editor for a number of international journals, as well as an editor and co-editor of three monographs.

Barbara Filipczyk is a lecturer in the Department of Communication Design and Analysis at the University of Economics in Katowice, Poland. She conducts scientific research and is also a teacher. She is the author of numerous scientific publications, articles, book chapters, and textbooks on the usage of information technology in organizational management. Her research interests include issues of knowledge engineering and knowledge management, and also the design and development of information systems for a variety of access platforms.

Grzegorz Filipczyk (PhD) is a lecturer in the Department of Communication Design and Analysis at The University of Economics in Katowice, Poland. His research interests include subjects of the acquisition of knowledge from data and the usage of serious games in knowledge management. Beyond scientific activity, he also has significant experience in teaching.

Monika Gębska (PhD) is a zoo technician and economist with a career in university research. She graduated from the Faculty of Animal Sciences at the Warsaw University of Life Sciences (WULS). She completed her postgraduation in Consultancy at Warsaw University of Economics. She has broad experience in teaching to adults: university students, farmers, and operators. She conducts classes in agricultural economics and management of agriculture. Since 1996, she has worked at the WULS in the Management Institute. Her main interest is animal welfare issues, including animal welfare during transport. For the last

10 years, she has researched the social and economic aspects of animal welfare, sustainable agriculture, and decision support tools. In this area, she has worked on many international projects.

Jerzy Gołuchowski has spent more than 40 years in the academic and business community. He is a full professor at the University of Economics in Katowice, Poland, where he is also the head of Communication Design and Analysis Department. Since 2012, he has been serving as the president of the Polish Society of Business Informatics. He is a member of the editorial board of the *Journal of Business Economics and Management, Polish Journal of Management Studies,* and *Business Informatics.* He has published over 100 articles and 10 books. His publications are related to decision support systems, trust and knowledge management, leadership, and information technology.

Teppo Heimo holds master's degrees both in Molecular Biotechnology and Diagnostics from the University of Turku and in Economics and Business Administration from the University of Vaasa. Currently, he works as a business developer in HyTest Ltd. He has specialized in innovation and technology management, especially in the life science and biotechnology scene.

Piotr Jałowiecki (PhD) completed his diploma of master's and engineer's studies in the field of Computer Science at the Faculty of Technical Physics and Applied Mathematics of the Lodz Technical University. He holds a master's degree in Information Technology. His master's thesis is entitled "Internet address-telephone book based on the X.400 communication protocol". The result of this work was an introduction to the first online tele-address book in Poland. He received his PhD in medical sciences in the field of medical biology at the Nofer Institute of Occupational Medicine in Łódź. His doctoral dissertation is titled "Development and verification of a toxicokinetic simulation model based on physiological parameters (PB-TK) for duren and isoduren". It was the first scientific study of tetramethyl benzene isomer toxicokinetics in the world, and the result of this work was the first computerized physiologically-based toxicokinetic models in Poland. He is the author and co-author of 5 monographs, 89 scientific articles and chapters in monographs, and scientific editor of 12 monographs. His main areas of scientific research include management and marketing, logistics, e-logistic systems, food markets and agri-food industry, data science, forecasting and simulation of economic processes, protection of public health, toxicokinetic and toxicodynamic modeling, biostatistics, defense, and national security.

Sławomir Jarka (PhD) works at the Warsaw University of Life Sciences (WULS) in the Management Institute. He graduated from postgraduate managerial studies at the Warsaw School of Economics and a course organized by Cornell University (USA) and the Mellon Foundation on "Experimental Economics". He has participated and spoken at many conferences and national and international seminars, including Mansholt Graduate School and Wageningen University. His areas of interest includes management problems in agricultural enterprises, the use of IoT, and blockchain technology in the process of building food safety and increasing their efficiency. He is the author of numerous articles in national and international scientific journals.

Anna Jasiulewicz (PhD) is an assistant professor at the Warsaw University of Life Sciences (WULS—SGGW) in the Management Institute. She is theme editor in the international journal *Annals of Marketing Management & Economics (AMME)*. She is an author of a few dozen articles and a researcher with a special interest in marketing, consumer behavior, marketing, innovative strategies.

Krzysztof Kania is a professor at the University of Economics in Katowice, Poland. He is a researcher and teacher at the Department of Knowledge Engineering. Professionally, he deals with the issues of improving business processes and the use of information and communication technologies in the management of organizations.

Paweł Kobus (PhD) is an assistant professor in the Department of Econometrics and Statistics, Institute of Economics and Finance, Warsaw University of Life Sciences (WULS). He is a lecturer on courses of Statistics and Econometrics. Presently, his research efforts are concentrated on modeling organization and performance of farms with the use of large datasets. He is the author of many articles dealing with the use of quantitative methods for analyzing the economics of the agricultural sector.

Anna Losa-Jonczyk (PhD) is a lecturer in the Department of Communication Design and Analysis at The University of Economics in Katowice, Poland. Her main topics of research are communication management, corporate responsibility, and CSR communication. She also serves as a certified tutor for students.

Katarzyna Łukasiewicz (PhD) works at the Warsaw University of Life Sciences (WULS) in the Management Institute. Her research interests focus on the issues of quality management, quality standards, and customer relationship management in the tourism industry. She is the author of many publications in this field. She is also the promoter of many master's theses in the field of Tourism and Recreation (two of them awarded the prize of the Minister of Sport and Tourism in 2009 and 2013). Outside of work, she is an animal lover.

Magdalena Mądra-Sawicka (PhD) is an academic from the Institute of Economics and Finance at the Warsaw University of Life Sciences (WULS—SGGW). She has worked as a scientist and academic teacher since 2006 and as an assistant professor since 2010. She was a participant and the director of research projects with national and international scopes. Her research interests are related to corporate finance, Big Data technologies in finance, internal financing issues, capital structure, and determinants of small and medium enterprises' growth. She is the author of numerous articles and book chapters and participant of many national and international conferences.

Edward Majewski is a full professor in the Department of Economics and Organisation of Enterprises, Institute of Economics and Finance, Warsaw University of Life Sciences (WULS). Main fields of his scientific interests are sustainable agriculture, farming systems, and impacts of CAP reforms on Polish agriculture. He plays a leading role in Poland in disseminating the sustainability concept, specific implementation of the Integrated Farming System (IFS). His research activities include studies on farm-level impacts of agricultural policy measures, farmers, strategies toward farm development and quality improvement, adoption of agro-environmental measures, and more sustainable farming practices and sustainability indicators. In recent years, he has been involved in the realization of a number of EU-funded research projects (e.g., Income Stabilization, Seamless, Cap-ire, Crop Rotations, Fadntool, Claim, Biogaz II) dealing with such issues as agricultural policy impacts, sustainable agriculture (including mitigation of environmental pressures), and risks in farming. He is also active in farmers' and agricultural advisors' training and consultancy.

Konrad Michalski (PhD) is an assistant professor at the Warsaw University of Life Sciences (WULS—SGGW), Institute of Management. He received his PhD degree in economics on the logistics from the University of Szczecin in 2010. His main scientific interests include logistics in public services, changes in processes of adjustment of organizational structures, and processes within the organization to requirements of innovative technologies and leadership in the organization. He has many years of experience in business project management.

Piotr Pietrzak (PhD) is an assistant professor at the Warsaw University of Life Sciences (WULS—SGGW), in the Management Institute. His main areas of interest include the efficiency of public sector institutions, public management, performance measurement, and Balanced Scorecard. He is the author of over 50 articles and 2 books.

Grzegorz Polok is a professor in the Department of Public Management and Social Sciences at The University of Economics in Katowice, Poland. He is an ethicist, pedagogue, and theologian. He is the author of five books and many other publications related to business ethics and ethics in public relations. His most important publication published in seven different languages is the book *Spread Your Wings*.

Marcin Ratajczak (PhD) is an adjunct professor at the Warsaw University of Life Sciences (WULS) in the Management Institute. He is conducting educational classes in the field of work psychology, entrepreneurship, and elements of human resource management. His scientific and research activity focuses on issues of small and medium-sized entrepreneurship and Corporate Social Responsibility (CSR). He is the author of many scientific publications in domestic and foreign journals, as well as the author of two monographs on responsible business on the example of agribusiness companies. He has been awarded at conferences for the best articles and the best presentations in terms of substance. He has participated in international internships. He was the laureate of the "Mazowiecki Doctoral Scholarship" awarded by the Marshal of the Mazowieckie Voivodeship and received the Rector's Award for scientific and publishing achievements several times.

Ewa Stawicka (PhD) is an assistant professor at the Warsaw University of Life Sciences (WULS) in the Management Institute. Her scientific and research activities focus on issues of human capital and corporate social responsibility (CSR). She has participated in foreign internships at Alanya Alaaddin Keykubat University in Turkey and Universitat Politecnica de Valencia in Spain. She has completed many training and scientific and didactic projects. She was the head of postgraduate studies: CSR-strategy of socially responsible business. She is the author of scientific publications in national and international journals as well as monographs on responsible business (on the example of agribusiness enterprises and in agriculture).

Janusz Strużyna is a full professor in the Department of Organizational Relationship Management at the University of Economics in Katowice, Poland. He currently teaches courses in HRM and Management at bachelor's, master's, and doctoral levels. His current research interests include aspects of HRM development in various types of organizations in the digital era and model of evolutionary changes in the organizations. He is the author or co-author of more than 300 scientific publications.

Piotr Sulewski (PhD) is an associate professor in the Department of Economics and Organisation of Enterprises, Institute of Economics and Finance, Warsaw University of Life Sciences (WULS). Main fields of his scientific interest are farm efficiency, risk production in agriculture, fertilizer market, agricultural biogas production, and the potential of reduction of GHG from the agricultural sector. He is the author of a number of articles and books in his field of study. He is a lecturer on courses in Agricultural Economics, Farm Management, Strategic Management, Risk Management in Agriculture, Risk Management in Logistics, and Organization and Management of Production Processes. He is a member of the European Association of Agricultural Economists and Association of Agricultural Economists and Agribusiness. He is the referee of several scientific journals and coordinator or partner in a number of research projects in the field of Sustainable

Development, Risk Management in Agriculture, Renewable Energy Sources, and Potential of Agricultural Biorefineries.

Hubert Szczepaniuk (PhD) is an assistant professor at the Warsaw University of Life Sciences (WULS—SGGW), Institute of Management. He completed his doctoral degree in the field of computer science on technical science in the Faculty of Cybernetics at the Military University of Technology in Warsaw, Poland, in 2015. His scientific interests include information security, application of NoSQL databases in intelligent systems, and programming machine learning algorithms. He is the author of numerous publications within this scope.

Josu Takala (Professor) has vast experience in both industry and academia. He worked for ABB (Asea Brown Boveri) Group in R&D and Quality Assurance within different application areas of automation as a researcher and a manager from 1979–1992. He received his M.Sc. in Electrical Engineering in 1980 at Tampere University of Technology, Finland; his Dr.Tech. in Electrical Engineering, and business studies at the University of Vaasa, Finland, in 1988; his Dr. HC in 2009 from the Technical University of Košice, Slovakia; and his Dr. HC at Universiti Tun Hussein Onn Malaysia in 2015. Currently, he is a professor of Industrial Management at the University of Vaasa (1988–), Finland, besides various other universities in Finland and abroad such as Thailand, Malaysia, China, Slovakia, Poland, and Slovenia. His field of interest is mainly technology management in the sustainable competitive strategies of private and public organizations in manufacturing networks by utilizing the generic fields of quality management (technology and operations) strategy, new product and service development, and environmental management. He has published over 600 scientific articles. He is the co-editor, special issue editor, member of Scientific Board in Journals (such as *Management and Production Engineering Review* and *Management*) and invited or keynote speaker and chairman or honored chairman in many international conferences. He has participated in international activities, mostly in Asia and Europe, within his area of expertise, e.g., within university society (industry) relationships (e.g., how to graduate PhD in the industry) and evaluations of international M.Sc. and PhD programs. He is the owner of some university startup businesses.

Sara Tilabi did her bachelor's degree in the field of industrial engineering and completed her master's degree in the field of economics and business administration. Sara Tilabi did her bachelor's degree in the field of industrial engineering at Iran University of Science and Technology and completed her master's degree in the field of economics and business administration at the University of Vaasa. She has been working as a project researcher since 2013 in different research and consultancy projects, and before this, she has worked as an engineer for 4 years in the manufacturing sector. Her areas of expertise are operation strategy, business analysis, and supply chain management.

Adam Wąs (PhD) is an associate professor in the Department of Economics and Organisation of Enterprises, Institute of Economics and Finance, Warsaw University of Life Sciences (WULS). The main fields of his scientific interest are building economic models for farms; assessing the impact of agricultural policy on farm organization and structure of the farm sector; estimating external effects of agricultural production; mitigating GHG emission in agriculture; and analyzing risk management in agricultural production. He is the author of a number of articles and books in his field of study. He is a lecturer on courses in Agricultural Economics, Farm Management, Quality Management in Agriculture, and Business Planning. He is the coordinator or partner in a number of research projects in the field of Structural Changes in the Farming Sector, Potential Effects of Agricultural Biorefineries, Risk Management in Agriculture, and Renewable Energy Sources. He is the referee of several scientific journals. He is a member of the European Association of Agricultural Economists and International Farm Management Association.

Agnieszka Werenowska (PhD) is an assistant professor at the Warsaw University of Life Sciences (WULS—SGGW) Management Institute. She is writing publications related to public relations, media communication, marketing in enterprises, and territorial self-government units. She is the author of over 80 publications.

Barbara Wyrzykowska (PhD) is an assistant professor at the Warsaw University of Life Sciences (WULS—SGGW) Management Institute. Her scientific and research activities focus on human resource management, human capital, competencies, and new management methods in the organization. She is the author of over 70 publications and co-author of 2 books.

BIG DATA AND MANAGEMENT: THEORETICAL FOUNDATIONS

Chapter 1

Big Data Analytics: Innovation Management and Value Creation

Anna Jasiulewicz, Piotr Pietrzak, and Barbara Wyrzykowska

Warsaw University of Life Sciences—SGGW

Contents

1.1 Introduction

Innovations are one of the key areas of enterprise activity (Kotler & Kotler, 2013). Many authors (including Davenport et al., 2012; Chen et al., 2012; McAfee & Brynjolfsson, 2012) believe that BDA can be a source for creating innovative products, services, and business opportunities. Gunther et al. (2017) claim that economic value arising from the use of Big Data Analytics (BDA) can be measured by organizations in terms of profit, business expansion, or an increased competitive advantage. Other economic and social values resulting from BDA can manifest themselves in more robust decision-making, improved business processes, and the creation of innovative business models (e-commerce, security) (Manyika et al., 2011; Das & Kumar, 2013), as well as tracking and monitoring various socio-economic phenomena (Wamba et al., 2015; Erickson & Rothberg, 2013; Schmarzo, 2013).

BDA is currently counted among the most dynamically developing research areas in the world (Davenport et al., 2012; Chen et al., 2012; Lavalle et al., 2011). The importance of the potential inherent in Big Data (BD) is indicated by representatives of both scientific institutions (Kailsler et al., 2013, Chen et al., 2014, Olszak, 2018), as well as those engaged in business (Manyika et al., 2011, Microsoft, 2016; The Data Warehousing Institute, 2013). They believe that the challenge for the coming years and, at the same time, one of the greatest needs of modern organizations is intelligent analytics, which allows business value to be distilled from BD (Ulru et al., 2014; Gunther et al., 2017). Until now, an overall value creation model based on BDA innovations has not been developed and validated. This issue is the focus of this chapter.

This chapter aims to present examples of innovative products derived from BD methods and to develop a model for creating value based on BDA innovations. Dissemination of knowledge on this subject is important from the perspective of modern technologies being implemented by enterprises and their innovativeness.

This chapter begins with a presentation of examples of innovative products and services created based on the implementation of BDA methods in various fields. This chapter's second part presents innovation-based value creation and a proposed model for creating value from BDA-based innovations based on a literature review and case studies. In the end, conclusions have been formulated regarding BD's potential in managing innovation and creating value.

1.2 Research Method

The primary research method was a critical evaluation of literature on the topic (Webster & Watson, 2002), which was aimed at identifying the key innovations shaping BDA-based value creation. This methodology included searching for source materials, their selection, analysis, and synthesis. It was used to develop a value creation model based on BDA innovations.

The critical evaluation included articles from such databases as EBSCO, ProQuest, Scopus, and Google Scholar. Over 120 different studies were collected for an initial review and subsequently subjected to a selection process (based on selected keywords, abstracts, and titles). Finally, over 90 articles were chosen for in-depth analysis. A synthesis of the collected research material made it possible to identify the research gap and propose a comprehensive BDA-based value creation model.

1.3 Big Data Analytics: The Innovation Driver

BDA has become a popular topic of discourse among industry executives, policy-makers, and even academics over the last 7 years (Persaud & Schillo, 2017). Madsen and Stenheim (2016) suggest that BDA may be of a longer duration and not just another short-term management fad or fashion. A range of metaphors and buzz-words have been used to promote the hype around BDA (Madsen & Stenheim, 2016). These include *a new era, a management revolution, the new oil, the next frontier,* and *a new economic asset* (Brown et al., 2011; McAfee & Brynjolfsson, 2012; Manyika et al., 2011; Syed et al., 2013). At the same time, Harford (2014, p. 14) points out that "as with so many buzzwords, 'Big Data' is a vague term, often thrown around by people with something to sell".

Despite the growth of the popularity of BDA, some scholars (Rigby & Bilodeau, 2011) claim that there is presently little conclusive proof of the adoption of BDA by governments, non-profit organizations, or even firms. According to Mazzei and Noble (2017), a great number of managers are still unsure of how to correctly apply BDA within their organizations. "With a billion-plus users on the online social graph doing what they like to do and leaving a digital trail, and with trillions of sensors now being connected in the so-called Internet of Things, organizations need clarity (…) into what lies ahead in deploying these capabilities" (Bapna, 2015, p. vi). The same BDA has become a key organizational asset, which forms a strategic basis for business competition.

This evolution is making companies look at new contemporary tools and methods on maximizing the potentials of BDA along with the challenges it generates (Wielki, 2013). However, the success of numerous organizations requires new abilities, as well as new perspectives on how the era of BD could accelerate the speed of business processes.

Many organizations are seeking better approaches to continuously innovate and develop their products and services in today's aggressive business environment (Piatetsky-Shapiro, 2013). Generally, innovation is seen as a factor of regular research and improvement processes using common manual procedures (Gobble, 2013). Due to the increase of BDA, companies are "gradually depending on accumulated computerized data acquired from different sources such as their suppliers, customers and shareholders for recognizing innovative products and service systems" (Morabito, 2015, p. 125).

Several experts have offered suggestions and guidelines for organizations to create innovative products and services from BDA applicable to different fields (e.g., Wielki, 2013; Groves et al., 2013). Of course, some industries have more potential in BDA than others (Manyika et al., 2011). The highest potential occurs in the insurance and finance industry (Sadovskyi et al., 2014). However, BDA can also be successfully used to accelerate innovation in the following industries: household appliances, automotive, healthcare and medicine, and even government. Selected examples are presented below.

There has been enormous advancement in sensor technologies that go into automobiles, machines, utility grids, or mobile devices. This has led to the generation of machine-to-machine (M2M) data at a unique speed and in real time (Ehret & Wirtz, 2017). For instance, Whirlpool, the home-appliances manufacturer, uses sensors in their products to follow how clients use their products, connect these data with user-generated content from social media platforms, and create insights into their clients' behaviors and preferences (Woerner & Wixom, 2015). Also, Volvo Cars Company, one of the most prominent players in the automotive industry, implements automatic fault monitoring through the analysis of data collected from sensors located inside the vehicles (Sadovskyi et al., 2014). This data, integrated with information acquired from maintenance workshops and results of customer analytics processes in social media, generates an important basis for the improvement of higher-quality products that better fit the needs of the clients (Van Horn et al., 2012).

In turn, BDA in healthcare and medicine includes various types and massive amounts of data generated from hospitals such as omics data, biomedical data, and electronic health records data (Ristevski & Chen, 2018). In other words, BDA in medicine is generated from historical clinical activities (Tsumoto et al., 2013) and has significant effects on the medical and healthcare industry. For instance, it can assist in processing clinical decision support, planning treatment paths for patients, and improving healthcare technology and systems (Jee & Kim, 2013). Moreover, Raghupathi and Raghupathi (2014) point out that BDA in healthcare can contribute to evidence-based medicine, genomic analytics, pre-adjudication fraud analysis, and patient profile analytics. In turn, Manyika et al. (2011) estimate that BDA can enable more than $300 billion in savings per year in U.S. healthcare. Also, in 2017, the Ministry of Health Malaysia has launched the Malaysian Health Data Warehouse to share information and medical records between private/public hospitals and clinics (Fatt & Ramadas, 2018). Besides, North York General Hospital in Toronto has implemented a scalable real-time analytics application to improve patient outcomes and acquire better insight into the operations of healthcare delivery (Raghupathi & Raghupathi, 2014).

Finally, BDA can also be used to create innovation in the government sector. Kim et al. (2014) have proposed ways governments can use BDA to help them serve their citizens and deal with national challenges involving the economy, job creation, natural disasters, and terrorism. The U.K. government was one of the earliest implementers among EU countries of BD programs, establishing the U.K. Horizon Scanning Centre (HSC) (Sherry, 2012). It began work in December 2004 with the aim to "feed directly into cross-government priority setting and strategy formation, improving Government's capacity to deal with cross-departmental and multi-disciplinary challenges" (Habegger, 2009, p. 14). Besides, in 2009, the U.S. government launched Data.gov as a "step toward government accountability and transparency" (Kim et al., 2014, p. 82). It is a warehouse containing 235,959 datasets (as of September 2019), covering education, agriculture, healthcare, or transportations. As we can read on the website, government data are "accessible, vetted, and available; and are, for the majority, free and do not require registration to use" (https://www.data.gov/. Download: 16.09.2019). Because it should be noted that corporations use BDA to pursue profits, "governments use it to promote public goods" (Kim et al., 2014, p. 78).

To sum up, BDA has the great potential to accelerate innovation and, consequently, to create value. Persaud and Schillo (2017, p. 10) admit that "the path from data to value creation is not automatic, as more data does not naturally lead to greater value. Several technical and organizational challenges must be overcome along the way". In the next part, the authors will focus on value creation.

1.4 Value Creation through Innovation

The concept of value creation is an interdisciplinary issue, combining sciences such as management, marketing, psychology, philosophy, and theology (Doyle, 2008; Waśkowski, 2018). The value should be treated as a multidimensional construction that can be considered from economic, functional, and emotional benefits provided to various actors (consumers or organizations) involved in the creation of the offer and/or its consumption (Storbacka, 2019; Waśkowski, 2018). Introducing innovation focused on creating value is now an important strategic imperative for many organizations (Zupok, 2015). Understanding the essence of value delivered/created through innovation, therefore, requires a distinction from the outset of three concepts: "value for the organization", "customer value", and "value for the customer". According to Della Corte and Del Guardio (2014), the concept of value creation regards financial performance, market competitiveness, human resources involvement, commitment and brand image, and reputation. At present, many organizations focus on value creation through innovations (with the use of BDA) both in the context of creating increased value for customers purchasing its goods, as well as for business shareholders who want to see their stake expressed in value.

1.4.1 Creating Value for an Organization Using Information Resources and ICT

The Resource-Based View (RBV) provides guidelines on how to create unique values for organizations based on information resources and information and communication technology (ICT) (Fink et al., 2017, Olszak & Kisielnicki, 2018). The issue of value creation has also been interestingly described by Ross et al. (1996). The authors analyzed ICT from the perspective of various assets: human assets (technical skills, business understanding, problem-solving orientation), technological assets (physical ICT infrastructure, databases, SI architecture, standards), and relationships between these assets (relationships with clients, management support, risk, and liability management).

Feeny and Willcocks (1998) identified nine key capabilities relevant to the development of business value with ICT that can be grouped into four interlocking areas. These are ICT business and vision, ICT architecture designing, ICT services delivery, and the network of capabilities related to ICT leadership and obtaining (purchasing) information. Bharadwaj (2000) proposed six dimensions of ICT, important from creating a value point of view. These are ICT/business partnership, external links in ICT, strategic thinking in the ICT area, ICT business processes integration, ICT management, and ICT infrastructure. Research carried out by these authors shows that the ICT infrastructure is the most comfortable asset to capture and copy by competitors and, therefore, represents the most "fragile" resource in creating business value. Organizations derive value mainly from intangible assets such as new skills, new products, and new business models (Wade & Hulland, 2004).

Value creation using BDA can be accomplished through various business models (Davenport & Hariss, 2007; Erickson & Rothberg, 2013; Ishikawa & Nakagawa, 2013; Schick et al., 2011). The delivery of specific products and services takes place in close connection with other organizations, e.g., telecommunication operators and enterprises from the financial sector. These organizations can operate more efficiently and optimize their supply chain and manage their innovation through BD platforms.

According to Shang and Seddon (2002), obtaining value (benefits) can be classified into five dimensions: ICT infrastructure (e.g., reduction of ICT costs), operational (e.g., improvement of customer service), managerial (e.g., better resource management), strategic (e.g., development of innovative business), and organizational (e.g., improvement of organizational learning).

However, it should be remembered that the value of the organization is mainly created by maximizing customer value for the company (Zupok, 2015). It is logical if, according to the definition proposed by Kotler (2004), we assume that "customer value" is a bundle of values (added value) provided by buyers to the enterprise, e.g., through revenues (through customer satisfaction), information and signals, trust, loyalty, and other values. According to Kaplan and Norton (2004, p. 30), "if customers value innovation and high performance, then the skills, systems, and processes that create new products and services with superior functionality take on high value. Consistent alignment of actions and capabilities with the customer value proposition is the core of strategy execution".

1.4.2 Creating Value for the Consumer through Innovation

Delivering value for customers is indisputably one of the significant determinants of business success (Martins & Fernandes 2015). According to Kotler et al. (2002), "value for the customer" is the difference between the total value of the product for the customer and the cost that must be incurred in connection with its acquisition. The overall value of the product for the customer is the sum of the benefits that he expects from the product or service. Value for customers also includes contacts maintained with them, the manner of service, company reputation, brand, and outstanding organization competences (Waśkowski, 2015).

Innovation is intrinsically connected with value (Lee et al., 2012). Also, these innovations are created using BDA. Creating value through innovation is visibly a winning strategy (Martinsuo, 2019; Špaček & Vacik, 2016; Martins & Fernades, 2015; Ritala et al., 2013). Moreover, organizations are putting considerable effort into creating value with their customers (co-creation) as part of the innovation process to achieve competitive advantages (Prahalad & Ramaswamy, 2004).

1.4.3 Value Creation through Innovation: Conceptual Model

The literature analysis became an inspiration to create a conceptual model of creating value for the enterprise through implemented innovations (Figure 1.1).

The proposed model was based on two assumptions:

1. The implemented innovations start the process of creating value for the enterprise.
2. Value creation is a process, and the value itself is the result of this process.

Based on the literature review, key components necessary for the proper functioning of a company that stimulates its innovativeness have been identified.

To implement and manage innovations, an organization must have:

a. Resources (De Witt & Mayer, 2014; Špaček & Vacik, 2016; West & Gallagher, 2006).
b. Developed mechanisms of operations (process) (Špaček & Vacik, 2016).
c. Relationships built in its surroundings (Rangus, 2017a).

The implemented (managed) company's innovations have a positive influence on its market position (e.g., Anning Dorson, 2018, Mañez et al., 2013). In turn, the market position has an impact on company perception by customers and other stakeholders (Waśkowski, 2018).

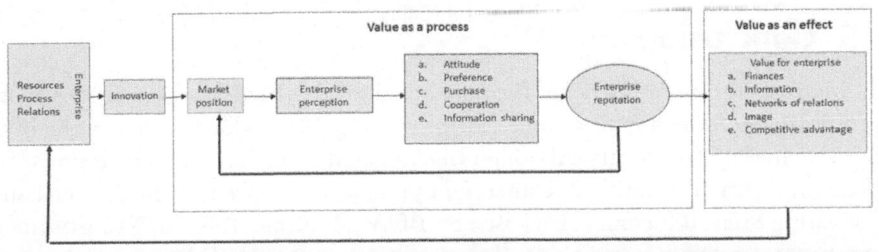

Figure 1.1   Model of value creation through innovation. (Own elaboration.)

This perception translates into:

a. The positive attitude of these stakeholders toward the company (Waśkowski, 2018).
b. Buyers' preference for a company's products (e.g., Kotler et al., 2002; Keller, 1993; Adil, 2012; Zhang, 2015).
c. An increase in purchases of these products by buyers (Ataman & Ülengin, 2003).
d. Willingness to cooperate and willingness to share information with the company and among stakeholders (Chariomonte, 2006; Usman & Vanhaverbeke, 2017).

Thanks to the benefits mentioned above, the company is gaining an increasingly strong reputation on the market. The reputation (positive opinion about the organization on the market) translates into further growth and strengthening of the company's market position. The entire process operates in a closed system.

The value for the company treated as an effect is manifested in the following elements:

a. Money from customers.
b. Information from customers and other stakeholders (Chesbrough et al., 2018; Repovienė, 2017; Roberts & Alpert, 2010).
c. Networks of relations between the enterprise and stakeholders and between the stakeholders themselves (because they share information) (Cheng & Huizingh, 2014; Hitchen et al., 2017; Huizingh, 2011; Lichtenthaler, 2011; Owner & Korelina, 2016).
d. A strong and positive image (Rangus, 2017b).
e. The emerging competitive advantage (e.g., McGrath et al., 1996; Sanchez-Gutierrez et al., 2019; Ungerman et al., 2018).

These effects, in turn, strengthen resources, processes, and relationships. Here again, we are dealing with a closed system, which can be a kind of flywheel to implement further innovations driving the process of creating value for the enterprise.

1.5 Conclusions

An increase in innovation is not the only advantage of BDA but possibly the most significant one, which makes it one of the most important global trends in the ICT industry in the 21st century. Although BDA-related issues have recently become an interesting area of scientific discourse, comprehensive research devoted to the issue of creating innovation and value based on BDA is lacking. This study constitutes a significant contribution to the development of research on BDA innovation management. It investigates the nature of BDA resources that create innovation and value for customers. The conducted research resulted in a proposed value creation model for organizations using BDA-based innovations. The conducted literature-based research points to the need for continued efforts focused on understanding the mechanisms used for extracting value from BDA.

This study is not devoid of limitations. The shortcomings of this chapter include the research method adopted by the authors. In the presented review, the authors used selected databases (EBSCO, ProQuest, Scopus, Google Scholar). The articles contained there do not exhaust the subject.

For future research, the authors propose conducting empirical research on generating value from BDA-based innovations. Based on the proposed model, studies can be conducted in various groups of entities, both in manufacturing and in services.

References

Adil, M. (2012). The influence of brand image on sales. *Journal of Basic and Applied Scientific Research, 2*(4), 3552–3556.

Anning-Dorson, T. (2018). Innovation and competitive advantage creation. *International Marketing Review, 35*(4), 580–600.

Ataman, B., & Ülengin, B. (2003). A note on effect of brand image on sales. *Journal of Product and Brand Management, 12*(4), 237–250.

Bapna, R. (2015). *Foreward*. In: V. Morabito (ed.), *Big Data and Analytics. Strategic and Organizational Impacts*. (pp. v–vi). Switzerland: Springer.

Bharadwaj, A. (2000). A resource-based perspective on information technology capability and firm performance: An empirical investigation. *MIS Quarterly, 24*(1), 169–196.

Brown, B., Chui, M., & Manyika, J. (2011). Are you ready for the era of 'big data'?. *McKinsey Quarterly, 4*, 24–35.

Chariomonte, F. (2006). Open innovation through alliances and partnership: Theory and practice. *International Journal of Technology Management, 33*(2–3), 111–114.

Chen, H., Chiang, R. H. L., & Storey, V. C. (2012). Business inteligence and analitycs: From big data to big impact. *MIS Quarterly, 36*(4), 1–24.

Chen, M., Mao, S., & Liu, Y. (2014). Big data: A survey. *Mobile Networks and Applications, 19*(2), 171–209.

Cheng, C. C. J., & Huizingh, E. K. R. E. (2014). When is open innovation beneficial? *The Journal of Product Innovation Management, 31*(5), 235–1253.

Chesbrough, H., Lettl, C., & Ritter, T. (2018). Value creation and value capture in open innovation. *The Journal of Product Innovation Management, 35*(6), 930–938.

Das, T. K., & Kumar, P. M. (2013). Big data analytics: A framework for unstructured data analysis. *International Journal of Engineering Science & Technology, 5*(1), 153–156.

Data Catalog. Retrieved from https://www.data.gov/. [September 16, 2019].

Davenport, T., Barth, P., & Bean, R. (2012). How big data is different. *MIT Sloan Management Review, 54*(1), 21–24.

Davenport, T. H., & Hariss, J. G., (2007). *Competing on Analytics. The New Science on Winning*. Boston, MA: Harvard Business School Press.

De Witt, B., & Meyer, R. (2014). *Strategy: An International Perspective, 5th Edition Perspective.* New Delhi: Cengage India.

Della Corte, V., & Del Guardio, G. (2014). A literature review on value creation and value capturing in strategic managing studies. *Corporate Ownership and Control, 11*(2), 328–346.

Doyle, P. (2008). *Value-based Marketing: Marketing Strategies for Corporate Growth and Shareholder Value.* West Sussex: John Wiley & Sons, Ltd.

Ehret, M., & Wirtz, J. (2017). Unlocking value from machines: Business models and the industrial internet of things. *Journal of Marketing Management, 33*(1–2), 111–130.

Erickson, G., & Rothberg, H. (2013). *Competitors, Intelligence, and Big Data,* In: J. Liebowitz (ed.), *Big Data and Business Analytics.* (pp. 103–115). Boca Raton, FL: CRC Press, Taylor & Francis Group.

Fatt, Q. K., & Ramadas, A. (2018). The usefulness and challenges of big data in healthcare. *Journal of Healthcare Communications, 3*(2), 21.

Feeny, D., & Willcocks, L. (1998). Core IS capabilities for exploiting information technology. *Sloan Management Review, 39*(3), 9–21.

Fink, L., Yogew, N., Evan, A. (2017). Business intelligence and organizational learning: An empirical investigation of value creation process. *Information & Management, 54*, 38–56.

Gobble, M. M. (2013). Big data: The next big thing in innovation. *Research-Technology Management, 56*, 64–67.

Groves, P., Kayyali, B., Knott, D., & Van Kuiken, S. (2013). *The "Big Data" Revolution in Healthcare Accelerating Value and Innovation.* Chicago, IL: McKinsey & Company.

Gunther, W. A., Mehrizi, R. H. R., Huysman, M., & Feldberg, F. (2017). Debating big data: A literature review on realizing value from big data. *Journal of Strategic Information Systems, 26*, 191–209.

Habegger, B. (2009). *Horizon Scanning in Government. Concept, Country Experiences, and Models for Switzerland.* Zurich: Center for Security Studies. Retrieved from https://www. files.ethz.ch/isn/96274/Horizon-Scanning-in-Government.pdf. [September 16, 2019].

Harford, T. (2014). Big data: A big mistake? *Significance, 11*, 14–19.

Hitchen, E. L., Nylund, P. A., Ferràs, X., & Mussons, S. (2017). Social media: Open innovation in SMEs finds new support. *The Journal of Business Strategy, 38*(3), 21–29.

Ishikawa, A., & Nakagawa, J. (2013). *An Introduction to Knowledge Information Strategy. From Business Intelligence to Knowledge Sciences.* London: World Scientific Publishing Co Pte Ltd.

Jee, K., & Kim, G-H. (2013). Potentiality of big data in the medical sector: Focus on how to reshape the healthcare system. *Healthcare Informatics Research, 19*(2), 79–85.

Kailsler, S., Armour, F., Epinosa, A., & Money, W. (2013). Big Data: Issues and Challenges Moving Forward. *Proceedings of 46th Hawaii International Conference on System Science*, 995–1004.

Kaplan, R. S., & Norton, D. P. (2004). *Strategy Maps: Converting Intangible Assets into Tangible Outcomes.* Cambridge, MA: Harvard Business School Press.

Keller, K. L. (1993). Conceptualizing, measuring, and managing customer-based brand equity. *Journal of Marketing, 57*, 1–22.

Kim, G-H., Trimi, S., & Chung, J-H. (2014). Big-data applications in the government sector: A comparative analysis among leading countries. *Communications of the ACM, 57*(3), 78–85.

Kotler, Ph. (2004). *Philip Kotler odpowiada na pytania na temat marketingu*. [Philip Kotler Answers Questions About Marketing]. Poznań: Rebis.

Kotler, Ph., Armstrong, J., & Wong, V. (2002). *Marketing. Podręcznik europejski*. Warszawa: PWE.

Kotler, Ph, & Kotler, M. (2013). *Przez marketing do wzrostu; 8 zwycięskich startegii*. [From Marketing to Growth; 8 Winning Strategies]. Poznań: Rebis.

LaValle, S., Lesser, E., Shockley, R., Hopkins, M., & Kruschwitz, N. (2011). Big data, analytics and the path from insights to value. *MIT Sloan Management Review, 52*(2), 21–23.

Lee, S.M., Olson, D.L., & Trimi, S. (2012). Co-innovation: Convergenomics collaboration, and co-creation for organizational values. *Management Decisions, 50*(5), 817–831.

Lichtenthaler, U. (2011). Open innovation: Past research, current debates, and future directions. *The Academy of Management Perspectives, 25*(1), 75.

Madsen, D. Ø., & Stenheim, T. (2016). Big data viewed through the lens of management fashion theory. *Cogent Business & Management, 3*(1), 1165072.

Manyika, J., Chui, M., Brown, B., Bughin, J., Dobbs, R., Roxburgh, C., & Byers, A. H. (2011). Big Data: The Next Frontier for Innovation, Competition, and Productivity. *Report*. Retrieved from https://bigdatawg.nist.gov/pdf/MGI_big_data_full_report. pdf. [September 16, 2019].

Mañez, J. A., Rochina-Barrachina, M. E., Sanchis, A., & Sanchis, J. A. (2013). Do process innovation boost SMEs productivity growth? *Empirical Economics, 44*, 1373–1405.

Mazzei, M. J., & Noble, D. (2017). Big data dreams: A framework for corporate strategy. *Business Horizons, 60*(3), 405–414.

Martins, M., & Fernandes, T. (2015). Too small to innovate? Creating value with fewer resources. *Journal of Business Strategy, 36*(2), 25–33.

Martinsuo, M. (2019). Strategic value at the front end of radical innovation program. *Project Management Journal, 50*(4), 431–446.

McAfee, A., & Brynjolfsson, E. (2012). Big data: The management revolution. *Harvard Business Review, 90*, 61–67.

McGrath, R. G., Tsai, M.-H., Venkataraman, S., & MacMillan, I. C. (1996). Innovation, competitive advantage and rent: A model and test. *Management Science, 42*(3), 389–403.

Microsoft (2016). Microsoft Analytics Platform System. Retrieved from https://docs.microsoft.com/en-us/sql/analytics-platform-system/home-analytics-platform-system-aps-pdw?view=aps-pdw-2016-au7. [September 10, 2019].

Morabito, V. (2015). *Big Data and Analytics. Strategic and Organizational Impacts*. Switzerland: Springer.

Olszak, C. M. (2018). Tworzenie wartości biznesowej z wykorzystaniem zasobów Big Data. [Generating business value using big data resources]. *Przegląd Organizacji, 7*, 35–39.

Olszak, C. M., & Kisielnicki, J. (2018). A conceptual framework of information systems for organizational creativity support. Lessons from empirical investigations. *Information Systems Management, 35*(1), 29–48.

Owner, O., & Korelina, A. (2016). The influence of customer engagement in value co-creation on customer satisfaction: Searching for new forms of co-creation in Russian hotel industry. *Worldwide Hospitality and Tourism Themes, 8*(3), 327–345.

Persaud, A., & Schillo, S. (2017). Big Data Analytics: Accelerating Innovation and Value Creation. Retrieved from https://ruor.uottawa.ca/handle/10393/37744 [September 16, 2019].

Piatetsky-Shapiro, G. (2013). Comment on "A revolution that will transform how we live, work, and think: An interview with the authors of big data". *Big Data, 1*(4), 193.

Prahalad, C., & Ramaswamy, V. (2004). Co-creating unique value with customers. *Strategy & Leadership, 32*(3), 4–9.

Raghupathi, W., & Raghupathi, V. (2014). Big data analytics in healthcare: Promise and potential. *Health Information Science and Systems, 2*(1), 3.

Rangus, K. (2017a). Does a firm's open innovation mode matter? *Economic and Business Review for Central and South – Eastern Europe, 19*(2), 181–201.

Rangus, K. (2017b). The relation between different open innovation practices and firm's innovation performance. *Managing Global Transitions, 15*(1), 61–79.

Repovienė, R. (2017). Role of content marketing in a value creation for customer context: Theoretical analysis. *International Journal on Global Business Management & Research, 6*(2), 37–48.

Rigby, D., & Bilodeau, B. (2011). *Management Tools & Trends 2011*. London: Bain & Company.

Ristevski, B., & Chen, M. (2018). Big data analytics in medicine and healthcare. *Journal of Integrative Bioinformatics, 15*(3), 1–5.

Ritala, P., Agouridas, D., Assimakopoulos, D., & Gies, O. (2013). Value creation and capture mechanism in innovation ecosystems: A comparative case study. *International Journal Technology Management, 63*(3/4), 248–267.

Roberts, H., & Alpert, F. (2010). Total customer engagement: Designing and aligning key strategic elements to achieve growth. *Journal of Product&Brand Management, 19*(3), 198–209.

Ross, J., Beath, C. M., & Goodhue, D. L. (1996). Develop long-term competitiveness trough IT Assets. *Sloan Management Review, 39*(1), 31–42.

Sadovskyi, O., Engel, T., Heininger, R., Böhm, M., and Krcmar, H. (2014). Analysis of big data enabled business models using a value chain perspective. In: D. Kundisch, L. Suhl, L. Beckmann (eds.), *Multikonferenz Wirtschaftsinformatik*. Paderborn: Electronic Book. Retrieved from http://mkwi2014.de/Content/Tagungsband_MKWI2014.pdf. [September 15, 2019].

Sanchez-Gutierrez, J., Cabanelas, P., Lampon, J. F., & Gonzalez-Alvarado, T. E. (2019). The impact of competitiveness of customer value creation through relationship capabilities and marketing innovation. *Journal of Bussiness & Industrial Marketing, 34*(3), 618–627.

Schick A., Frolick, M., & Ariyachandra T. (2011). Competing with BI and Analytics at Monster Worldwide. *Proceedings of the 44th Hawaii International Conference on System Sciences, Hawaii*, 1–10.

Schmarzo, B., (2013). *Big Data: Understanding How Data Powers Big Business*. Indianapolis, IN: John Wiley and Sons.

Shang, S., & Seddon, P. B. (2002). Assessing and managing the benefits of enterprise systems: The business manager's perspective. *Information Systems Journal, 12*(2), 271–229.

Sherry, S. (2012). 33B Pounds Drive U.K. Government Big Data Agenda. Big Data Republic. Retrieved from http://www.bigdatarepublic.com/author.asp?section_id=2642&doc_id=254471. [September 15, 2019].

Špaček, M., Vacik, E. (2016). Company value creation through effective innovation process management. *Journal of Innovation Management, 4*(3), 65–78.

Storbacka, K. (2019). Actor engagement, value creation and market innovation. *Industrial Marketing Management, 80*, 4–10.

Syed, A., Gillela, K., & Venugopal, C. (2013). The future revolution on big data. *International Journal of Advanced Research in Computer and Communication Engineering, 2,* 2446–2451.

The Data Warehousing Institute (2013). TDWI Launches Big Data Maturity Model Assessment Too. Retrieved from https://tdwi.org/pages/maturity-model/big-data-maturity-model-assessment-tool.aspx?m=1 [September 14, 2019].

Tsumoto, S., Hirano, S., & Iwata, H. (2013). Mining Nursing Care Plan from Data Extracted from Hospital Information System. *Proceedings of the* 2013 *IEEE/ACM International Conference on Advances in Social Networks Analysis and Mining,* 956–961.

U.S. Government. Data.gov. Retrieved from https://www.data.gov. [September 16, 2019].

Ungerman, O., Dedkova J., & Gurinova, K. (2018). The impact of marketing innovation on the competitiveness of enterprises in the context of industry 4.0. *Journal of Competitiveness, 10*(2), 132–148.

Ulru, E.G. Apostu, A., Puican, F.C., & Velicanum, M. (2012). Perspectives on big data and big data analytics. *Database Systems Journal, 3*(4), 3–13.

Usman, M., & Vanhaverbeke, W. (2017). How start-ups successfully organize and manage open innovation with large companies. *European Journal of Innovation Management, 20*(1), 171–186.

Van Horn, D., Olewnik, A., & Lewis, K. (2012). Design Analytics: Capturing, Understanding, and Meeting Customer Needs Using Big Data. *Proceedings of the ASME International Design Engineering Technical Conference & Computers and Information in Engineering Conference,* 1–13.

Wade, M., & Hulland, J. (2004). Review: The resource-based view and information systems research: Review, extension, and suggestions for future research. *MIS Quarterly, 28*(1), 107–142.

Wamba, S., Akter, S., Edwards, A., Chopina, G., & Gnazou, D. (2015). How big data can make big impact: Findings from a systematic review and a longitudinal case study. *International Journal of Production Economics, 165,* 234–246.

Waśkowski, Z. (2015). Creating value for mass event organisers' stakeholders – model approache. *Problemy Zarządzania, Finansów i Marketingu, 41*(1), 187–198.

Waśkowski, Z. (2018). Managing corporate competences in the process of creating customer value. *Handel Wewnętrzny, 5*(376), 300–309.

Webster, J., & Watson, R. T. (2002). Analyzing the past to prepare for the future: Writing a literature review. *MIS Quarterly, 26*(2), 13–23.

West, J., & Gallagher, S. (2006). Challenges of open innovation: The paradox of firm' investment on open source software. *R&D Management, 36*(3), 319–331.

Wielki, J. (2013). Implementation of the Big Data Concept in Organizations - Possibilities, Impediments and Challenges. *Proceedings of the 2013 Federated Conference on Computer Science and Information Systems,* 985–989.

Woerner, S. L., & Wixom, B. H. (2015). Big data: Extending the business strategy toolbox. *Journal of Information Technology, 1*(30), 60–62.

Zhang, Y. (2015). The impact of brand image on Consumer behaviour: A literature review. *Open Journal of Business and Management, 3,* 58–62.

Zupok, S. (2015). Impact of innovation in creating value for customer. *Studia i Prace Wydziału Nauk Ekonomicznych i Zarządzania, 39*(2), 37–47.

Chapter 2

Human Resource Management in the Era of Big Data

Janusz Strużyna and Krzysztof Kania

University of Economics in Katowice

Contents

2.1 Introduction

Big Data (BD) technology presents human resource (HR) managers with another challenge. It is one of those new technologies that can change human resource management (HRM) the most. On the other hand, HR is also one of the most critical and sensitive areas, where individual people face new, unknown, and overwhelming solutions. The direct motive for addressing the topic is the identified and constantly filled knowledge gap regarding the effects of the application of this technology in HRM. The purpose of this chapter is to present the impact that BD technology has on HRM, as well as to identify the benefits, challenges, threats, and dilemmas that arise as a result of using BD technology in the area of HRM.

This chapter begins with a description of the impact of BD on HRM through the analysis of the attributes ascribed to this technology and determination of the scope of HRM as the basis for research (including the identification of the most frequently distinguished HRM practices). Next, the application of BD in HR practice is briefly presented, as well as the group of dilemmas and challenges that arise as a result of the attempts to use BD in HRM. The essential element of the analysis is based on the literature and the recognition of use cases, a summary of HRM practices with BD, and the indication of opportunities and benefits as well as threats and dilemmas related to it. This research permitted the next step, i.e., providing conclusions and possible further research directions in this area.

2.2 Influence of Big Data on HRM

In a broad sense, HRM covers all issues concerning the people employed and managed in different types of organizations (Armstrong & Taylor, 2014, p. 4). Due to the significant impact of the human factor and HRM on the organization's successes (Schneider et al., 2003; Pološki Vokić & Vidović, 2008), it is possible to identify an abundance of topics that HRM researchers currently deal with, however, a microscopic space on the map of interest is occupied by issues associated with the use of "Big Data" in HRM (Markoulli et al., 2017). This little interest may be surprising because today, the adjective "Big" refers to the strength of its influence on society and organization (Ward & Baker, 2013) and not just to the infrastructure needed for data storage and processing. BD is a change in the ways of solving problems (Mayer-Schönberger & Cukier, 2013), a new industry (Martin, 2015), a new organizational strategy (Mazzei & Noble, 2017), a new paradigm in science and the humanities (Kitchin, 2014). Changes in the perception of BD can also be observed by analyzing the set of features that describe this concept. Starting from the 3V model (Volume, Variety, and Velocity) (Laney, 2001) through the 7V model (3V + Veracity, Validity, Volatility, and Value) (Khan et al., 2014), the 10V model (7V + Venue, Vocabulary, and Vagueness) (Borne, 2014) up to the 17V model (10V + Visualization, Virality, Viscosity, Variability, Verbosity, Voluntariness, and Versatility) (Arockia et al., 2017) and the 42V model of BD and Data Science (Shafer, 2017), one can see the shifting of the accents from purely technical issues (volume, speed, different types of data) to the issues of BD use and their usefulness and suitability in various contexts (social, economic, etc.). Also, from HRM perspective, the features/attributes of BD can be treated as indicators of problems and chances for the improvement of practices; however, in many cases, they can be perceived both as an opportunity and as a threat. BD can also be considered from the process perspective. According to the five phases of BD processing (Krishnan, 2013, p. 37; Curry, 2015) and the aforementioned 17V attributes model, the most obvious consequences of BD for HRM are presented in Table 2.1.

Table 2.1 Possible Consequences of Big Data for HRM Indicated by Big Data Features

Big Data Processing Phase	*Big Data Attribute*	*HRM Consequences*	
		Opportunities	*Threats*
Collect (data acquisition)	Volume Velocity Variety Venue	• Employee dataset extension, • More complete picture of the social world, human being and the organization.	• Redundancy, overload, • High cost, • Crossing the borders of privacy, • Entering the employee's private sphere.
Discover (data analysis)	Variety Variability Vagueness	• Describing the world in new categories, • Thinking about what can be learned from these data, • Discovering new rules, patterns, etc.	• Ethical and law challenges, • Knowledge quickly becoming outdated, • Using data to answer unauthorized or unethical questions.
Process (data curation)	Variety Verbosity Vocabulary	• Integration of data from different sources requires cooperation between experts and practitioners, • Interdisciplinary approach, • The wider picture of the world.	• No common language.
Manage (data storage)	Volatility Vulnerability Veracity Validity	• New functions and roles in organization.	• More IT problems, • Sensitive data leakage.

(Continued)

Table 2.1 (*Continued*)   Possible Consequences of Big Data for HRM Indicated by Big Data Features

Big Data Processing Phase	Big Data Attribute	HRM Consequences	
		Opportunities	Threats
Generate (data usage)	Value Validity Visualization Vagueness Virality	• New questions and answers, • New, independent, and not the human-biased view of the world, • Automation, simulations, and micro-simulations, • Forecasts, predictive, and prescriptive analytics, • Capturing weak signals predicting people's behavior, • Exception identification, clarification of anomalies, and nonlinear dependences between variables, • Better justification, supporting intuition with hard facts.	• Stigmatization, • Sophistication, complicated methods, • Blurred and unclear responsibility, • New human–machine relationships, • Difficulties in explaining personnel decisions based on machine algorithms, • Problems with social and personal consequences of domination of model of exploration and elaboration of data.

The identified theoretical knowledge gap in the BD–HRM relationship can have serious consequences in recognizing the management processes. The HRM reality is then driven by practices dictated by IT companies and corporations rich enough to start deploying this idea. About two-thirds of HR executives agree that HR has undergone or is undergoing a digital transformation. However, only 40% of HR leaders confirmed having a digital work plan in place at the enterprise or HR level. Barely a third—37%—feel "very confident" about HR's actual ability to transform and move them forward via key capabilities like analytics and AI (Bolton et al., 2019). Although the first scientific works have already appeared (Scholz, 2017) and the theoretical foundations of research have been formulated, the need for further discussion and research is not weakening (Baig et al., 2019; Raguseo, 2018; Calvard & Jeske, 2018; Tursunbayevaa et al., 2018). Huselid and Minbaeva (2019) directed several thematic questions on this issue to the researchers:

1. Is the BD trend a positive development for the HRM field?
2. Will BD and analytics transform the HRM practice as we know it?
3. Where is the biggest value-added of BD and analytics for HRM?
4. What are the key priorities for the development of workforce analytics?

Following these intellectual challenges, the authors of this chapter undertook to realize twofold aims:

1. The identification of HR specialists' expectations and the conducting of rational scientific speculation to recognize and evaluate the potential impact of BD on HRM practices based on the review of both literature and practice cases.
2. The identification of challenges and problems of using BD in the improvement of HRM practices with a simple and universal method of cross-matching.

2.3 HRM and Big Data As a Subject of Interests

Building a convincing and universal definition of the subject of research in the field of HRM is hampered by (Keenoy, 1999; Thompson, 2011; Greenwood & Van Buren 2017):

■ The multiplicity and diversity of proposed/used definitions and terms
■ The diversity of approaches, interdisciplinary assumptions, various research methods, etc.
■ The imperative of contextual interpretation of research results, guidelines, and principles (due to labor law, history, national culture, etc.)
■ The theory-practice gap

Therefore, despite justified doubts about the division of commonly used activities of HRM specialists (Cassar & Bezzina 2017), a traditional set of HR practices was adopted as a framework for analyzing the possible impact of the BD idea on HRM. These are:

■ HR planning (Bratton & Gold, 2007; Jacobson, 2010; Pilbeam & Corbridge 2010)
■ Recruitment and selection (Price, 2007; DeCenzo et al., 2010)
■ Adaptation (White et al., 1997; De Vos et al., 2003; Levesque, 2005)

- Performance appraisal (Van Dijk & Schodl 2015)
- Training and development (Khawaja & Nadeem 2013)
- Rewarding and motivating (Anku et al., 2018)
- Career development (Sun et al., 2012)
- Layoffs and voluntary resignations (Karren & Sherman 2012; Cascio, 2002)

Determining the subject by HRM practices allows the next steps of the analysis:

1. Preparation of the analytical matrix through crossing the HR practices with BD opportunities and risks.
2. Completion of the matrix based on the literature review.
3. Identification of poorly developed areas.
4. Scientific speculation.
5. Formulation of analytical conclusions and synthesis.

The sources of the reviewed literature were Ebsco, ProQuest, and Google. The search criteria consisted of the co-occurrence of the "HRM" and "BD" terms in the content of a scientific publication, full-text access, and the English language. The main criterion for article selection was the method of argumentation, i.e., the role of references and a way of documentation of practical examples.

In the literature, there are many examples of the use of BD HRM and discovering rules useful in the improvement of HRM functions. Already in 2010, Davenport et al. (2010) gave six examples of using employee data in talent management. The most known cases of BD technology use include:

- The Oxygene project, initiated by Google in 2009, the purpose of which was to identify the success factors of good management (Morrison, 2012; Marr, 2013).
- Microsoft, based on data on 90,000 employees collected over 9 years, calculated the costs of leaving the employee as well as the minimum employment time in which one can expect that the cost of recruitment, introduction to the company, training, etc. will be returned (CIPD, 2014b).
- ArcelorMittal (steel producer), based on the analysis of data including employee rankings, their aspirations, expectations, and competences, improved the management of career paths and increased employee involvement (CIPD, 2014a).
- Tesco used analytical tools to study staff behavior (Marr, 2013).
- McDonald's used HR analytics to investigate the relationship between employee age, management styles, and staff attitudes to optimize restaurant operations (Sparrow et al., 2015).
- Sodexo used employee data to improve Quality of Life programs, organization of the work environment conducive to employee development and

satisfaction, and health-oriented programs (well-being Facility Management) (Conklin et al., 2016; Ware, 2016).

▪ Credit Suisse and Wal-Mart used employee data to predict who might quit the company (employee churn analytics) (Silverman & Waller, 2015).

▪ IBM used the Watson analytical system for retaining valuable employees (Forsyth, 2016).

▪ Walmart used advanced data analysis to manage products, customers, and employees (Marr, 2016a).

▪ McDonald's used Alexa (a versatile digital assistant from Amazon) for pre-selection in the hiring process (McDonald's, 2019).

▪ Unilever used HireVue application in the hiring process and for talent acquisition (Feloni, 2017; HireVue, 2019).

Other, numerous examples of the use of BD in the practice of HRM can be found in the works of Marr (2016b), Scholz (2017), and Levenson and Pillans (2017). Successes and positive examples of the use of BD and analytical methods give hope for better implementation of the HRM function but also raise strong concerns and fears:

▪ Ethical and law

BD is not morally neutral (Martin, 2015). Even only gathering detailed, personal data raises many doubts and questions. From the technological point of view, an individual can be reduced to merely a source of data for further operations. Data can be processed for good or bad intentions (e.g., search for signs of burnout or disease to dismiss the employee before they become less efficient or to help them and protect them from danger). In particular, excessive interference with privacy, feelings of deterioration of working conditions, dehumanization, and an approach in which a person is perceived only as a source of data should be avoided (McLean et al., 2015). The rapid emergence of new technologies and the possibility of observation (and in a more pejorative sense—surveillance) are ahead of not only our knowledge in the field of psychology, management, or sociology but also legal regulations.

▪ Delegation of authority and decisions to algorithms

Algorithms are crucial in the interpretation of the data in a manner that has the potential to add value (Cheng & Hackett, 2019). One of the biggest threats of using BD and machine learning methods lies deep in their nature. Algorithms working on data taken from the past reflect not only good but also bad practices. Algorithms by themselves do not know what is good and beneficial and what is bad. They learn using assessments that come from people, so they are subjective and burdened by human weaknesses, biases, prejudices, and inclinations. Machine learning, based on small datasets (which most companies have), has an even greater risk of error. One of the most spectacular examples of failed implementation is the recruitment system supported by AI in Amazon. The entire 4-year project was closed because the algorithms could not be stopped from discriminating against women (Dastin, 2018). In general, there is a fundamental threat to this approach. We try to predict and act for the future, but we use methods that learn from historical data. This makes the whole process to be driven by the past. Besides, statistics are not able to consider sudden changes, so an assumption of continuity of trends is taken.

Another, often raised an argument against the use of AI systems is that they work as "black boxes" (Pasquale, 2015), and one is not able to determine what factors caused, for example, the acceptance/rejection, hiring/firing of a particular person. Everyone has the right to obtain the answer to the question "Why?", but many AI tools (especially neural networks) do not provide it. This suggests that the use of AI in HRM may cause problems with the justification of personal decisions, and this, in turn, may cause the fear of violations of social norms. A broad and detailed analysis of the algorithms used in HRM is presented in the work by Cheng and Hackett (2019).

◾ Reorganization of the HR process, changing organizational attitude and culture, and managing the inter-organizational trust.

The greater dependence on data means that most companies have no chance to obtain benefits from BD technologies as they are not able to build their own data centers, do not have access to the necessary external data resources, or do not have skilled HR analysts and statisticians. This means that an increasing number of HRM processes will have to be outsourced. Entrusting sensitive personal data to external companies can be the first insurmountable mental barrier. For many, the whole idea can be perceived as dehumanizing HRM processes and pushing responsibility for making decisions to anonymous external companies and machines.

2.4 Results of the Analysis

The results of the analysis of the selected publications are presented in Table 2.2. The last column indicates theoretical sources and examples of practical use. As some of these works discuss issues regarding the impact of BD on various HRM practices, it was decided arbitrarily to place a reference in one or more table rows. This way, numerous repetitions of literary sources were omitted. In the case of the absence of references, scientific speculation was used (Johnson et al., 2009) based on a logical combination of knowledge about HRM and BD (Alexander, 2006). In the "Threats/Risks/Dilemmas" column, the repeated elements have been replaced by the numbers explained under the table.

The implementation of BD in HRM is a breakthrough for both processes and managers who have been working for many years using similar cognitive, interpretative, decision-making, stimulating, and control patterns. Thanks to BD, new or hidden patterns can be discovered, and subsequently, recognized rules, rituals,

Table 2.2 Combination of HRM Practices and Big Data Consequences

HRM Practices	Opportunities/ Challenges	Threats/Risks/ Dilemmas *	Theoretical Foundations
			Practical Examples
HR planning	• Meeting with a new language • A new order, a new description of the world and a new reality • Experimenting with new methods of analysis, new models and new structures of data, constant learning to ask new questions, and building hypotheses • New tools and methods to draw conclusions • Maintaining a still-open mind • Taking into account the broader context, e.g., demographic or macroeconomic phenomena	[4], [5] • The pressure of facilitating • Simplifications and surrendering to the hidden assumptions of can cause social conflicts and disclosed specialists' incompetence • Incomprehensible language of argumentation that justifies sophisticated calculations • The temptation of continuously increasing analytical demands	Kaiser and Kraus (2014) Du Plessis and De Wet Fourie (2016) CIPD (2014b)
Recruitment and selection	• "Tracking recruitment" forces recruiters to renew contact with the candidate and the organization • Finding talents before they reach the labor market • Wider sources of knowledge about candidates	[1], [3], [4], [5] • The process of transferring responsibility for person–organization alignment violates the known organizational order and structure of power	Peck (2013) Kaiser and Kraus (2014) Forsyth (2016) Davenport et al. (2010) Dastin (2018) McDonald's (2019)

(Continued)

Table 2.2 (*Continued*) Combination of HRM Practices and Big Data Consequences

HRM Practices	Opportunities/ Challenges	Threats/Risks/ Dilemmas *	Theoretical Foundations
			Practical Examples
	• Permanent recognition, matching, and adaptation to the flowing "person-organization fit" pattern • Deeper insight into the labor market	• The need for extension of the communication system with candidates and extension of HRIS functionality raises costs • New patterns for these process are required • Various data may make recruitment more difficult than traditional recruitment and selection process	
Adaptation	• Confronting the behavior of a new employee with the organizational procedures and behavior of other employees • Quick response to conflicts • Removal of dangerous habits of "old" employees • Setting new organization improvement goals	[1], [6], [7] • Employee resistance and unpredictable organizational changes • Social tensions and economic losses • Deepening divisions and worsening intergenerational relations • Excessive adaptation of employees to algorithms	Not found CIPD (2014a), Marr (2013), Sparrow et al. (2015) Conklin et al. (2016)

(Continued)

Table 2.2 (*Continued*)   Combination of HRM Practices and Big Data Consequences

HRM Practices	Opportunities/ Challenges	Threats/Risks/ Dilemmas *	Theoretical Foundations Practical Examples
Appraisal	• Enriching the image of the employee's achievements, competencies, the possibility of continuous assessment • Finding outstanding employees • Finding new appraisal criteria and individualization • Bolstering the role of intuition based on weak premises • Constant monitoring of employee's achievements and behaviors to verifying intuitive assessments • Implementation of multi-criteria assessment process theory	[6], [7], [8] • Assessment system instability caused by changes in algorithms • New social competences are required to (re) shape human–new technology relationships	Kaiser and Kraus (2014) Sparrow et al. (2015)
Training and development	• A better understanding of the manner of the transformation of the employee development programs' effects into new ideas and the evolution of the organization	[7], [1], [2], [4], [9] • The necessity of reinvention of the organizational patterns of change management, entrepreneurship, intrapreneurship, and innovation discovering	Pentland (2014) Kaiser and Kraus (2014) CIPD (2014b), Sparrow et al. (2015)

(*Continued*)

Table 2.2 (*Continued*)   Combination of HRM Practices and Big Data Consequences

HRM Practices	Opportunities/ Challenges	Threats/Risks/ Dilemmas *	Theoretical Foundations
			Practical Examples
	• Chances for discovering the success factors of training • Better measurement of education techniques and methods, talents of trainers, coaches, managers, etc • Identifying opportunities and anticipating risks arising with employee's track of development by discovering tendencies and latent relations between different variables of the education process • Working with long time-series of observations allows discovering opportunities and risks by comparison between a plan of training and development	• Reverse mentoring and other similar techniques of organizational improvement require a special complex program of implementation and shaping organizational culture (especially bureaucratic one)	
Rewards and incentives	• Detailed data instead of aggregates • Individualization and adjustment to personal preferences	[1], [2], [6], [8], [9] • Difficulties in building one overall organizational, transparent reward system	Not found
			Sparrow et al. (2015), Conklin et al. (2016)

Table 2.2 (*Continued*)   Combination of HRM Practices and Big Data Consequences

HRM Practices	Opportunities/ Challenges	Threats/Risks/ Dilemmas *	Theoretical Foundations
			Practical Examples
	• The flexibility of assessment criteria and reward methods by creating a multidimensional image of activity and lifestyle of a person • Testing of the link between the incentives set and the reward system begins the construction of a specific form of micro-theory	• Permanent changes of rules lead to miscomprehensions between employees and activation of trade unions • Experimenting with the reward system can be very expensive and dangerous to the survival of an organization	
Career development	• Forming the basis for a broader presentation of the advantages and weaknesses of the person, • Individualization of employee career paths • Increasing the degree of utilization of employees' potential • Correction of previous wrong decisions • Detection of pathological career paths	[1], [3], [6], [9] • Failure to take into account those elements of human nature that are not recognized by algorithms but decide about leadership and management skills	O'Neil (2016), Peck (2013), Kaiser and Kraus (2014) CIPD (2014a) Forsyth (2016)

(*Continued*)

Table 2.2 (*Continued*)   Combination of HRM Practices and Big Data Consequences

HRM Practices	Opportunities/ Challenges	Threats/Risks/ Dilemmas *	Theoretical Foundations / Practical Examples
Layoff and voluntary turnover	• Preventing valuable employees from leaving • Early warning, • Churn analysis • Finding the best way to terminate the contract (e.g., severance relevant to the current situation of the dismissed person, treated as a member of the community) • Tracking the careers of former employees • Maintaining contact even after leaving work	[5], [1], [2], [4], [8] • Dehumanizing employee–organization relations, • No sense of responsibility • Lack of support in difficult moments of employees' lives	Peck (2013) Linkedin's congratulation mechanism CIPD (2014b)

* *Where:*

[1] Privacy issues.

[2] Ethical and law issues.

[3] Working analytics tools as a "black box" and hidden bias.

[4] Lack of information system and infrastructure support, excessive data diversity, overloading, redundancy, chaos.

[5] Lack of skilled HR analysts—troubles with measurement and interpretation of results.

[6] Patterns based on the past data do not reflect the current needs and situations.

[7] Inclusion of external standards in the analysis causes the disappearance of individual characteristics.

[8] Transferring responsibility outside the organization and to the machine.

[9] Discovered that new patterns require radical changes in organizational culture.

habits, etc. can be questioned. This leads to the inevitable confrontation of old solutions with a new picture of the world, new knowledge, and new possibilities. To achieve the desired improvement, it is necessary to undertake the challenges of reconciling two contradictions. On the one hand, due to costs, technical requirements, human limitations, and organizational potential, it is natural to collect and use data in accordance with the previously adopted models, concepts, formulas, tradition, etc. In this way, existing HRM practices can only be slightly improved. On the other hand, BD creates an opportunity for continuous searching and discovering new models, patterns, and methods, which leads to the reorganization of processes or even the initiation of new ones. Only then, as a result, real innovations will be introduced in HRM. However, these changes are always inhibited by organizational inertia and social resistance. Introducing BD to HRM practices creates a need for radical change at three levels.

At the personal level, leaders of change must ensure that the employee is aware of the gathering and processing of data and the purposes for which it is used. She/he should also be able to obtain an explanation of the decisions and even question the results of the analysis. The use of BD in HRM deepens the imbalance in relations between employees and organizations because the employer has a deeper insight, wider knowledge, and stronger tools. The task of the HR manager is to build a new kind of relationship between the employee and the organization in which the alignment is based on dynamically changing expectations, emerging opportunities, and mutual respect and trust. The benefits of implementing BD in HRM must be the joint participation of employees and organizations based on fair and simple principles.

At the organizational level, there is a need for a rethinking of the Human Resource Information System (HRIS) concepts, principles, and methods (Bondarouk et al., 2017). HRIS should not only meet the expectations of HR specialists but also encourage continuous improvement of HRM practices, models, and concepts. The emphasis on maintaining constant contact with employees, candidates, and the social environment is the first and simple but important improvement. HRIS must provoke HR managers to open minds and build an open HR information system. The BD implementation in HRM practices also forces HR managers to assume social responsibility and ethical challenges far beyond today's legal requirements.

The individual becomes more and more helpless against technology. Tracking and automatic data analysis allow finding any weaknesses or deficiencies that someone who has malicious intent and power can use (Calvard & Jeske, 2018). Hence, at a regional/national level, the new institutional, organizational, and law instruments should be created for equalizing the chances of using BD by big corporations, micro-enterprises, and individual employees.

Addressing the challenges mentioned above will cause the gap between practice and theory to decrease, and this is a huge benefit that has not yet been achieved in implementing HR management practices.

2.5 Conclusions and Future Research

The potential impact of BD on HRM practices identified above indicates serious personal and institutional, practical, and theoretical challenges that all subjects of economic and social relations will face. The proposals formulated above, especially those related to the establishing of new public institutions, as well as combining data from many existing ones, can be considered as idealization. However, without such institutions, the poor will become even poorer, and sustainable development will be unreal.

The presented method of analysis, especially the proposal to cross HRM practices with BD, provides a simple and universal way to identify challenges and problems using BD in HRM improvement in a specific company. General postulates formulated in Table 2.2 can be adapted to the priorities of the HRM strategy and analyzed from the perspectives of attributes of the possessed tools, characteristics of resources, details of practices, or bundle of practices. The application in this text and the approach based on practices, especially in the field of BD, can be considered as a simplified experiment. In further studies, it is possible to test other approaches (e.g., based on crossing types of resources: data segmentation and HR segmentation). Focusing on practices is the one, but not the only, way to create an analysis matrix.

References

Alexander, P. A. (2006). Evolution of a learning theory: A case study. *Educational Psychologist, 41*(4), 257–264.

Anku, J. S., Amewugah, B. K., Glover, M. K. (2018). Concept of reward management, reward system and corporate efficiency. *International Journal of Economics, Commerce and Management, 6*(2), 621–637.

Armstrong, M., Taylor, S. (2014). *Armstrong's Handbook of Human Resource Management Practice*. London: Kogan Page.

Arockia, S., Varnekha, S., Veneshia, A. (2017). The 17 V's of big data. *International Research Journal of Engineering and Technology, 4*(9), 329–333.

Baig, M., Shuib, L., Yadegaridehkordi, E. (2019). Big data adoption: State of the art and research challenges. *Information Processing and Management, 56*(6), 102095.

Bolton, R., Dongrie, V., Saran, C., Ferrier, S., Mukherjee, R., Söderström, J., Brisson, S. (2019). The Future of HR 2019: In the Know or in the No, *The Gulf between Action and Inertia*. [KPMG report]. Retrieved September 25, 2019, from https://assets. kpmg/content/dam/kpmg/pl/pdf/2019/05/pl-Raport-KPMG-The-future-of-HR-2019-In-the-Know-or-in-the-No.pdf

Bondarouk, T., Parry, E., Furtmueller, E. (2017). Electronic HRM: Four decades of research on adoption and consequences. *International Journal of Human Resource Management. 28*(1), 98–131.

Borne, K. (2014, April 12). Top 10 List – The V's of Big Data, *Data Science Central* [Blog post]. Retrieved October 5, 2019, from https://www.datasciencecentral.com/profiles/blogs/top-10-list-the-v-s-of-big-data

Bratton, J., Gold, J. (2007). *Human Resource Management: Theory and Practice*. Basingstoke: Macmillan.

Calvard, T., Jeske, D. (2018). Developing human resource data risk management in the age of big data. *International Journal of Information Management*, *43*, 159–164.

Cascio, W. F. (2002). *Responsible Restructuring: Creative and Profitable Alternatives to Layoffs*. San Francisco, CA: BerrettKoehler Publishers.

Cassar, V., Bezzina, F. (2017). Evidence-based HRM through analytics: Reducing the propensity of HRM to become a cinderella. *Management Sciences*, *32*(4), 3–10.

Cheng, M., Hackett, R. (2019). A critical review of algorithms in HRM: Definition, theory, and practice. *Human Resource Management Review*, Available online 21 June, 2019, doi: 10.1016/j.hrmr.2019.100698

CIPD. (2014a). Talent's Talent for Creating Talent at ArcelorMittal, *Chartered Institute of Personnel and Development* [White paper]. Retrieved October 2, 2019, from https://www.cipd.co.uk/Images/case-study-arcelormittal-260516_tcm18-19984.pdf

CIPD. (2014b). Microsoft: The Four Stages of Analytical Life: HRBI at Microsoft, *Chartered Institute of Personnel and Development* [White paper]. Retrieved October 2, 2019, from https://www.cipd.co.uk/Images/case-study-microsoft-260516_tcm18-19990.pdf

Conklin, C., Abebe, N., Petrelli, J. (2016). Population Health Management: A New Business Model for a Healthier Workforce, *2016 Workplace trends*, [Sodexo white paper]. Retrieved October 12, 2019, from http://sodexoinsights.com/wp-content/uploads/2016/03/Workplace%20Trends%202016%20Final.pdf

Curry, E. (2015). The big data value chain: Definitions, concepts, and theoretical approaches. In: J. Cavanillas, J. Curry, E. Wahlster (Eds.), *New Horizons for a Data-Driven Economy: A Roadmap for Usage and Exploitation of Big Data in Europe*. Heidelberg: Springer.

Dastin, J. (2018). Amazon Scraps Secret AI Recruiting Tool That Showed Bias Against Women. Retrieved October 8, 2019, from https://uk.reuters.com/article/us-amazon-com-jobs-automation-insight/amazon-scraps-secret-ai-recruiting-tool-that-showed-bias-against-women-idUKKCN1MK08G

Davenport, T., Harris, J., Shapiro, J. (2010). Competing on talent analytics. *Harvard Business Review*. *88*, 52–58.

DeCenzo, D. A., Robbins, S. P., Verhuls, S. L. (2010). *Fundamentals of Human Resource Management*. Chichester: Wiley.

De Vos, A., Buyens, D., Schalk, R. (2003). Psychological contract development during organizational socialization: Adaptation to reality and the role of reciprocity. *Journal of Organizational Behavior*, *24*(5), 537–559.

Du Plessis, A. J., De Wet Fourie, L. (2016). Big data and HRIS used by HR practitioners: Empirical evidence from a longitudinal study. *Journal of Global Business & Technology*, *12*(2), 44–55.

Feloni R. (2017). Consumer-goods Giant Unilever Has Been Hiring Employees Using Brain Games and Artificial Intelligence — And It's a Huge Success, *Business Insider*, June 28. Retrieved October 12, 2019, from https://www.businessinsider.com/unilever-artificial-intelligence-hiring-process-2017-6?IR=T

Forsyth, A. (2016, February 2). Watson Analytics Use Case for HR: Retaining valuable employees, *IBM Watson Analyst Community* [Blog post]. Retrieved October 11, 2019, from https://www.ibm.com/blogs/business-analytics/watson-analytics-use-case-for-hr-retaining-valuable-employees/

Greenwood, M., Van Buren, H. (2017). Ideology in HRM scholarship: interrogating the ideological performativity of 'New Unitarism'. *Journal of Business Ethics*, *142*(4), 663–678.

HireVue. (2019). Unilever Finds Top Talent Faster with HireVue Assessments. Retrieved October 21, 2019, from https://www.hirevue.com/customers/global-talent-acquisition-unilever-case-study

Huselid, M., Minbaeva, D. (2019). Big data and human resource management. In: A. Wilkinson, N. Bacon, L. Lepak, S. Snell (Eds.), *Sage Handbook of Human Resource Management*. Los Angeles, London, New Delhi, Singapore, Washington DC, Melbourne: SAGE Publications Ltd.

Jacobson, W. (2010). Preparing for tomorrow: A case study of workforce planning in North Carolina municipal governments. *Public Personnel Management, 39*(4), 1–21.

Johnson, W., Carothers, A., Deary, I. J. (2009). Speculation to inform and speculation to explore, response to Craig et al., (2009) and Turkheimer & Halpern. *Perspectives on Psychological Science, 4*(6), 622–623.

Kaiser, S., Kraus, H. (2014). Big data im personal-management. *Zeitschrift Führung + Organisation, 83*(6), 379–385.

Karren, R., Sherman, K. (2012). Layoffs and unemployment discrimination: A new stigma. *Journal of Managerial Psychology, 27*(8), 848–863.

Keenoy, T. (1999). HRM as hologram: A polemic. *Journal of Management Studies, 36*(1), 1–23.

Khan, M., Uddin, M., Gupta, N. (2014). Seven V's of Big Data: Understanding Big Data to Extract Value, *Proceedings of the 2014 Zone 1 Conference of the American Society for Engineering Education*, Bridgeport, CT, April 3–5, 1–5. doi: 10.1109/ASEEZone1.2014.6820689

Khawaja, J., Nadeem, A. B. (2013). Training and development program and its benefits to employee and organization: A conceptual study. *European Journal of Business and Management, 5*(2), 243–252.

Kitchin, R. (2014). Big data, new epistemologies and paradigm shifts. *Big Data & Society, 1*(1), 1–12.

Krishnan, K. (2013). *Data Warehousing in the Age of Big Data*, Waltham, MA: Morgan Kaufman.

Laney, D. (2001). 3D Data Management: Controlling Data Volume, Velocity, and Variety, Application Delivery Strategies, Meta Group Inc., whitepaper, File: 949. Retrieved October 10, 2019, from https://blogs.gartner.com/doug-laney/files/2012/01/ad949-3D-Data-Management-Controlling-Data-Volume-Velocity-and-Variety.pdf

Levenson, A., Pillans, G. (2017). Strategic Workforce Analytics, *Corporate Research Forum*. Retrieved October 10, 2019, from https://www.concentra.co.uk/uploads/2019/04/strategic-workforce-analytics-report.pdf

Levesque, L. L. (2005). Opportunistic hiring and employee fit. *Human Resource Management, 44*(3), 301–317.

Markoulli, M., Lee, C., Byington, E., Felps, W. A. (2017). Mapping human resource management: Reviewing the field and charting future directions. *Human Resource Management Review, 27*(3), 367–396.

Marr, B. (2013). From Data to Decisions. Lessons from the field, *Chartered Professional Accountants of Canada*. Retrieved October 16, 2019, from https://www.cpacanada.ca/en/business-and-accounting-resources/management-accounting/management-reporting-needs-and-systems/publications/evidence-based-management-a-three-part-series/evidence-based-management-case-studies

Marr, B. (2016a). The Most Practical Big Data Use Cases of 2016. *Forbes*, August 25.

Marr, B. (2016b). *Big Data in Practice: How 45 Successful Companies Used Big Data Analytics to Deliver Extraordinary Results*. Chichester: John Wiley & Sons, Ltd.

Martin, K. E. (2015). Ethical issues in the big data industry. *MIS Quarterly Executive, 14*(2), 67–85.

Mayer-Schönberger V., Cukier K. (2013). *Big Data: A Revolution That Will Transform How We Live, Work, and Think*. London: John Murray Publishers.

Mazzei, M., Noble D. (2017). Big data dreams: A framework for corporate strategy. *Business Horizons, 60*(3), 405–414.

McDonald's. (2019). Finding a Job at McDonald's is Now as Simple as Asking Alexa. Retrieved October 25, 2019, from https://news.mcdonalds.com/Introducing-McDonald%E2%80%99s-Apply-Thru/

McLean, S., Stakim, C., Timner, H., Lyon, C. (2015). *Big Data and Human Resources: Letting the Computer Decide?* Washington, DC: The Bureau of National Affairs Inc., Retrieved November 10, 2019, from https://www.jdsupra.com/legalnews/big-data-and-human-resourcesletting-the-91679/

Morrison, M. (2012). Google's Project Oxygen – 8 Point Plan to Help Managers Improve. RapidBi. Retrieved September 26, 2019, from https://rapidbi.com/google-project-oxygen-8-point-plan-to-help-managers/

O'Neil, C. (2016). *Weapons of Math Destruction: How Big Data Increases Inequality and Threatens Democracy*. New York: Crown.

Pasquale, F. (2015). *The Black Box Society: The Secret Algorithms that Control Money and Information*. Cambridge, MA: Harvard University Press.

Peck, D. (2013). They're Watching You at Work. What Happens When Big Data Meets Human Resources? The emerging practice of "people analytics" is already transforming how employers hire, fire, and promote. Retrieved October 2, 2019, from https://www.theatlantic.com/magazine/archive/2013/12/theyre-watching-you-at-work/354681/

Pentland, A. (2014). *Social Physics. How Good Ideas Spreed – The Lesson from a New Science*. New York: The Penguin Press.

Pilbeam, S., Corbridge M. (2010). *People Resourcing and Talent Planning. Human Resource in Practice*. London: Prentice Hall.

Pološki Vokić N., Vidović, M. (2008). HRM as a significant factor for achieving competitiveness through people: The croatian case. *International Advances in Economic Research. 14*(3), 303–315.

Price, A. (2007). *Human Resource Management in a Business Context*. London: Thomson Learning.

Raguseo, E. (2018). Big data technologies: An empirical investigation on their adoption, benefits and risks for companies. *International Journal of Information Management, 38*(1), 187–195.

Schneider, B., Hanges, P. J., Smith, D. B., Salvaggio, A. N. (2003). Which comes first: Employee attitudes or organizational financial and market performance? *Journal of Applied Psychology, 88*(5), 836–851.

Scholz, T. M. (2017). *Big Data in Organizations and the Role of Human Resource Management: A Complex Systems Theory-Based Conceptualization*. Frankfurt: International Academic Publishers, Peter Lang.

Shafer, T. (2017). The 42 V's of Big Data and Data Science. Retrieved September 29, 2019, from https://www.kdnuggets.com/2017/04/42-vs-Big-Data-Data-science.html

Silverman, R., Waller, N. (2015). The Algorithm That Tells the Boss Who Might Quit, Wal-Mart, Credit Suisse Crunch Data to See Which Workers Are Likely to Leave or Stay. *Wall Street Journal*, March 13. Retrieved October 12, 2019, from https://www.wsj.com/articles/the-algorithm-that-tells-the-boss-who-might-quit-1426287935

Sparrow, P., Hird, M., Cooper, C. (2015). *Do We Need HR? Repositioning People Management for Success*. Basingstoke: Palgrave Macmillan.

Sun, J. Y., Wang, G. G. (2012). Career development. In: W. J. Rothwell, R. K. Prescott (Eds.), *The Encyclopedia of Human Resource Management*, *1*, 98–102. Short Entries. San Francisco, CA: John Wiley and Sons.

Thompson, P. (2011). The trouble with HRM. *Human Resource Management Journal*, *21*(4), 355–367.

Tursunbayevaa, A., Di Lauroc, S., Pagliaria, C. (2018). People analytics—A scoping review of conceptual boundaries and value propositions. *International Journal of Information Management*, *43*, 224–247.

Van Dijk, D., Schodl, M. M. (2015). Performance appraisal and evaluation. In: J. D. Wright (Ed.), *International Encyclopedia of the Social & Behavioral Sciences*, *17*, 716–721. Oxford: Elsevier.

Ward J., Barker A. (2013). Undefined by Data: A Survey of Big Data Definitions, preprint arXiv:1309.5821, Retrieved October 13, 2019, from http://www.adambarker.org/papers/BigData_definition.pdf

Ware J. (2016). Big Data in the Workplace: Can It Enhance Employee Productivity and Quality of Life? In: 2016 Workplace trends, online: http://sodexoinsights.com/wp-content/uploads/2016/03/Workplace%20Trends%202016%20Final.pdf

White, M. C., Marin, D. B., Brazeal, D. V., Friedman, W. H. (1997). The evolution of organizations: Suggestions from complexity theory about the interplay between natur-alselection and adaptation. *Human Relations, 50*(11), 1383–1401.

Chapter 3

Knowledge Management and Big Data in Business

Jerzy Gołuchowski and Barbara Filipczyk

University of Economics in Katowice

Contents

3.1 Introduction

Organizations operating in a dynamic, complex, and sometimes hard to predict business and social environment need up-to-date knowledge to conduct their business best (Abhishek & Divyashree, 2019; Soniewicki & Paliszkiewicz, 2019; Ying-Yen, 2019).

As a result of progressive digitization and related profound changes—not only technological but also social—the "parameters" of known situations as well as the framework ("boundary") conditions of business activity change; new, previously unknown situations appear and are unlike the previous ones (Obitade, 2019).

This chapter aims to present the perspectives on the use of Big Data as evidence in the management of the knowledge necessary to improve business processes. In this chapter, we initially focus on the challenges within the area of knowledge management that the organizations face during the time of Big Data and AI Analytics. It is followed by the presentation of the approach toward knowledge management in the context of Big Data. In order to illustrate the presented theoretical solutions and emerging technological possibilities of improving knowledge management, we outline a conception that targeted for the acquisition and utilization of Big Data to improve knowledge management in the student onboarding process. This chapter ends with a conclusion summarizing the undertaken considerations.

3.2 Situation and Challenges in Theory and Practice of Knowledge Management in the Era of the Big Data

Organizations today also acquire the resources they need to conduct business, including not only raw materials, machines (tools), capital but also knowledge (Al-Azzam & Al-Qura'an, 2019; Hidalgo-Peñate et al., 2019). Do they do it differently than before? Do they have new possibilities, and what are they? How do organizations acquire knowledge? How do they procure it from the outside, and how do they create it inside? What processes do they realize based on knowledge? How do they manage knowledge resources and processes based knowledge? What knowledge management strategies, technologies, and IT tools do they use? Where do organizations obtain the knowledge necessary to operate and conduct business? How are the processes of generating new knowledge organized, leading to innovation in organizations? How are these processes managed? How to improve the management of knowledge, resources, and knowledge processes? These are only selected questions that bother the organizations' practitioners and theoreticians.

The management's thinking, even when they consider the past and the present, is focused on shaping the future either by adapting to the perceived changes or by conducting innovative interventions. Thus, each of the above questions regarding knowledge management, when formulated by a practitioner (a manager), has a subtext regarding the future. For example, by asking the question of how organizations acquire new knowledge from Big Data, they are trying to determine how their organization is to do it in the future.

Running a business can be considered not only through the prism of resource management but also through the prism of managing business processes implemented in the organization, and process patterns can be treated as a significant knowledge resource.

Undoubtedly, changes in the environment should be seen and analyzed as soon as possible to optimize business processes and get the best direction for the organization. Managers of organizations must, therefore, analyze the processes or commission analyzes. This is seen in the example of conducting e-commerce: it is possible to dynamically change prices depending on the state of balance of demand and supply of individual goods. In the case of e-commerce, the knowledge about what and how to analyze and how to decide based on these results (at least part of these decisions) is built into the sales system.

Knowledge is necessary not only for efficient business processes but also to improve them. In order to improve the business process, e.g., customer service (sales) processes, you need a different kind of knowledge: knowledge about the course of processes, about potential changes in the attitudes or preferences of potential customers, the undertaken and planned activities of competitors, etc. The changes mentioned above in the area of e-commerce are an example of new trends initiated by the digital revolution. Digital technologies cause not only the transformation of the organization toward a so-called digital organization, affect not only the change in the implementation of many business processes implemented so far but they also affect the processes of analyzing business processes. Such opportunities arise due to the accumulation of rich knowledge about the course of business processes and the conditioning of these processes in a digital form, Big Data, and the access to new analysis tools (data processing) based on artificial intelligence and deep learning. The digital form increases the availability of knowledge and greatly facilitates the analysis of large data sets.

The need for current knowledge in management is not something new that only appeared in the 20th or 21st century. Information (knowledge) has always been valuable and necessary to make meaningful decisions. However, relatively recently, it has been realized that it is an important resource of the organization, and therefore, like any other resource of the organization, it should be managed. Such an approach to the organization's information and knowledge is new in both management research and management practice. The perspective of knowledge management of an organization allows to perceive new management situations and propose new, more relevant solutions for the efficient running of the business by business and non-business organizations.

The list of questions that knowledge management researchers are trying to answer is open. The first research questions in this theoretical and managerial perspectives were formulated by Drucker (1992, 2012), Probst, Raub and Romhardt (2000), Nonaka and Takeuchi (1995), Liebowitz and Wilcox (1997), Liebowitz (1999, 2005), Davenport and Prusak (2000), and Gasparski (2007). After approximately 20 years of research work on knowledge management, many of them are still valid, and new ones have appeared. New research issues are not only the result of obtaining answers to existing ones, but they also result from a change in the reality of business at the threshold of the third decade of the 21st century. The business reality is constantly evolving, also under the influence of technological changes, so new research challenges and the need to re-think on the questions that were once formulated are understandable. Such issues include the issue of organizational knowledge management in the era of almost universal access to Big Data.

Answers to research questions posed on the organization's knowledge management are formulated as part of three basic theoretical approaches: the resource approach, the process approach, and the system (Japanese) approach (see Paliszkiewicz, 2017, 2019). Sometimes, the integrated approach is also mentioned, e.g., Pourdehnad, Wexler and Wilson (2011). Each of them presents research problems differently, assesses them differently, and, as a result, receives different answers. Accepting research perspectives is like observing a room from different places and reporting what we see, e.g., when we look at it through a keyhole, the door ajar, or a slightly exposed window.

Both managers and scientists must not only study but also shape (study and shape) the organizational reality. The scientists do this, especially utilizing the formulation of postulative theories, in the postulate, normative movement. The managers do this through decisions, most fully in the processes of designing a future organizational reality, including designing patterns of future business processes. We treat design, after Gasparski (1978, 1991, 2007), as a conceptual preparation of activities (work). Therefore, it applies not only to physical artifacts but also to services, ideas, strategies, and business processes.

Based on the data and knowledge about the situation in the past and present, organizations want to "construct a future", which we only partially influence. It seems that the system and design approach aids in dealing with the challenges of thinking about the future. System thinking supports what is being constructed. Design thinking supports both how the future is being constructed (designed) and how to construct it (future activities, products, services, messages, etc.). In literature, one can also encounter considerations that integrate both approaches— integrated thinking (e.g., Douglas, 2003; Martin, 2009).

As shown above, in terms of improving business processes as well as managing knowledge in business processes, knowledge is necessary in order not only to utilize resources optimally but also to improve organizational processes, also taking into account the resources required for their implementation. The starting point of the optimization of processes of effective usage of available data and information is the stocktaking of knowledge regarding all business processes or the ones selected for improvement. Their course can be documented by, among others, Big Data. This approach to the usage of available knowledge leads to the application of the idea of evidence-based management in the area of business process management (BPM), including in the area of knowledge management, and the improvement of these processes.

3.3 Evidence-Based Management versus Knowledge Management in the Big Data Era

The term "evidence-based" was originally developed in the 1990s in the field of medicine (see Sackett et al., 2000). Today, the term is used in various disciplines, such as education, criminology, public politics, social work, and (recently) management. The concept of **evidence-based practice** refers to it. The starting point for the concept of evidence-based management is the belief that decisions in the field of organization management should be based on the connection (integration) of critical thinking with the collection of the best available evidence (see Rousseau, 2006). "Evidence" means information, facts, or data confirming (or negating) an assertion, an assumption, or a hypothesis (Steglitz et al., 2015). Evidence can come from scientific research, but it can also be created by internal business information and work experience. Undoubtedly, Big Data are perspective evidence for process management and knowledge management. This is illustrated by the success of IBM's Watson system, i.a. in diagnosing diseases and the development of epidemics. The Watson system is a cognitive computer system—capable of answering questions asked in natural language. It was developed as part of the IBM-DeepQA project by a research team led by David Ferrucci. The system was named after IBM's first president, Thomas J. Watson. Answers are formulated based on evidence (e.g., in the form of cases collected in practice, test results, etc.).

All managers base their decisions on some "evidence". One could, therefore, consider that all management is evidence-based. However, many managers do not pay enough attention or pay insufficient attention to the quality of evidence on which they base their decisions. There is a deficiency in their thinking and action, as well as the reflection on the sources of knowledge that they use in the decision-making processes. As a result, management decisions are often based on so-called "best practices" or storytelling about the reasons for the success of famous or known managers. The management practice-based/founded on the concept of evidence-based management aims to remedy this state of affairs, helping managers to critically assess the legitimacy, generalization, and usefulness of their evidence and how to find the "best available evidence". This also applies to the "treatment" of business processes and the improvement of knowledge management processes using Big Data.

In order to use Big Data as a source of evidence in making decisions that shape business processes, managers should make better use of both their knowledge management achievements as well as Big Data and business intelligence or have employees with such competences at their disposal. For example, they should know how to search for evidence (e.g., research results) in online databases, how to analyze Big Data to extract valuable knowledge, and how to assess the validity and usefulness of the research found. Knowledge managers, and in particular participants in improving business processes, should be aware of making assumptions in practice—consciously or not fully consciously—and of the need to reflect on the assumptions mentioned above. This includes not only knowledge in the field of research and methodology, in particular, knowledge management and critical thinking methods to balance the subjectivity of their assessments and cognitive limitations (see Filipczyk & Gołuchowski, 2019). They must be aware of the need to understand what type of situation is being analyzed (e.g., ordinary or extraordinary). Understanding the situation conditions the use of Big Data when the situation is ordinary and when it is extraordinary (VUCA—four dimensions of a situation: Volatility, Uncertainty, Complexity, Ambiguity)? What knowledge of the past can be used to construct the future of the organization? What will Big Data analyses be useful for this?

3.4 Improvement of Business Processes Using the Management Concept Based on Big Data

In recent years, many scientific studies have been conducted on various issues related to management practice. The research topics include i.a. employment, employee motivation, setting goals (especially strategic), entrepreneurship, merger management, conducting management training, process improvement methods or employee selection, evaluation, and onboarding. In terms of processes, these topics are related to BPM.

Traditional Enterprise Resource Planning (ERP) systems support the management of company resources in individual, organizational departments, e.g., human resources. BPM systems also support the management of defined organization activities—processes. This way of computerizing the company is consistent with its natural functioning. Repeatable processes can be automated. BPM shows that progress in management improvement is possible due to both process automation and the automation of analysis of their course, acquiring the necessary knowledge from Big Data created in the course of business processes. However, new technologies provide further opportunities for improving processes using evidence-based management ideas.

Organizations use BPM to model and manage existing processes.

It would seem that having large data sets on past activities, organizations had tools that allow them to formulate—based on the data on the past and present—an answer to every new question about the future. However, the situation is more complicated. The analysis and design of future reality (construction and operation of the system under consideration) require ontological, epistemological, axiological, and even technological assumptions (Filipczyk & Gołuchowski, 2019). The need to analyze the assumptions made, also in the course of Big Data analysis, results from the fact that there is no raw data—they are always entangled in certain world views, world visions, theories, or ideologies. Big Data are an objective result of the digitization of the organization and the environment, but they were created as a result of people's decisions and sometimes as a result of not making decisions. Thus, intentions, goals, and value systems affect knowledge management processes as well as real analysis and design processes. The manner of their influence is not entirely known and unambiguous, as it concerns the future that what will emerge from the actions of the organization and activities in its environment. Therefore, managers looking to the future must anticipate the direction of its change, make assumptions about the direction of these changes, their depth, etc. Sometimes these changes are consistent with the VUCA situation model described by Bennett and Lemoine (2014).

As shown in many publications, i.a. to improve organizational reality neither Big Data alone nor only intuition manifested in adopting model assumptions, assumptions about the possible shape of a variable future are enough. As shown, i.a. in the book by Liebowitz, Paliszkiewicz, Gołuchowski (2018) "Intuition, trust, and analytics", a skillful combination of intuition and analytics is needed. Intuition must relate to the adequate organizational model, which in a given situation, is the most appropriate. The selection of the organizational model to adopt requires analysis, but also intuition resulting from experience, the acquired tacit knowledge. For example, which metaphor best supports the change and process improvement? The organism metaphor (Morgan, 1998; Sułkowski, 2011) directs our thinking toward adaptive actions, or the incorporation of new cells into the organism to trigger the adaptive mechanism. The metaphor of the game makes focuses on the motivations and rules of the game. It is a mix of analysis and intuition that suggests a solution that can prove effective. What is more, it encourages the use of serious games to improve management.

When analyzing and designing organizational reality (e.g., business process patterns) based on Big Data, the manager and the analyst:

1. Think at the ontological level, considering what exists, what will exist in the future, what should exist (be constructed). Manovich (2014) writes about a community rooted in software, about a software culture. This also applies to construct organizational reality. They distinguish not only specific objects but also changes, activities, processes, states, and situations.
2. Treat the analyzed fragment of reality as a system. They organize the knowledge in the form of a designed system but also think about specific situations and also want to manage the knowledge for its solution.
3. Set the system boundaries and its relationships with the environment, set the limits of interest in reality. Apart from that, they separate what is interesting for the organization from what is not interesting.
4. Are not free from evaluative judgments. On the axiology and ethics level, they decide what is acceptable and valuable to the organization and its stakeholders.
5. At the epistemological level, they adopt what knowledge is, what knowledge, and where to obtain it from (sources of knowledge).
6. On the methodological level, they choose the methodology, decide how to organize the analysis or system design.

7. On the organizational/management level, they decide how to manage change and the process of its preparation using the selected metaphor of the organization (e.g., modeling the organization as a game).
8. At the technological level, they choose which tools to use in the process of analyzing and designing changes.

Scientific experience confirms that there is no raw data or pure facts. Is this true in the age of Big Data? Are they always entangled in theories, interpretations, and models of reality? We see that the issues of using and analyzing Big Data fit into the broader decision-making context. The technological aspect of data modeling, and therefore, their formalization and operationalization for the needs of analysis, especially automated, is only one of many areas of knowledge management using Big Data analytics, where there are limitations that require good solutions. However, even in this area, there are many challenges. One of them is that, according to IBM research, as much as 80% of the data available in the organization is unstructured (George et al., 2014). So, there is a significant opportunity to leverage in the analysis of unstructured data. Unlocking this potential represents the next Big Data challenge for businesses, concerning how to use Big Data to extract useful information to make more informed decisions and develop a competitive advantage.

This makes their use a significant challenge. Unlocking this potential in making more informed decisions and in developing a competitive advantage by analyzing this data is another challenge for companies in terms of using large data sets to obtain useful information (Rajaraman & Ullman, 2011). Moreover, another technological challenge arises from the fact that Big Data that can be used in the decision-making situation under consideration is usually incomplete because no one in the organization has previously thought that Big Data can be used in a new and innovative way to improve business processes. Yet another challenge is using Big Data regularly. How should a system learn from Big Data analysis when each new situation different from the previous one? How to improve learning algorithms using knowledge and communication management theories?

Big Data analyses use both the notions of states and situations. However, we consciously (or unconsciously) evaluate them, even in terms of ordinary and extraordinary situations. Modeling reality in accordance with the VUCA model shows that due to the available knowledge about changes in reality both in the environment and in the organization (the analyzed situation), only in specific situations and through creative methods one can infer—from the knowledge of the past and the present—about the future and obtain new knowledge useful to act in the future states of the analyzed reality. It seems that new technologies come to aid in process improvement, even in emergencies considered in the VUCA model.

It is impossible to show all of the challenges posed by Big Data analysis in organizations. Therefore, we shall limit ourselves to an example.

3.5 Improving Student Onboarding Using the Knowledge Management Conception Based on Big Data Analysis and Gamification

To illustrate the considerations on the transformation of knowledge management when connected with the use of Big Data (to improve processes), we will present a selected example from the reality of Polish universities. We present the prospects of using Big Data following the concept of evidence-based management in improving students' onboarding process. The improvement is focused on personalizing the knowledge provided to students starting studies at a selected university.

3.5.1 Situation Analysis

In management theory, it is recommended to follow the principle of providing the right information (knowledge), at the right time and in the right form, to the right users. Difficulties in maintaining a specific information balance, or in following the just-in-time principles in providing knowledge are noticeable to all who start a cooperation with the organization, including students who have undergone the recruitment process and begin their studies at the university. Adaptation of new students in a new environment encounters difficulties in providing them with knowledge and acquiring it by them in the course of the conducted communication processes also for this group of university stakeholders. Students come from various social, more, and more often, cultural backgrounds and have different experiences and expectations. According to Gazeta Prawna (2019), in the 2018/2019 academic year, as many as 78.3 thousand foreigners applied for studies in Poland. The majority of foreigners came from European countries, with the largest group consisting of people from Ukraine (39.2 thousand). The next largest are students from Belarus (7.3 thousand) and India (3.6 thousand).

This leads to the search for solutions that improve students' start at the university (student onboarding). The complexity of student onboarding is reinforced by a large number of students starting their studies at the same time.

Onboarding students is not an activity that amounts merely to the so-called orientation, socialization, or adaptation of students in the new environment. Orientation is an effort aimed at ensuring the successful transition of new students from high school learning to a college education. The goal of orientation is to facilitate the transition to university and to transfer key institutional expectations to students (see, e.g., Boening & Miller, 2005; Mayhew et al., 2016). By becoming students, the applicants change their role from external to internal stakeholders.

The publication (Sandoval-Lucero et al., 2017) describes the process of implementing the compulsory orientation of students of a selected university—the university in Colorado. Studies have shown that the implemented orientation program has contributed to increasing the effects of student retention and more effective studying from the very beginning of their higher education. This illustrates the potential of student onboarding processes.

However, it is worth noting that the orientation run by universities usually lasts one, two, or three days and is usually the event beginning the "onboarding" the university. Student onboarding is conceptualized as a continuous process that aims to achieve several goals. The notion of onboarding and its models were presented i.a. in Van Maanen and Schein (1979) and Bauer and Erdogan (2011). Onboarding is a continuous process that usually lasts for at least the entire first year and sometimes extends to the second year of study.

Onboarding for students is one of the most important elements of talent development at the university. Therefore, the "boarding" requires an efficient communication process to transfer the knowledge necessary to understand the new environment relatively quickly and in a convenient form, so that new students can function efficiently and achieve their set goals. What often transpires is that talented and vulnerable people do not function well in a new environment, and in the first days, they decide to quit their studies.

3.5.2 Shortcomings of the Current Onboarding System

Employee onboarding research presented among others in an article (Bauer & Erdogan, 2011) confirms that "onboarding" is of key importance for building relationships between a new employee (more broadly the organization's stakeholder) and the organization. The study showed that organized and continuous support had a significant positive impact on work results. When the level of support from the team and the leaders was high, new employees often had a more positive attitude to their work and worked more effectively. When support was not offered, the opposite situation arose, leading to the production of disappointed and less productive employees who left the organization more often than those who experienced effective onboarding processes. The sooner new employees feel welcome in the organization and are better prepared to start work, the sooner they can effectively contribute to the organization's mission. Undoubtedly, this also applies to students who constitute a specific group of internal stakeholders of the university.

When starting studies at a Polish university, students receive a variety of support. Meetings are organized, leaflets are delivered, information is available on the university and student parliament website. Students gain access to the virtual university system. They start communicating on Facebook by creating their groups. No matter how effective one-day or several-day orientation can be, it is hard to believe (it is unbelievable) that the assumed goals can be achieved in just one and the first week of study.

As already mentioned, the preparation, attitude, and students' expectations toward universities are different, and thus students expect a different range of support in the adaptation process. Interviews with administration employees show that there is insufficient knowledge of what students expect. Moreover, expectations are variable. Each subsequent year does not necessarily expect the same support as its predecessors. Often, real needs are not taken into account when preparing materials for onboarding, as no research on the needs is carried out. The current onboarding system does not take into account the diversity of expectations of new students, and there is no possibility of personalizing the transferred knowledge. This system does not support maintaining the specific information balance—the just-in-time principle in providing knowledge.

3.5.3 The Conception of Student Onboarding Improvement Using Big Data Acquired in the Serious Game

While analyzing the onboarding process at selected Polish universities, it was noticed that the main problem is the dispersion of knowledge available to students and, as a consequence, the inability to personalize the knowledge necessary in the onboarding process. This makes it difficult or even impossible, to provide the right knowledge to the right students at the right time. To a large extent, this applies to many universities, including foreign ones. This is also confirmed by the research conducted by the authors using the participatory method and focus interviews among students.

The noticed problem in providing knowledge that is necessary for the onboarding process is a consequence of the adopted approach to knowledge and communication management for students as well as the maladjustment of technologies and processes to the needs of students in the onboarding process. To overcome the indicated problem, it is necessary to acquire knowledge about the expectations (conscious and unconscious), and the behavior of students. This requires an audit of both knowledge and communication as well as a proposal for new solutions. It is necessary to reach new sources of knowledge and innovative methods of student involvement. The conducted surveys turn out to be too expensive and delayed in time in relation to the needs in terms of the expected knowledge. Acquiring knowledge about the needs and preferences of students in a different way than previously used is an important challenge for knowledge management theory and practice.

The preliminary research work undertaken by the authors shows that a computer game simulating a university and made available to candidates for studies can be a source of reliable knowledge necessary for students. As part of this game, the individuals learn about the organization, receive specific tasks related to the implementation of their roles. Students leaving digital traces of their activities in the virtual world allow the analysis of their needs and difficulties. Contact with the game can start before the start of studies, before the orientation event. It is possible to provide students with materials for independent learning before their arrival at universities on adaptation days. This enables students to assimilate knowledge at their own pace, at a convenient time and, if necessary, return to the materials provided to them whenever they see such a need. Of course, orientation before arrival cannot wholly replace orientation when students appear within the walls of the university. However, it can be much more useful, especially when their motivation to familiarize themselves with the material will be strengthened by game mechanisms.

It is also possible to use the best practices applied at universities in the game implementation. They show the benefits of continuous student onboarding for at least the first semester. Topics ideal for such a program, possible in the form of tasks in the game, include taking notes, time management, dealing with culture shock, getting along and communicating on sensitive topics, learning skills, useful learning applications, additional writing support—in particular highlighting how to avoid plagiarism, and general question and answer sessions on academic or cultural topics.

The interface of the university prototype game is shown in Figure 3.1. It is assumed that the player takes on the role of a student. His task is to complete the studies on time. Indicators that allow the tracking of game progress include, among others:

■ Progress of the semester dissertation
■ Group acceptance level
■ Additional activities (e.g., science club, the Silesianie song, and dance ensemble)
■ Position on the scholarship list
■ The number of the remaining semesters

The interface was designed by Przemysław Piwoni, Daniel Rejman, Arleta Stekla, Patryk Zbiciak. It is the result of the project developed on the course Game Interface and Multimedia Applications Design class led by dr Barbara Filipczyk during the third semester of the bachelor studies in Computer Science.

Figure 3.1 **The interface of the prototype university game.**

The game can be treated as part of a system that collects data about students, equipped with mechanisms of analysis, classification, and categorization. Based on the players' (students') behavior, it will allow building their profiles according to which it will be possible to provide them with appropriate support tailored to their expectations. The use of the game as a tool for gathering knowledge about the needs of students is an element of the matching of activities associated with the management of knowledge for students to the students' habits for whom games are almost natural activity environments. Big Data collected during the game will be a tool to improve the management of students' onboarding process.

3.6 Conclusion

This chapter is the short presentation of the results of literature research and considerations in the field of improvement of knowledge management using Big Data and should be treated as the starting point for the approach and further scientific research. The inclusion of the concept of an evidence-based approach in the considerations of Big Data seems to be a challenge for further research.

The outlined idea of using serious play, used in the student onboarding process, shows in practice how the ideas of evidence-based management can be realized in knowledge management and the management of the realized business processes. Serious play is treated as a tool for obtaining Big Data about the needs and preferences of students in terms of onboarding. Their analysis can lead to the improvement of knowledge management for students and the improvement of university management.

References

Abhishek, N., & Divyashree, M. S. (2019). Perception of knowledge management practices among HR managers: An analysis. *IUP Journal of Knowledge Management, 17*(3), 44–54.

Al-Azzam, Z., & Al-Qura'an, A. B. (2019). How knowledge management mediates the strategic role of talent management in enhancing customer's satisfaction. *Independent Journal of Management & Production, 10*(2), 334–354.

Bauer, T. N., & Erdogan, B. (2011). Organizational socialization: The effective onboarding of new employees. In S. Zedeck (Ed.), *APA Handbooks in Psychology®. APA Handbook of Industrial and Organizational Psychology*, Vol. 3. Maintaining, expanding, and contracting the organization (pp. 51–64). Washington, DC: American Psychological Association.

Bennett, N., & Lemoine, G. J. (2014). What a difference a word makes: Understanding threats to performance in a VUCA world. *Business Horizons, 57*(3), 311–317.

Boening, C. H., & Miller, M. T. (2005). New student orientation programs promoting diversity. *The Community College Enterprise, 11*(2), 41–50.

Davenport, T. H., & Prusak, L. (2000). *Working Knowledge: How Organizations Manage What They Know*. Boston, MA: Harvard Business School Press.

Douglas, G. (2003). Integrative thinking. *Innovative Leader, 11*, 589.

Drucker, P. F. (1992). The new society of organizations. *Harvard Business Review, 20*, 281–293.

Drucker, P. F. (2012). *The Practice of Management*. London: Routledge.

Filipczyk, B., Gołuchowski, J. (2018). Koncepcja zaangażowania menedżerów HR w zmianie procedury wyboru promotora pracy dyplomowej w uczelni [The concept of the involvement of HR managers in changing the procedure for selecting the thesis supervisor at the University]. *Zarządzanie Zasobami Ludzkimi, 5*, 11–26.

Gasparski, W. (1978). *Projektowanie koncepcyjne przygotowanie działań [Conceptual Design Preparation of Activities]*. Warszawa, PL: PWN.

Gasparski, W. (1991). Metodologia projektowania a metodologia ogólna i metodologia nauk praktycznych [Design methodology versus general methodology and methodology of practical sciences]. In: W. Gasparski, A. Strzałecki (eds.), *Logika, praktyka, etyka: Przesłania filozofii Tadeusza Kotarbińskiego*. Warszawa, PL: Towarzystwo Naukowe Prakseologii.

Gasparski, W. (2007). Wiedza o organizacji i zarządzaniu oraz jej poznawcze ugruntowanie [Knowledge of organisation and management and its cognitive consolidation]. *Współczesne Zarządzanie, 1*, 34–47.

George, G., Haas, M., & Pentland, A. (2014). Big data and management: From the editors. *Academy of Management Journal, 57*(2), 321–326.

Hidalgo-Peñate, A., Padrón-Robaina, V., & Nieves, J. (2019). Knowledge as a driver of dynamic capabilities and learning outcomes. *Journal of Hospitality, Leisure, Sports and Tourism Education, 24*, 143–154.

Liebowitz, J. (2005). Conceptualizing and implementing knowledge management. In P. E. D. Love, P. S. W. Fong, Z. Irani, *Management of Knowledge in Project Environments* (pp. 1–18). Oxford: Butterworth-Heinemann.

Liebowitz, J. (Ed.). (1999). *Knowledge Management Handbook*. Boca Raton, FL: CRC Press.

Liebowitz, J., Paliszkiewicz, J., Gołuchowski, J., (Eds), (2018). *Intuition, Trust, and Analytics*. Boca Raton, FL: CRC Press, Taylor & Francis Group, Auerbach Publications.

Liebowitz, J., & Wilcox, L. C. (1997). *Knowledge Management and Its Integrative Elements*. Boca Raton, FL: CRC Press.

Manovich, L. (2014). Software is the message. *Journal of Visual Culture, 13*(1), 79–81.

Martin, R. (2009). *The Design of Business: Why Design Thinking Is the Next Competitive Advantage*. Boston, MA: Harvard Business Press.

Mayhew, M. J., Rockenbach, A.B., Seifert, T.A., Bowman, N.A., & Wolniak, G.C. (2016). *How College Affects Students: A Third Decade of Research*. San Francisco, CA: Jossey-Bass.

Morgan, G. (1998). *Images of Organization: The Executive Edition*. San Francisco, CA: Better-Koehler Publishers and SAGE Publications.

Nonaka, I., & Takeuchi, H. (1995). *The Knowledge-Creating Company: How Japanese Companies Create the Dynamics of Innovation*. New York: Oxford University Press.

Obitade, P. O. (2019). Big data analytics: A link between knowledge management capabilities and superior cyber protection. *Journal of Big Data, 6*(1), 1–28.

Paliszkiewicz J. (2017). The Future of Knowledge Management. *Proceedings of the IFLA*, Satellite Meeting – Knowledge Management Section, Wroclaw.

Paliszkiewicz, J. (2019). *Przywództwo, zaufanie i zarządzanie wiedzą w innowacyjnych przedsiębiorstwach [Leadership, Trust and Knowledge Management in Innovative Enterprises]*. Warszawa, PL: CeDeWu.

Pourdehnad, J, Wexler, E. R. & Wilson, D. V. (2011). Integrating systems thinking and design thinking. *The Systems Thinker, 22*(9). Available at: https://thesystemsthinker. com/integrating-systems-thinking-and-design-thinking/ [Accessed 01.02.2020].

Probst, G., Raub, S., & Romhardt, K. (2000). *Managing Knowledge: Building Blocks for Success* (Vol. 360). Chichester: John Wiley & Sons.

Rajaraman, A. & Ullman, J. D. (2011). *Mining of Massive Datasets*. Cambridge: Cambridge University Press.

Rousseau, D. M. (2006). Is there such a thing as "Evidence-Based Management"? *Academy of Management Review*, 31, 256–269.

Sackett, D. L., Straus, S. E., Richardson, W. S., Rosenberg, W., & Haynes, R. B. (2000). *Evidence-Based Medicine: How to Practice and Teach EBM*. New York: Churchill Livingstone.

Sandoval-Lucero, E., Antony, K., Hepworth, W. (2017). Co-curricular learning and assessment in new student orientation at a community college. *Creative Education, 8*(10), 1638–1655.

Soniewicki, M., & Paliszkiewicz, J. (2019). The importance of knowledge management processes for the creation of competitive advantage by companies of varying size. *Entrepreneurial Business and Economics Review, 7*(3), 43–63.

Steglitz J., Warnick, J. L., Hoffman, S. A., Johnston, W., Spring, B. (2015). Evidence-based practice. In: *International Encyclopedia of Social and Behavioral Sciences, Vol 8*. (pp. 332–338). London: Oxford Elsevier.

Sułkowski, Ł. (2011). Metafory, archetypy i paradoksy organizacji [Metaphors, archetypes and organization paradoxes] *Organization and Management, 2*(145), 55–68.

Van Maanen, J., & Schein, E. H. (1979). Toward a theory of organizational socialization. *Research in Organizational Behavior, 1*, 209–264.

Ying-Yen, L. (2019). Knowledge management exploring the fundamental theory effect of corporate knowledge management for strengthening marketing strategy applications. *International Journal of Organizational Innovation (Online), 12*(1), 220–241.

Chapter 4

Information Management and the Role of Information Technology in a Big Data Era

Hubert Szczepaniuk and Konrad Michalski

Warsaw University of Life Sciences—SGGW

Contents

4.1 Introduction

Computer science and management face a data revolution. The emergence of new formats and databases of unprecedented scale poses new challenges for organizations' information systems. Common transferring of services to cyberspace requires companies to function within a distributed environment, and simultaneously, it defines requirements both for information systems and an organization itself, within the scope of effective management of information originating from various sources, often unstructured.

This chapter aims to review the literature and to identify the significance of information management and the role of information technology in the era of Big Data. This chapter structure is arranged in a way so that the stated research problem is realized systemically. The first point contains a definition and description of the key attributes related to Big Data. Next, a review of the literature is realized, according to the challenges posed by Big Data. The following points consider the synergetic fields related to the effective use of Big Data in an organization, distinguished by the authors: information management and the role of information technologies. This chapter ends with conclusions containing directions for further research and source literature. The authors use the method of literature analysis and synthesis.

4.2 The Big Data Perspective

Effective management of organization, both on the operational and strategic levels, requires reliable information, on time, precise, integral, and safe. Development of technology has been reflected in the improvement of the organization information system, and on the other hand, it has generated the issue of hardware, time and algorithmic limitations, related to the analysis of large, unstructured sets; processed, transferred and stored by an organization. The indicated issue was already known over two decades ago, and it was defined as early as in the year 1997 by M. Cox and D. Ellsworth in *Managing Big Data for Scientific Visualization*. The authors pointed out, among others, the issue of extraction of information from data, and they have proposed the concept of layered visualization and data management to the architecture of information systems. Specific layers, starting from the lowest one, included network file system, data management, data models, and visualization algorithms (Cox, Ellsworth, 1997). The proposed layered architecture enabled systemic analysis of the complexity of the issue of Big Data within the context of the main fields of information systems.

The contemporary perception of the term Big Data is often based on the characteristic provided by Laney (2001), which is based on the 3V model, which encompasses the following attributes: volume, speed, and diversity. Within the 3V model, the first attribute signifies data sets of high volume, which require new database-like technologies, to enable their effective management. It must be pointed out, that there is no precise definition of a large data set, as expressed in a specific information unit. The speed attribute refers to the data processing time, often data streaming, and provided that the processing carries additional information value, for organization management. The diversity attribute stresses the fact of the presence of inhomogeneous, unstructured and highly heterogeneous data sets. Data processed by an organization may originate from multiple, varying sources, and it may be stored in various formats. This may include flat files, semi-structural sets, and structural data sources. Storing of such data structures is highly straitened using the classic data models, i.e., the relational databases (RDB). The Big Data technologies and techniques must enable integration, structuring, and processing of the indicated data sources.

The model developed by Lanley was expanded with more attributes, thus becoming the 4V model (see Witkowski, 2017); and next, with the following characteristic: reliability and value, which has enabled to define Big Data based on of the 5V model (Lomotey, Deters, 2014). The reliability attribute considers the integrity and authenticity of data, while the reliability of data constitutes a basis for its further analysis, exploration, and extraction. On the other hand, the value attribute states the requirement of selection on a set of valuable data that is to be analyzed.

Within this chapter, the authors have indicated two synergically related research fields in the aspect of their significance and role in the processing of Big Data sets within an organization:

1. Information management: information system and managerial information system, decision-making processes and decision-makers, organizational culture.
2. Information technologies: data warehouses, distributed and parallel processing, machine learning.

Information management defines a set of requirements and guidelines for information technologies that support the processing of data realizing the Big Data attributes. On the other hand, the proper use of information technologies enables the extraction of information from data sets, which renders an opportunity to increase the effectiveness of management processes in an organization.

4.3 Literature Review and Synthesis

The authors performed the literature review according to the distinguished research fields, i.e., information management and information technologies within the scope of Big Data. For the literature review, primarily, Elsevier and EBSCO databases were used; moreover, also Research Gate and Google Scholar databases. In the order of priority, positions of the years 2017–2019 were focused on, but some older ones were also utilized. As keywords for the organization aspect, the following ones were used: "information management", "management information system", and "decision-making process" (updating with the "Big Data" expression in the second step). On the other hand, for the review in the aspect of information technologies, an approach based on the following keywords was used: "data warehouses", "distributed processing", "parallel processing", "machine learning", updated with the "Big Data" expression.

The literature aimed to specify thematically the distinguished research fields within the established range by using keywords. The assumption was that mentioning a given thematical field within a publication attests its significance and importance for information management in an organization, in the Big Data context. The results of the literature review are depicted in Table 4.1.

The results of the performed literature review indicate that the contemporary research studies in the field of Big Data concentrate mainly on the systemic approach to information management within an organization, while including information system, decision-making processes, and the so-called human factor, which constitutes a part of organizational culture. On the other hand, in the aspect of information technologies, research focuses mainly on utilization of data warehouses, distributed processing, and machine learning in the implementation of solutions enabling realization of specific attributes of Big Data sets.

4.4 Information Management in the Big Data Perspective

Sheng, Amankwah-Amoah, and Wang (2017) distinguish multiple general perspectives of analyzing Big Data for the impact on organization management: organization and its attributes (organizational structure, hierarchy, interpersonal relations, etc.), operations realized, and also the information management itself. The efficient management of any information, the more enormous data sets are, should be supported by three, more specified dimensions of the functioning of an organization: technology, people, and processes (Rossi, Hirama, 2015). One may assume that the key determinants in the aspect of Big Data are: systems (information systems and managerial information systems), processes (decision-making) and their performers, as well as the organizational culture supporting analysis.

4.4.1 Information System and Managerial Information System

The aim of information management in an organization is to provide an organization with a continuous inflow of information necessary for making efficient decisions. Tallon, Queiroz, Coltman, and Sharma (2019) state that the superior aim of any organization is to move toward a proper direction in proper time, toward a proper state, while having at disposal proper resources. Among the resources of contemporary organizations, information comes to the fore, which is as important

Table 4.1 Literature Review Synthesis

Quotation	Information Management			Technologies and Techniques of Information Management		
	Information System and Managerial Information System	Decision-Making Processes and Decision-Makers	Organizational Culture	Data Warehouses	Machine Learning	Distributed and Parallel Processing
Review in the Information Management Layer						
Adeoti-Adekeye (1997)	+	+				
Eroshkin, Kameneva, Kovkov, Sukhorukov (2017)	+					
Janssen, van der Voort, Wahyudi (2017)		+				
Jones (2019)			+			
Kościelniak, Puto (2015)		+				
McAffe, Brynjolfsson (2012)		+	+			
Merendino et al. (2018)		+				
Nedelko (2009)	+					

(Continued)

Table 4.1 (Continued) Literature Review Synthesis

Quotation	Information Management			Technologies and Techniques of Information Management		
	Information System and Managerial Information System	*Decision-Making Processes and Decision-Makers*	*Organizational Culture*	*Data Warehouses*	*Machine Learning*	*Distributed and Parallel Processing*
Review in the Information Management Layer						
Rossi, Hirama (2015)	+	+	+			
Sheng, Amankwah-Amoah, Wang (2017)	+		+			
Szymonik (2015)	+					
Tabesh, Mousavidin, Hasani (2019)		+				
Tallon, Queiroz, Coltman, Sharma (2019)			+			
Thirathon, Wieder, Matolcsy, Ossimitz (2017)		+	+			
Vyas, Vyas, Kundan (2014)	+	+				

(Continued)

Table 4.1 (Continued) Literature Review Synthesis

Quotation	Information Management			Technologies and Techniques of Information Management		
	Information System and Managerial Information System	*Decision-Making Processes and Decision-Makers*	*Organizational Culture*	*Data Warehouses*	*Machine Learning*	*Distributed and Parallel Processing*
Review in the Information Technologies Layer						
Bouaziz, Nabli, Gargouri (2017)				+		
Buthukuri, Rajeyyagari (2018)						+
Costa, Andrade, Santos (2018)				+	+	+
El Houari, El Asri, Rhanoui (2017)				+		+
Erraissi, Belangour, Tragha (2018)						+
Fonseca, Cabral (2017)					+	

(Continued)

Table 4.1 (*Continued*) Literature Review Synthesis

Quotation	Information Management			Technologies and Techniques of Information Management		
	Information System and Managerial Information System	Decision-Making Processes and Decision-Makers	Organizational Culture	Data Warehouses	Machine Learning	Distributed and Parallel Processing
Review in the Information Technologies Layer						
Gronwald (2017)						+
Hasan, Shamsuddin, Lopes (2014)					+	
Jan et al. (2017)					+	
Motwani, Madan (2015)						+
Rouse (2019)						+
Sree Divya, Bhargavi, Jyothi (2018)					+	

Source: Own work.

and critical at the same time, as it supports managers in the processes of searching for answers for questions regarding directions of actions themselves; the crucial matter for each organization. Managers responsible for the management of information resources of an organization utilize an organization information system, in which the cybernetic approach is depicted in Figure 4.1.

Information system of an organization is the area of its functioning which has no formal borders in practice, due to the fact that in practice it encompasses not only an entirety of organization but also its environment, which is the source of information, or the data, directly speaking, utilized in the process of management. However, taking the functional perspective of perceiving an information system of an organization, it is its area, into which information is being acquired to, where it is gathered and processed, analyzed, and transformed and shared with consumers, both within and outside of an organization (Szymonik, 2015). In the age of common process automation, even more so, in the age of Big Data, which requires an organization to act in pace even faster than thus far, the effectiveness and efficiency of its functioning depends on whether an organization has a managerial information system, which constitutes a part of an organization information system.

A managerial information system provides managers with the information necessary for the entirety of functions and specified tasks they realize. This system is a formalized, contemporarily already digitized, systemic domain of an organization which integrates information and specific data originating from many sources, and delivering it to decision-makers (Nedelko, 2009). MIC (Management Information Systems) class solutions contain IT tools utilized for these purposes.

Attributes of information expected by managers, for example: being up-to-date, precision, accuracy, adequacy, completeness, etc. (Vyas, Vyas, Kunda, 2014), are determined, among others, by the level of decision-making in an organization, as well as the nature of the decision itself.

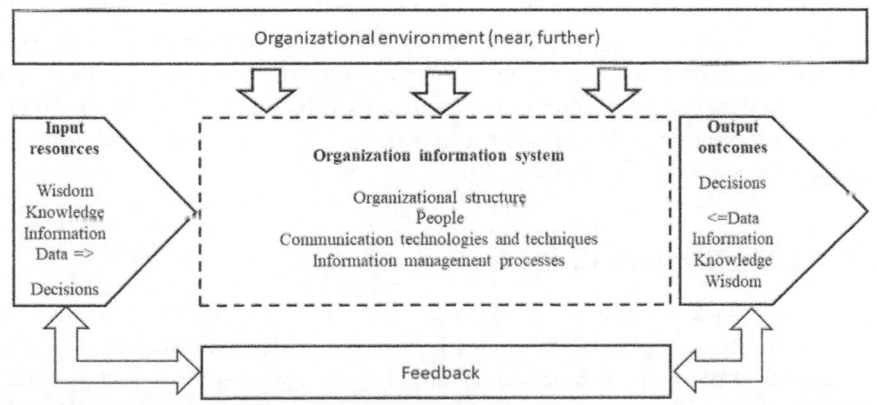

Figure 4.1 The cybernetic approach of an organization information system. (Own work: Buytenen, Christopher, Wils, 1976, p. 23.)

4.4.2 Decision-Making Processes and Decision-Makers

Management encompasses functions that can be related also to information: planning, decision-making, organizing, leadership, motivating and control (Adeoti-Adekeye, 1997). Among the indicated functions, the decision-making processes come to the fore; thus, they become the direct recipients of information, of which the source is an organization information system, and the transmitter—managerial information system.

General activities regarding utilization of Big Data in a decision-making process, proceeding selection of final decision, are gathering, development and analysis of information (Janssen, van der Voort, Wahyudi, 2017), and they are considered typical steps within workflow related to use of any data set. Details of information demand, as well as of the course of a decision-making process, depend primarily on the decision level in an organization (strategic, tactical, operational), as well as on the fact, whether a decision is of structured nature (Nedelko, 2009; Vyas, Vyas, Kundan, 2014). In principle, the higher level of decision-making, the less structured information is required (see: Nedelko, 2009, p. 221).

On specific levels of organization, different systems and dedicated IT tools are present (see: Eroshkin, Kameneva, Kovkov, Sukhorukov, 2017). The key to achieving synergic effects is to properly define the role which a given type of support is to perform in the entirety of an information system so that it is aligned with a holistic concept of organization support.

The key actors in decision-making processes utilizing large data sets are not only managers taking business decisions. Those are also the ones responsible for information management and the dedicated technical and communication infrastructure (information and communication technology, ICT), e.g., on the level of Data Scientist Manager (Tabesh, Mousavidin, Hasani, 2019) or other under a senior manager, e.g., CIO (Chief Information Officer).

Also, the manager-decision-maker himself, which is characterized with competence also analytical, responsibility for the undertaken steps, ability to take risk, to cooperate, to reach an agreement in cooperation, which is aware of the nature of issues and challenges, certain of reality of the decisions to be taken, also in the aspect of information gathering and transformation, has an impact on the decision-making process (Kościelniak, Puto, 2015).

4.4.3 Organization Culture

According to the knowledge pyramid (Jones, 2019), data acquired from the environment constitute information that builds knowledge, which leads to wisdom. If we merge wisdom of an organization, understood as the ability to utilize all resources (including information) optimally for the continuous improvement with agility in everyday operations, the generated image of an organization will be the one most desired. Modern information technologies support organization in the process of development—we read in work by Tallon, Queiroz, Coltman, and Sharma (2019), distinguishing, aside from technological and organizational management determinants included in the area of organizational culture, also environmental and human determinants.

Operating in the context of Big Data carries specific challenges for the whole ecosystem of an organization. These are, except the aspects of adjustment of new, disruptive technologies and efficient decision-making process, also proper leadership, management of talents (analytical in this case) and organization's culture, supporting advanced analysis (see: McAffe, Brynjolfsson, 2012). Babaei and Beikzad (2013) mention several highly detailed challenges within human, organizational and environmental areas, which determine the functioning of a managerial information system, the main beneficiary of the advantages resulting from access to enormous data sets and their analysis. Most of the diagnosed factors contain the "lack of something", e.g., understanding, cooperation, coordination, data flow, etc.

Implementing of culture that supports operations in the Big Data context (analytic culture) in an organization requires time and it is difficult; however, developing such culture may give a strategic advantage (Thirathon, Wieder, Matolcsy, Ossimitz, 2017). Traditional organizational cultures based on functional relations and hierarchy within an organization are not the ones considered adjusted to operating in conditions of distributed resources and cooperation, which exceeds the structure itself and the already developed action schemes. Organizational relations and behavior, which assume higher freedom in work and possibility to utilize unlimited information resources, are the ones considered agile. However; implementation of rules of agile operating is not possible in every organization or industry, and certainly, it requires time and involves high risk and costs.

4.5 Role of Information Technologies in the Era of Big Data

Uses of information technologies in the processing of Big Data sets are identified in the area of extraction of knowledge and information from data sets that realize the Big Data attributes. Analysis based on Big Data renders an opportunity to develop new or to reorganize the current business models, due to utilization of the potential available within possessed data sets. IT offers a spectrum of technologies that may be used in support within an organization in analysis in the context of Big Data. The authors have specified three main pillars of solutions out of the discussed field: data warehouses, distributed processing of large data sets, and machine learning.

4.5.1 Date Warehouses

Data warehouses and Big Data are different but synergetic concepts. In contrast to the operational databases, the purpose of data warehouses is the extraction of knowledge and information from large data sets, for analysis and management. Big Data generates the problem of storing data originating from multiple, heterogeneous, distributed systems. A solution for this issue consists of platforms that enable the possibility to integrate data originating from various sources by developing a common data model and storing it in a single system referred to as a data warehouse. The process of feeding the warehouses with data originating from various sources relies on the ETL (extract, transform, and load) processes. An ETL process covers also data cleaning, providing coherence and automation of identification of changes. In the highest level of a data warehouse, analytical applications are operating, which support decision-making, uncovering hidden relations within data, and new knowledge.

Requirements posed by Big Data sets led to the emergence of a new class of solutions referred to as the Big Data Warehouse (BDW). BDW can be defined as a scalable, efficient, and flexible system of storing of processing, able to operate on data sets realizing the attributes of Big Data, while simultaneously enabling the possibility to lower costs of traditional data warehouses via utilization of commodity hardware (Costa, Andrade, Santos, 2018). The key elements of the BDW architecture consist in a distributed query engine, which can be used, among others, for utilization of data stored in a warehouse, as well as delivering it to other elements of a system, and the data recipients component which represents stakeholders interested in access to the data (Costa, Andrade, Santos, 2018).

In the aspect of the speed attribute of the 3V Laney models, a necessity to implement a real-time data warehouse is proposed. Bouaziz, Nabli, and Gargouri (2017) emphasize that data processing in time approximating a real time will reduce the delay between business transactions, which will facilitate analysis of the latest data and speed up decision-making. Architecture of a real-time data warehouse comprises of three main components: sources operating the data manufacturing systems, which are being loaded into the data warehouses; indirect data processing area, in which the processes of cleaning, extraction, and transformation of data are realized; and the data warehouse (Bouaziz, Nabli, Gargouri, 2017).

An extension of the architecture of a data warehouse for Big Data may be a hybrid approach of merging a Classical Data Warehouse with solutions of distributed processing in the aspect of data processing, multi-dimensional processing, and decision maturity (Rhanoui, El Asri, 2017).

4.5.2 Distributed and Parallel Processing of Big Data Sets

A growing number of organizations that are willing to gather, process, and analyze Big Data sets are moving to a new class of information technologies. Search for solutions of parallel processing of large data sets, independent of their structure, leads to Apache Hadoop and MapReduce. In the aspect of potential possibilities regarding uses of Apache Hadoop and MapReduce, among others, the following can be indicated: text (e.g., text search on Twitter), image analysis and visualization, mood analysis, and identification of outliers (Gronwald, 2017).

Apache Hadoop library available via open-source license enables distributed Big Data processing using programming tools. Apache Hadoop also enables storing large data sets and management of their processing, basing its functionality on cluster architecture. The library comprises of the following modules containing a wide spectrum of analytical tools facilitating processing of Big Data sets: a platform to integrating specific modules of the system, a distributed file system, a framework that enables management of calculation cluster resources, a platform to providing parallel computation tools for processing of Big Data sets, a repository of objects, and a machine learning engine (see: Apache Hadoop, 2019).

The above indicate that integration of the Apache Hadoop module enables realization of advances predictive analysis scenarios, data exploration, and machine learning. Additionally, it must be pointed out that the platform offers support for data of various levels of structure. Due to the characterized functionality, Apache Hadoop can provide better flexibility of processing of Big Data sets than the classic relational data models and data warehouses (Rouse, 2019).

Apache Hadoop can be also utilized for the implementation of stream processing systems and Big Data sets real-time processing. Buthukuri and Rajeyyagari (2018) delivered two basic solutions in this aspect: processing in memory and real-time queries on Big Data sets.

4.5.3 Machine Learning

Machine learning and Big Data can function independent of each other. Machine learning is a part of the field of science concerned with artificial intelligence, and its aim is the implementation of systems able to generate new knowledge automatically and to self-improve based on available data sources. Machine learning systems are capable of learning on the basis of data. Although the technologies are not correlated, Big Data can deliver data sets to a machine learning system in real time, based on which, predictive models can improve the accuracy of predictions. An organization can use machine learning systems to increase the effectiveness of Big Data sets analysis. On the other hand, it must be pointed out that Big Data sets are not required for proper implementation and utilization of machine learning systems. In the aspect of machine learning algorithms which may be used in Big Data sets processing, there are, among others, decisions trees, neural networks, Bayesian networks, k-nearest neighbors algorithms, support vector machines, and algorithm based on rules (see: Sree Divya, Bhargavi, Jyothi, 2018). It is worth mentioning that some of the machine learning algorithms, such as neural networks, are expensive in the aspect of computing; therefore, it is worth to search for possibilities offered by high-efficiency GPUs (graphics processing unit) (Hasan, Shamsuddin, Lopes, 2014).

Machine learning provides advantages for an organization at the end of a process, and they result from predictive models, not from the Big Data sets themselves.

Advantages of machine learning emerge in a situation where Big Data sets do not fit the classic warehouses based on RDB due to incompatible data formats, lack of structure, or real-time data transfer.

4.6 Conclusions

It is anticipated that due to its enormous potential, Big Data may immeasurably affect pace and mode of decision-making; this considers especially senior-level decision-making (Merendino et al., 2018). Such change may be a revolution in operating an organization of the future is assumed, that even more decision-making will be performed on the lower levels of an organization. This would result in, on the one hand, weakening the position of senior managers, and on the other hand, an increase of expectations regarding the mode of work of decision-makers on the lowest levels and their responsibility for results of their actions. Moreover, work with enormous data sets itself, in practice, takes the form of matrix cooperation within an organization, which results from the necessity of continuous communication with various participants of the decision-making processes, also outside of organization. Therefore, significant directions of further research in the aspect of organization management is the impact of Big Data on transformations of organizational structures in the process of adjusting to operations in the context of distributed information and its unstructured nature. That is due to the fact, one must assume, that progressively more necessary information will "circle" around an organization, instead of being permanently present within a sealed information system. Increasingly, information must be "reached for" outside of an organization, even each time for realization of a specific task. Possibility of fast, efficient, and effective "grabbing" of the necessary information may be provided via properly selected information technologies.

The advantages resulting from the literature review conducted within this chapter is a statement, that the theme of the impact of distribution and inhomogeneity of information, its enormous range and potential scale of usability for improvement of the functioning of an organization, is discussed relatively rare. That is due to the fact, one must remember, that it is an organization and its needs that dictate the requirements toward technologies that it utilizes. Meanwhile, operating of an organization in the context of Big Data is not the same as an activity within stable and predictable frames resulting from the relative stability of the phenomena in its environment. Big Data sets may have a breaking impact on the processes of an organization, thus affecting the necessity to change fixed operating methods, including decision-making processes. On the other hand, information or communication technologies, introduced into an organization, speed up, improve, make more flexible, and increase the effectiveness of those processes. This results in a conclusion that operating of an organization in the context of Big Data can be studied in two directions: from the inside of an organization (as a research issue, assuming adjustment challenges, e.g., in the aspect of organizational culture) and toward the inside of an organization (for breaking technological changes, e.g., decision-making process in an organization).

A limitation for the conducted study is the fact that only a few of the available databases were used. In the following step, it would be worth the further analysis and to quote the results of the already conducted empirical studies and to identify any research gap(s). Therefore, like a road sign for future actions, significant directions for further research in the field of impact of modern communication technologies on the functioning of an organization can be assumed:

- Impact of distribution and lack of structure of information within the environment of modern organizations on the shaping of their internal processes, hierarchy, and work processes
- Integration of external organization processes in the aspect of Big Data analysis with business processes, including client activities
- Organizational behavior, including the required leadership attitudes of managers in a distributed work environment
- Framework in the aspect of adjustment of information technologies supporting Big Data sets processing according to requirements and specificity of a given organization and its information needs
- Data structures and models in the aspect of their optimization regarding Big Data attributes
- Security threats in distributed and parallel data processing technologies (such as Apache Hadoop)

In conclusion, this chapter indicates that contemporary organizations cannot remain unaffected in the face of the potential anticipated in the age of Big Data. Proper information management and selection of proper IT tool classes constitutes a necessary improvement direction for every organization, and perhaps, for some of them, a condition for further existence.

References

Adeoti-Adekeye, W.B. (1997). The importance of management information systems *Library Review*, 46(5), 318–327.

Babaei, M., Beikzad, J. (2013). Management information system, challenges and solution. *European Online Journal of Natural and Social Sciences*, 2(3s), 374–381.

Bouaziz, A., Nabli, A., Gargouri F. (2017). From Traditional Data Warehouse to Real Time Data Warehouse, *Conference Paper in Advances in Intelligent Systems and Computing*. DOI: 10.1007/978-3-319-53480-0_46.

Buthukuri, B., Rajeyyagari, S. (2018). Investigation on processing of real-time streaming big data. *International Journal of Engineering & Technology*, 7(3.13).

Buytenen, V., Christopher, M.G., Wils, G.C. (1976). *Business Logistics*. Hague: Martinus Nijhoff.

Costa, C., Andrade, C., Santos, M.Y. (2018). Big data warehouses for smart industries. In: Sakr, S., Zomaya, A. (Eds). *Encyclopedia of Big Data Technologies*. Cham: Springer.

Cox, M., Ellsworth, D. (1997). Managing big data for scientific visualization. *ACM Siggraph*, *97*, 21–38.

El Houari, M., El Asri, B., Rhanoui, B. (2017). Hybrid Big Data Warehouse for On-demand decision needs, *Conference Paper: 2017 International Conference on Electrical and Information Technologies (ICEIT)*. DOI: 10.1109/EITech.2017.8255261.

Erraissi, A., Belangour, A., Tragha, A. (2018). Meta-modeling of data sources and ingestion big data layers. *SSRN Electronic Journal*. DOI: 10.2139/ssrn.3185342.

Fonseca, A., Cabral, B. (2017). Prototyping a GPGPU neural network for deep-learning big data analysis. *Big Data Research*, *7*, 50–56.

George, G., Hass, R. M. (2014). Big data and management. *The Academy of Management Journal*, *57*(2), 321–326.

Gronwald, K. D. (2017). Big data analytics. In: K. D. Gronwald (ed.) *Integrated Business Information Systems*, (pp. 127–157). Berlin: Springer.

Hasan, S., Shamsuddin, S. M., Lopes N. (2014). Machine learning big data framework and analytics for big data problems. *International Journal of Advances in Soft Computing & Its Applications*, *6*(2), 1–17.

Jan, B., Farman, H., Khan, M., Imran, M., Ul Islam, I., Ahmad, A., Ali, S., Jeon, G. (2017). Deep learning in big data analytics: A comparative study. *Computers and Electrical Engineering*, *75*, 275–287.

Kościelniak, H., Puto, A., (2015). BIG DATA in decision making processes of enterprises. *Procedia Computer Science*, *65*, 1052–1058.

Laney, D. (2001). 3D Data Management: Controlling Data Volume, Velocity, and Variety. Retrieved from: https://blogs.gartner.com/doug-laney/files/2012/01/ad949-3D-Data-Management-Controlling-Data-Volume-Velocity-and-Variety.pdf (Accessed 26 September 2019).

Lomotey, R. K., Deters R. (2014). Towards Knowledge Discovery in Big Data. *Proceeding of the 8th International Symposium on Service Oriented System Engineering, SOSE 2014*. Oxford: IEEE Computer Society.

McAffe, A., Brynjolfsson, E., (2012). Big Data: The Management Revolution. *Harvard Business Review*, 10, 3–9. Retrieved from: https://hbr.org/2012/10/big-data-the-management-revolution.

Merendino, A., Dibb, S., Meadows, M., Quinn, L., Wilson, D., Simkin, L., Canhoto, A. (2018). Big data, big decisions: The impact of big data on board level decision-making, *Journal of Business Research*, 93, 67–78.

Motwani, D., Lal Madan, M. (2015). Information retrieval using Hadoop big data analysis. In: V. Lakshminarayanan, I. Bhattacharya (eds). *Advances in Optical Science and Engineering*. Springer Proceedings in Physics, 166. (pp. 409–415) New Delhi: Springer.

Nedelko, Z. (2009). Management Information Systems and Information Needs of Managers in the Frame of Managerial Decision Making, *Proceedings of the 20th Central European Conference on Information and Intelligent Systems*, 219–224.

Rossi, R., Hirama, K. (2015). Characterizing big data management, *Issues in Informing Science and Information Technology*, *12*, 165–180.

Rouse, M. (2019). Hadoop. Retrieved from: https://searchdatamanagement.techtarget.com/definition/Hadoop (Accessed 30 September 2019).

Sheng, J., Amankwah-Amoah, J., Wang, X. (2017). A multidisciplinary perspective of big data in management research, *International Journal of Production Economics*, *191*, 97–112.

Sree Divya, K., Bhargavi, P., Jyothi, S. (2018). Machine learning algorithms in big data analytics. *International Journal of Computer Sciences and Engineering*, *6(1)*.

Szymonik, A. (2015). *Informatyka dla potrzeb logistyka(i) [Informatics for the needs of logistician (logistics)]*. Warsaw: Difin.

Tallon, P.P., Queroiz M., Coltman, T., Sharma, R. (2019). Information technology and the search for organization agility: A systematic review with the future research possibilities, *Journal of Strategic Information Systems*, *28*, 218–237.

Witkowski, K. (2017). Internet of things, big data, industry 4.0 – innovative solutions in logistics and supply chain management, *Procedia Engineering*, *182*, 763–769.

Vyas, V., Vyas, S., Kundan, A. (2014). Management information system: Information needs of organization, *International Journal of Information & Computation Technology*, *4(17)*. 1903–1908.

Chapter 5

Financial Management in the Big Data Era

Magdalena Mądra-Sawicka

Warsaw University of Life Sciences—SGGW

Contents

5.1 Introduction

In recent years, several authors have undertaken international research on Big Data in finance and its possible implementation and application in practice. This chapter presents the results of the synthesized literature review of Big Data used by managers in the financial management of financial and non-financial organizations.

In the area of financial management, we can notice a greater need for Big Data technology and data for services such as data warehouse, decision analysis, inquiry statistics, and customer analysis (SMB World Asia, 2015). According to IBM research, around 70% of banking and financial market firms report to use Big Data analytics is creating a competitive advantage for their organization (Turner, Schroeck, & Rebecca, 2013). The use of these technologies becomes the basis for conducting productive operational activity. The purpose of this chapter was also the present concepts and new trends in financial management in the Big Data era.

This chapter proceeds as follows. Section 5.2 introduces Big Data techniques used in financial management. Section 5.3 presents the systematic literature review of different areas where Big Data technologies are being implemented and support financial managers' decisions. Section 5.4 concludes this chapter with essential recommendations for the use of Big Data in financial management.

5.2 Big Data Characteristics in Financial Management

The era of "digital economy" brings digital technologies almost to every sector. Big Data opens new perspectives in finance by bringing the evolutionary breakthrough; thus, the world of finance has the unique ability to combine real-world data with online world data.

Big Data technologies in financial management give support to the decision-making process due to a higher level of automation that makes company performance more efficient in case of lowering cost, increasing productivity, improving customer relation, risk detecting, and legal action data processing. Big Data implementation helps in the long run to increase the company's operational efficiency. It benefits in increasing profitability, growing market share, and lowering risk losses. Big Data technology gives the ability to manage vast amounts of diverse data at the right speed and at the right time to enable them to react in real time. The information technologies market in the financial sphere is one of the fastest-growing ones (Bataev, 2018), with data production that concerns daily operations. The data analysis technique discovers more patterns by involving machine learning that extracts proper information and transforms it by using different models for the defined task. The machine learning is supportive by artificial intelligence that imitates human intelligence by computer. These technologies allow better data management and its analytics across financial technology that implements automation before complex decision-making processes.

Big Data system joins the aspect of size and speed of data processing. Big Data is a combination of old and new technologies as part of a new data management concept that supports financial and non-financial institutions in developing corporate knowledge about customers, services, market activities, and creating firm's value.

The leader in the digital transformation of the economy is the technology for processing and analyzing Big Data that developed in recent years (Bataev, 2018). Big Data have three main characteristics: volume—are measurable, velocity—need to be processed quickly, and variety—represents a different type of data (time-series, semi-structured, metadata, and so on). Big Data technologies provided a more natural way to collect data and joined them into massive dynamic databases (Choi, Chan, & Yue, 2017).

Big Data in finance also include structured and unstructured data. Big Data are constituted by techniques and processes, information, privacy/security/ethics, professional competencies, and dedicated modern application. Applications that use Big Data could be used in trading signals, fraud prevention, the Internet of Things, and customer insights (Cockcroft & Russell, 2018; Tian, Han, Wang, Lu, & Zhan, 2015). Big Data technologies in finance have a core topic that could be divided into business intelligence and data mining, system that could be used in industries and security systems, and risk management operating systems. Big Data areas also concern financial distress modeling, financial fraud modeling, and stock market prediction and quantitative modeling (Gepp, Linnenluecke, O'Neill, & Smith, 2018).

According to Bataev (2018), Big Data technologies are being introduced in the financial sphere in targeted mobile marketing, detecting signs of fraud, or managing cash to attract customers.

5.3 Implementation of Big Data Technologies for Supporting Financial Management Decision

Different approach of Big Data management constitutes from the company status: financial institution or not. In addition, the use of Big Data in financial management occurs at various levels of the organization's functioning.

5.3.1 Financial and Non-Financial Organizations

5.3.1.1 Financial Institutions

Investment bankers, financial advisors, loan officers must have accurate customer information to make better decisions. These organizations are extracting new insights from existing and available internal sources of information to define the most useful Big Data technology that will be accurate for organization strategy (Turner et al., 2013). Big Data solution in the banking sector introduces a higher level of automation, which provides a higher-quality information concerning the return on investment, better model of personnel management, and risk identification. In the aspect of financial management, Big Data in banks improve their operational, efficiency, customer service, risk management (Bataev, 2018). Furthermore, Big Data in the case of the banking system ensure better data protection and confidentially and substitute the lack of qualified personnel while the ongoing data is processed automatically and analyses by created algorithms. Financial institutions can forecast the bankruptcy of a firm better and predict defaulters of loans by introducing the Big Data predictive analytics (Huttunen et al., 2019). In the case of banks, Big Data are used in cybersecurity solutions and customer knowledge management.

The cost of financial fraud has obvious economic implications. Thus, fraud detection is quicker and more effective, especially in the case of financial institutions like banks. Banks identify suspicious connections and present them graphically in the form of networks of contacts. Through visualization, it is possible to diagnose new types and ways of scams faster and more effectively. Banks analytics monitor and track transactions with a high risk of fraud, mostly because they know specific facts beyond (Debenham, 2016). It allows blocking a transaction before the funds are taken out of the client's account.

The integration of the Internet with Big Data technology supports financial institutions with opportunities to link unstructured data from publicly available sources with records of transactions. These smart analytics provide a solution for identifying fraud by monitoring websites that contain allegations of fraud (Debenham, 2016). Lending firms exchange information about their customers and process a growing amount of personal data thanks to Big Data analytics. Lenders access databases and other data managed by third-party providers to evaluate a consumer's credit application to assess the creditworthiness (Ferretti, 2018).

The Big Data technology gives the possibility to design rules and strategies in the finance area and helps to achieve a balance between flexibility and efficiency (Choi, Wallace, & Wang, 2018).

5.3.1.2 Non-Financial Companies

Big Data help enterprises in profit maximization by optimizing the business process (Vera-Baquero, Colomo-Palacios, & Molloy, 2013) by leading toward customer retention (ur Rehman, Chang, Batool, & Yinh Wah, 2016). Big Data implementation in the finance sphere of a company helps to modernize the company's financial transactions. Many businesses rely on a data system that creates the view of customers, products, and suppliers by using a variety of sources. Big Data in finance allows for increasing the visibility of process information to create a clear understanding of the market and support the trading strategies (Fang & Zhang, 2016). Bigger firms have/produce more data and hence benefit more than smaller firms from Big Data analysis. It is consistent with the statement that large companies shape Big Data.

Big Data in financial management can influence corporate activity via operations (assets) or funding (debt and equity) (Begenau, Farboodi, & Veldkamp, 2018). These are important in case of decisions on granting trade credit. It also helps to reduce unnecessary outflow from companies. Big Data tools help to optimize the cash management in the company, which is especially important in the case of a big group of clients and developed a structure of trade credit. These tools become more wildly practice; thus, it could open up the option for obtaining higher revenues.

The possibility to join private companies databased with external one gives new options for better client risk management and thus a better chance to increase sales. Thus, Big Data analysis systems help make better business decisions and react quickly to the market situation. This information primarily creates the opportunity to adapt to customer expectations and improve the quality of products, and increases the company's competitiveness in the long run. Massive data resources can also help recover lost clients by creating advertising campaigns or long-term strategies.

Non-financial enterprises use Big Data technology by including data sources directly from operating activities. The direct data sources in companies are gathered from operational information related to supply chain management, production, fleet management, marketing strategies, behavior analysis of employees, etc. (ur Rehman et al., 2016). Big Data help non-financial companies to integrate and consolidates various economic and environmental data into one comprehensive, live-automated data warehouse. This technology could be used in agricultural finance, natural resource, and environmental fields of companies' operation. It can be accessed by data visualization tools that support the analyses of commodity futures used for selecting the most beneficial contracts, spot price interpolation to set the commodity spot price (Woodard, 2016). Big Data analytics support also decision in inventories transactions, inventory receipts, issues, valuations, frequency identification, and financial statement report creation.

Big Data also support customer preference identification by text analysis on the posted opinion of customers that induce the study of negative words with lower stock returns (Subrahmanyam, 2019). The advanced analytical algorithms based on Big Data enable building a detailed customer profile, which will include their needs, preferences, and capabilities. The personalized offer depends on the current context and contact channel.

5.3.2 Capital Market Investments

The Big Data model is used on capital market in various ways like enhancing the capital investment thanks to real-time predictive modeling, decreasing the cost of capital by selecting the most optimal financial resources, used market stock prediction model (that used the fundamental information and sentiment measure or information from social media (O'Connor, 2013)). The investment choices of financial managers affect the prices, cost of capital on the market. Thus, Big Data analysis improves investors' forecasts and reduces equity uncertainty (Begenau et al., 2018). The advantage of using these technologies in financial management underlines the importance of real-time predictive modeling. This approach also includes proper classification, clustering, and association rules, which helps to switch managers from retrospective analytical techniques to predictive financial outcomes.

Stock market prices are from a technical perspective modeled by using machine learning algorithm (Nayak, Pai, & Pai, 2016; Cockcroft & Russell, 2018). Machine learning forecasts stock returns based on a large number of documented anomalies (Subrahmanyam, 2019) and thus provide manager information. Another approach of Big Data used in finance shows the aggregated rankings of stock, according to the level of forecasted returns of different securities (Da, Huang, & Jin, 2018). That's why Big Data technologies impact on decreasing cost of capital. It is supported by faster-processed data that cover the macro announcements, financial statements, competitors' performance, and other industry results. High-speed data processing lowers uncertainty, which reduces risk and makes investments more attractive (Begenau et al., 2018).

The stock predicting model of market valuation in the Big Data era based on the media pessimism measures are more popular than the fundamental values of equities (Bollen, Mao, & Zeng, 2011; Tetlock, 2007). This approach includes using social media, news articles, Twitter, and historical data series variables in fundamental analysis of stock prices (Attigeri et al., 2015). It changes the perspective of decisions taken by managers in the area of company finances.

5.3.3 Risk Management

All financial transactions and credit transactions involve risks or uncertainties. Financial risk prevention and financial fraud identification have been the essential aspects that financial companies need to focus on and manage (Zhang, Li, Shen, Sun, & Yang, 2015). Risk management in banks is more developed via bid data. Its usage allows building a portfolio of owned financial instruments, which helps to reduce customer risk and improve credit risk management.

The other option is the optimization of bank investments by using up-to-date data that help you to choose the best investment options. It supports financial managers moving toward a more strategic and proactive role in the finance area.

Financial risk management uses different financial instruments to manage various types of risk, such as operational, credit, market, foreign exchange, or liquidity risk (Huttunen et al., 2019). Credit intermediaries are exploiting the mechanisms of data collection under Big Data. Data for the analysis of creditworthiness come, among others, from social media portals, where not only the client information but also friends' social status and financial situation are assessed (Yu, Huang, Hu, & Cai, 2010). In the case of risk management, Big Data technology decreases the problem of asymmetric information by reducing the cost for both financial institutions and enterprises (Cao, 2015; Ferretti, 2018).

5.3.4 Financial Markets

Financial markets are characterized by a large number of heterogeneous participants interacting with one another in nonlinear ways (Tang, Xiong, Luo, & Zhang, 2019). Big Data views in the analyses of the capital market include its volatility, portfolio development, risk analysis, and market transparency (Ferreira & da Costa, 2017). The volatility concerns the dispersion of the assets price.

Big Data technology supports managers' decision by implementing advance prediction model that provide higher gains for investor due to more reliable analyses when the models have access to high-frequency data with continuity data production. Building an investment portfolio and risk analysis thanks to that Big Data enhances fundamental analysis by processing and quantification different business valuation models, which help to consider the best market opportunities for financial management. Machine learning techniques and statistical modeling are supporting Big Data solutions (James, Witten, Hastie, & Tibshirani, 2013). Market is transparently investigated by using business intelligence to identify market liquidity and thus its efficiency. Further development of this application Big Data usage on information disclosure is important for the functioning of financial systems across different markets (Ferreira & da Costa, 2017), as well as significant due to changes in the regulations.

Data from the financial market data are accessible on a real-time basis and could be used with a business intelligence system. This solution is joined mostly with cloud services that can be used to store data in remote locations. Other Big Data technologies are based on data extraction and algorithm creation, which is crucial for machine learning. It reduces the risk and creates new business value to financial management date from a more comprehensive perspective.

5.3.5 Accounting Data Processing

The whole data-generating process as a result of purchases, sales, and other transactions is related to companies accounting system. Only by integrating (compiling multiple data), selecting (extracting relative data), cleaning (removing conflicting data), transforming (transforming into easy-to-extract forms), searching (extracting data model in an intelligent way), and estimating (assessing its value) technology transform accounting data into relevant and useful information for managers (Ke & Shi, 2014). These applications become standard tools in the case of large companies.

5.3.6 Budget Management

The budget performance evaluation is a kind of innovation in financial management methods. Quick data analysis through Big Data technologies and tool provide up-to-date information that notifies managers to locate money in more effective financial instruments and capital resources. Big Data technologies support the application of budget performance management and analysis techniques (Liu, 2014), both in the case of government and private companies. Budgets can provide a report that presents limited resources of the company and requires control. The company data platform undertakes data analysis and could improve budget performance by focusing on data collection, conversion, integration, and storage (Liu, 2014). Big Data technologies support budget adjustment and analysis. After integration budgets with the business information system, the budget report will be quickly available for further decisions, and the budget evaluation could be performed at every moment. Financial managers can compare multiple future outcomes and customize the budgeting model to various assets and portfolios that the company possesses (Huttunen et al., 2019). Data science supports budgeting optimization and allows companies to combine diverse financial and non-financial data and produce more comprehensive reporting systems.

5.3.7 Controlling and Audits

Big Data has been used in many areas to enhance the process of inspecting, transforming, and modeling (Cao, Chychyla, & Stewart, 2015). It is already applied in formal auditing, data analysis in continuous auditing, and risk management (Zhang, Yang, & Appelbaum, 2015). In the auditing profession, both quantitative and textual data are being used. Big Data analysis improves corporate finance, controlling, and financial audits. Auditors use Big Data models to predict financial distress and detect financial fraud. Big Data also refers to the techniques and technology used to uncover patterns in data by prepared algorithms. External auditors can improve their fraud risk assessments by using Big Data financial fraud models (Gepp et al., 2018). As a background for model creation, Big Data systems use historical data about previous frauds.

Auditors could use Big Data techniques and methods for forecasting financial distress. Data mining techniques in the form of neural networks are used to build and test distress modeling (Chen & Du, 2009). Auditors are reluctant to use techniques and technology that are more advance comparing to those used by clients of firms (Alles, 2015). Real-time auditing processes are required. Thus, continuous auditing refers to a constant cycle of auditing (Gepp et al., 2018; Routledge, 2018).

5.4 Conclusions

The application of Big Data is transforming the entire financial industry and the characteristics and role of financial managers' decisions by breaking the data barriers and ensuring new quality. Big Data in financial management is becoming one of the most promising areas of management (Sun, Shi, & Zhang, 2019). However, its proper application needs to be supported by the higher cost of its implementation. Big Data technologies also include higher pressure on data protection and training of personnel. Furthermore, it also includes the higher level of the distrust of new technologies, continuing changes in the structure of the data, and other external data, which brings the problem with proper integration of the data and the quality from different providers.

Big Data technology provides alternatives for asset valuation and thus creates the business knowledge for managers (Huttunen et al., 2019). The use of the data should reflect the investor's expectations that reduce their uncertainty about investment outcomes.

The key challenges are the problems with data integration and data collection (Cao et al., 2015). The Big Data implementation impacts on closer cooperation of non-financial companies with financial institutions (Vera-Baquero et al., 2013). The data protection becomes a problem of Big Data development and thus creates a complex and multifaceted concept from a societal and legal obligation (Ferretti, 2018).

The Big Data analytics in financial management stand in front of many changes, like how to effectively extract valuable information and design a highly efficient computing system. These systems need to process distributed historical and incoming data. Another problem is the creation of data centers (Big Data parking with cloud solutions), a system that will deploy thousands of computers effectively (Tian et al., 2015). Big Data requires a diverse range of tools, including data warehousing and providing for data anonymity (Cockcroft & Russell, 2018).

The financial manager will receive thus ready dashboard of data and information that are connected with graphs and standardized models and taxonomies. It will improve operations and the creation of further business opportunities. This approach will change manager involvement in optimizing operational efficiency.

References

Alles, M. G. (2015). Drivers of the use and facilitators and obstacles of the evolution of big data by the audit profession. *Accounting Horizons, 29*(2), 439–449.

Attigeri, G. V., MM, M. P., Pai, R. M., & Nayak, A. (2015). Stock market prediction: A big data approach. In *Tencon 2015-2015, IEEE Region 10 Conference*, IEEE 1–5.

Bataev, A. V. (2018). Analysis of the Application of Big Data Technologies in the Financial Sphere. *Proceedings of the 2018 International Conference 'Quality Management, Transport and Information Security, Information Technologies', IT and QM and IS 2018*, 568–572.

Begenau, J., Farboodi, M., & Veldkamp, L. (2018). Big data in finance and the growth of large firms. *Journal of Monetary Economics, 97*, 71–87.

Bollen, J., Mao, H., & Zeng, X. (2011). Twitter mood predicts the stock market. *Journal of Computational Science, 2*(1), 1–8.

Cao, D. (2015). The Application of Big Data Technology in Banks. *Conference Proceedings of the G20 Youth Forum 2015, Economics and Finance*, 1–13.

Cao, M., Chychyla, R., & Stewart, T. (2015). Big data analytics in financial statement audits. *Accounting Horizons, 29*(2), 423–429. doi: 10.1145/3132847.3132886.

Chen, W. S. & Du, Y. K. (2009). Using neural networks and data mining techniques for the financial distress prediction model. *Expert Systems with Applications, 36*(2), 4075–4086.

Choi, T. M., Chan, H. K., & Yue, X. (2017). Recent development in big data analytics for business operations and risk management. *IEEE Transactions on Cybernetics, 47*(1), 81–92.

Choi, T. M., Wallace, S. W., & Wang, Y. (2018). Big data analytics in operations management. *Production and Operations Management, 27*(10), 1868–1883.

Cockcroft, S., & Russell, M. (2018). Big data opportunities for accounting and finance practice and research. *Australian Accounting Review, 28*(3), 323–333.

Da, Z., Huang, X., & Jin, L. J. (2018). Extrapolative beliefs in the cross-section: What can we learn from the crowds? *SSRN Electronic Journal, 1*(574), 1–53.

Debenham, D. (2016). Big data analytics, big financial institutions, and big money fraud litigation. *Banking & Finance Law Review, 32*(1), 103–143.

Fang, B., & Zhang, P. (2016). Big data in finance. In: Yu, S., & Guo, S. (Eds.), *Big Data Concepts, Theories, and Applications* (pp. 391–412). Cham: Springer.

Ferretti, F. (2018). Not-so-big and big credit data between traditional consumer finance, FinTechs, and the banking union: Old and new challenges in an enduring EU policy and legal conundrum. *Global Jurist, 18*(1), 1–42.

Ferreira, T. S. V., & da Costa, F. J. (2017). Big data: Epistemological reflections and impacts in finance and capital market studies. *Revista de Educação e Pesquisa Em Contabilidade, 11*(4), 385–395.

Gepp, A., Linnenluecke, M. K., O'Neill, T. J., & Smith, T. (2018). Big data techniques in auditing research and practice: Current trends and future opportunities. *Journal of Accounting Literature, 40*(5), 102–115.

Huttunen, J., Jauhiainen, J., Lehti, L., Nylund, A., Martikainen, M., & Lehner, O. M. (2019). Big data, cloud computing and data science applications in finance and accounting. *ACRN Oxford Journal of Finance and Risk Perspectives, 8*, 16–30.

James, G., Witten, D., Hastie, T., & Tibshirani, R. (2013). *An Introduction to Statistical Learning*. New York: Springer.

Ke, M., & Shi, Y. (2014). Big data, big change: In the financial management. *Open Journal of Accounting, 03*(04), 77–82.

Liu, Q. (2014). Study on the implementation of budget performance evaluation from the perspective of big data. *Management & Engineering, 17*(17), 6–12.

O'Connor, A. J. (2013). The power of popularity: An empirical study of the relationship between social media fan counts and brand company stock prices. *Social Science Computer Review, 31*(2), 229–235.

Nayak, A., Pai, M. M., & Pai, R. M. (2016). Prediction models for Indian stock market. *Procedia Computer Science, 89*, 441–449.

ur Rehman, M. H., Chang, V., Batool, A., & Yinh Wah, T. (2016). Big data reduction framework for value creation in sustainable enterprises. *International Journal of Information Management, 36*(6), 917–928.

Routledge, B. R. (2018). Comments on: Big data in finance and the growth of large firms, by Juliane Begenau & Maryam Farboodi & Laura Veldkamp. *Journal of Monetary Economics, 97*, 88–90.

SMB World Asia. (2015). *Big Data in Finance Industry to Drive Analytics Demand in China Says IDC. SMB World Asia (Online)*. Newton: Questex, LLC.

Subrahmanyam, A. (2019). Big data in finance: Evidence and challenges. *Borsa Istanbul Review, 19*(4), 283–287.

Sun, Y., Shi, Y., & Zhang, Z. (2019). Finance big data: Management, analysis, and applications. *International Journal of Electronic Commerce, 23*(1), 9–11.

Tang, Y., Xiong, J. J., Luo, Y., & Zhang, Y. C. (2019). How do the global stock markets influence one another? Evidence from finance big data and granger causality directed network. *International Journal of Electronic Commerce, 23*(1), 85–109.

Tetlock, P. C. (2007). Giving content to investor sentiment : The role of media in the stock market published by : Wiley for the American Finance Association Stable. *Journal of Finance, 62*(3), 1139–1168.

Tian, X., Han, R., Wang, L., Lu, G., & Zhan, J. (2015). Latency critical big data computing in finance. *The Journal of Finance and Data Science, 1*(1), 33–41.

Turner, D., Schroeck, M., & Rebecca, S. (2013). Analytics : The real-world use of big data in financial services. *IBM Institute for Business Value*, 16, 1–12.

Vera-Baquero, A., Colomo-Palacios, R., & Molloy, O. (2013). Business process analytics using a big data approach. *IT Professional, 15*(6), 29–35.

Woodard, J. (2016). Big data and Ag-Analytics: An open source, open data platform for agricultural & environmental finance, insurance, and risk. *Agricultural Finance Review, 76*(1), 15–26.

Yu, H., Huang, X., Hu, X., & Cai, H. (2010). A Comparative Study on Data Mining Algorithms for Individual Credit Risk Evaluation. *Proceedings - 2010 International Conference on Management of e-Commerce and e-Government, ICMeCG 2010*, 35–38.

Zhang, H., Li, Y., Shen, C., Sun, H., & Yang, Y. (2015). The Application of Data Mining in Finance Industry Based on Big Data Background. *Proceedings - 2015 IEEE 17th International Conference on High Performance Computing and Communications, H*, 1536–1539.

Zhang, J., Yang, X., & Appelbaum, D. (2015). Toward effective big data analysis in continuous auditing. *Accounting Horizons, 29*(2), 469–476.

Chapter 6

Ethics and Trust to Big Data in Management: Balancing Risk and Innovation

Grzegorz Polok, Grzegorz Filipczyk, and Anna Losa-Jonczyk

University of Economics in Katowice

Contents

6.1 Introduction

Management based on large data sets nowadays seems to be increasingly more common. Creating Big Data sets and striving for using them to extract the sought knowledge is a challenge and opportunity in the era of the digital economy. The users of digital technologies, both as consumers of digital content and services as well as employees and associates of the organizations, leave many digital traces while using common digital technologies. These collections are created from digital data streams (often already collected in the cloud) out of which – using analytical systems – knowledge can be extracted to be incorporated in business processes and made available in the organizations' communication processes using digital media.

The purpose of this chapter is to depict the correlation between the use of Big Data in management, and the aspects of their ethical use in the context of risk and innovation in the organization. This chapter begins by discussing the place of Big Data in the concept of digital risk. Next, the problem of trust in Big Data and the building of reasonable trust in Big Data were characterized. This chapter ends with an analysis of the impact of solutions in the field of Big Data ethics on organizational innovation and the balancing of the security of the organizations and the digital risk and innovation in organizations that utilize the concept of evidence-based management. The conclusion indicates the importance of the considerations made for management practice and the possibilities of resolving the conflict between risk and confidence in data, and innovative management of the organization.

6.2 The Digital Risk Associated with Big Data

Digital technologies that are undoubtedly developing dynamically offer huge benefits for the companies. The list of benefits is long and includes, among others, higher business intelligence, faster product launch, better customer relationships, greater work productivity, and the greater profitability of the entire organization. However, as the pace of digital transformation increases, threats and, consequently, the risks of conducting business by organizations increase (Mayer-Schonberger, Cukier, 2013).

The business has always been and still is associated with risks. A new type of risk has emerged since organizations began using computers to process data, information, and knowledge: the digital risk (Davis, Patterson, 2012). In the past, the concept of digital risk was largely limited to the area of cybersecurity threats. The digital risk was related to the problems of hacker attacks and computer fraud. These threats remain ubiquitous. However, today, in the era of Big Data and Artificial Intelligence, new threats appear, e.g., the security of digital footprints extends beyond ensuring the right infrastructure (e.g., network, data center, cloud). Digital footprints leave data that is shared with customers, suppliers and partners, official and fake social media accounts, websites, and applications representing employees and the company. However, threats and risks also result from the effects of data centralization due to a change in consumer preferences and the widespread use of mobile devices. Uploading data into the so-called cloud means that several huge financial databases will be created in the near future. Yet, the process of creating Big Data does not only affect the area of finance (Zwitter, 2014; Herschel, Miori, 2017).

The digitization of business and the emergence of Big Data introduce completely new digital risk classes for individuals and organizations. They include, among others, threats such as:

- Making incorrect, inaccurate assumptions not only in the data modeling process but throughout the data lifecycle
- Data theft for unauthorized use
- Creating and distributing fake news not only by people but also by software agents
- Making decisions by the organization and its stakeholders based on the analysis of false data and fake news
- Reinforcement of prejudice, discrimination, and exclusion (through algorithms) that reinforce social and economic injustice, preferring specific groups and discriminating against others
- Unethical or even unlawful use of data insight
- Use of the data for purposes that the individuals that originally disclosed them would not have agreed to, without their consent

These digital threats cannot be remedied solely by ensuring strong security through technological solutions. New technologies, including blockchain, aim to minimize fraud and increase data security. However, especially when using the Internet of Things to attract investors and customers to achieve organizational goals, organizations must use completely transparent, auditable, and rather unchanging solutions. Solutions covering the entire data lifecycle "trusted from the very beginning" are necessary, which contribute to building trust in Big Data and the organization.

6.3 Trust in Big Data

Young people who make use of the benefits of the Internet and mobile phones, with confidence and even carefree, leave a lot of digital traces. On their basis, among others, Big Data is created. Research shows that trust in Big Data collected in organizations is also high, although no analysis of their creation is carried out. Many users of digital technologies (the Internet) are not aware of how the data they create is being used or of the threats they generate. This, of course, also applies to the (security of) employees of organizations and the organizations themselves.

Mitigating internal and external threats is crucial for any organization. The new threats mentioned above require the adoption of solutions at the level of organizational framework (including the introduction of a code of data ethics), at the strategic level (including the introduction of a catalog of best practices), and at the operational level (including the application of best practices at every stage of the lifecycle of projects, products, and services). The analysis of threats and risks arising from (associated with) Big Data should be included in (integrated with) each implemented project, every offer, and every new business venture based on Big Data.

Digital trust is, in fact, a widely expressed and accepted belief that an organization is trustworthy and that the promoted image of the organization or brand is credible, secure, transparent, and consistent with reality in terms of its digital practices. A simultaneous introduction of this, relatively new in organizations, the perspective of the business building will provide the organization with the opportunity to simultaneously manage risk and build trust by consistently assessing how ethics are taken into account in decisions based on Big Data.

The threats mentioned above can be identified, managed, and effectively controlled when organizations, not ignoring technical safeguards, prioritize ethical practices regarding data and algorithms for their processing throughout the decision-making process (in other words: throughout the entire data lifecycle or the entire chain of their supply). Big Data ethical aspects should the organizations aim for their activities are to be effective, cannot be limited to the last stages of the cycle. The data lifecycle includes:

■ Recording data (and their origin) from sensors, systems, or people and obtaining permission for their use wherever possible
■ Saving data in a trusted area that is both secure and easily accessible for further processing
■ Combining different data sets to create a larger data set that is larger than the sum of its parts
■ Applying the knowledge acquired through data analysis to make decisions, make changes, or provide a product or service
■ Providing owners with access to data sets or new consumers with insight into the data
■ Researching and transforming data to extract information and discover new knowledge
■ Deleting data from servers to prevent their sharing or future use

The development of sound ethical control throughout the entire supply chain of data, information, and knowledge applies to all types of digital risk throughout the whole lifecycle of data used in the organization. With the right solutions for data ethics and algorithms at the corporate governance level, at the strategic management level, and the operational level, organizations can build digital trust. An alternative approach, thus leaving data and algorithms unsupervised, can permanently damage consumers' confidence in the brand or stakeholders' trust in the organization.

6.4 Building a Sensible Trust in Big Data in Organization Management

The data is merely the starting point for decisions and actions. Similar to a surgeon performing an operation (before they perform an operation), the manager plans, organizes, and makes changes to the organization. Similar to a surgeon, they not only remove "sick" cells and organs but also implement new (similarly to the surgeon – implant) and motivate others to accept the plan, undergoing implementation or already implemented changes (therapies). By analyzing the data, one seeks to extract from it the knowledge necessary to make decisions based on it and subsequently take actions to achieve the organization's goals.

Organizations, considering data ethics in their activities, are able to improve their clients' trust in the organizations and strengthen the legitimacy of their business activities (Crane et al., 2008). This is particularly important for organizations that have undergone a digital transformation and become publishers or participants of digital platforms and ecosystems. In the digital market, where consumers differentiate (discriminate) suppliers based on their ability to build trust, achieving a high level of trust by an organization increases the attraction toward the brand and becomes a strong distinguishing feature for companies. This applies to all industries and sectors of the economy – nowadays especially to the financial sector (electronic banking services, payments, insurance), but increasingly more to other industries, including media and tourism.

Data ethics affect not only the organizations' activities. Organizations rely on external data. Therefore, trust in this data is an important problem for organizations. Their main source is data created on social media. It is obvious that fake news, especially created by bots, should not constitute the basis for the organizations' decisions and actions. Including them in big textual data is a serious threat, and their detection and elimination is a serious challenge for the organizations. Their creation is, to a large extent, beyond the control of the organization and its managers. However, the rest of the large data lifecycle can be controlled. This allows it to be considered trustworthy and consistent with the principles of its ethical use in the management of the organization. This is related not only to the application of codes of ethics but also to corporate social responsibility programs (of the organization).

Digital trust is hard to build but surprisingly easy to lose. This makes it an increasingly more significant factor in differentiating organizations in the digital economy. Trust in the brand facilitates the development of the organization through product development, cooperation with partners, expansion into new markets, and increasing the share in existing markets. Hence, it translates into measurable financial results. Therefore, devoting attention to ethics in data, information, knowledge (and thus evidence) management brings financial benefits – it is not just an attitude for naive philanthropists.

6.5 The Impact of Data Ethics Solutions on Organizational Innovation and Organization Management in the Digital Age

Data ethics is part of business ethics. Business ethics is a scientific discipline that is nowadays widely developed, having a broad institutional base. Business ethics undertakes theoretical reflection and multi-faceted historical, methodological, axiological analyzes, etc. The subject of business ethics is the moral practice in the business world, as well as the influence of market mechanisms on the hierarchy of values and vice versa, the influence of moral values on market functioning. It is a systematic study of moral issues in the business world. Business ethics also means real moral practice in the business world, postulating real behavior that defines its principles (Dahl, 2009). On this plane, the concept of "business ethics" includes, in a positive sense, a set of values and norms recognized and respected in the business world, in its mentality and activity. Basic tools of using business ethics in practice are ethical programs, ethical codes, professional ethics, and programs of corporate social responsibility. It seems that data ethics (Big Data) can be classified as professional ethics, which incorporates moral principles that are most often determined by ethical codes.

The ethical treatment of data throughout the entire supply chain of data, knowledge, or products and services requires a fundamental change in the way data is perceived in organizations. A security perspective, which focuses on the confidentiality, integrity, and availability of data, or a privacy perspective, emphasizing data control in the context of meeting the requirements of legal and organizational regulations by users using the data is not enough. For the success of activities in both perspectives, an additional view becomes crucial: ensuring ethical activities amounting to the application of data ethics, ensuring building trust in data and the knowledge extracted from it.

Organizations must begin to apply ethics to data collection, manipulation, and use processes. Only ethical actions lead to confidence building. This requires focusing attention on these activities at every stage of the data supply chain and cooperation with each stakeholder. Creating a Big Data code of ethics facilitates the implementation of this principle by the organizations. From the point of view of the code of ethics, a specific type of document can be considered, containing principles, assumptions, rules of behavior, and action of the organization toward the external environment and toward internal groups (Kryk, 2001). The code of ethics is a written set of rules for behavior that management and employees are required to comply with it. The standards contained in the code apply to all employees irrespective of their position in the professional hierarchy (Gasparski et al., 2002). They are not, of course, a decalogue, where all principles are timeless and inviolable. Standards in the data codes must be updated as knowledge of new threats and the ability to calculate the risks associated with them are acquired. The fundamental values and general principles contained therein should remain unchanged. In contrast, the more detailed principles must be held up-to-date, and therefore updated along with changes in culture and technology (Gasparski et al., 2002). In essence, the code contains a set of rules and principles in force in a given environment and a set of restrictions (often associated with sanctions). It is expedient that these principles are rooted in employee value systems and organizational culture (Zbiegień-Maciąg, 1994).

The code, including the data code, is designed to assist employees in ethical behavior. It, therefore, indicates how general moral principles apply to what an organization does (Gasparski, 2001). The ethical code has the nature of separate moral regulations for employees' behavior, constituting an important element of professional ethics (Walkowiak, 1998). The code takes a form that emphasizes the most important principles of general ethics (Pietrzkiewicz, 1997) while concretizing them in terms of subject and object aspects (Banajski, 2001). Often, the code is an element of ethical programs, which also contain, among others, organizational principles, the strategy of behavior, standards of behavior, or constant ethical evaluation of activities (Szulczewski, 2003).

The code in its content may be general or detailed. Sometimes, it formulates general, basic aspirations of the organization, its mission, and relations with the environment. In other cases, it contains very detailed instructions and behavioral standards for the employees (Klimczak, 2013). The widest code has general principles as well as specific directives of conduct. The volume of the code varies, ranging from a single-page document to extensive multi-page records (Gasparski, 2002).

When analyzing the construction of the code, one may notice that some examples of them have an introductory part containing the basic principles that the organization follows in its conduct. It usually consists of the address signed by the unit's "head" and the preamble. The preambles to the code are the "profession of faith", sometimes referred to as the "philosophy" of the company. The introduction to the code may also include the mission, vision, and goals of the organization as well as its fundamental values (Gasparski, 2001). The mission of an organization or company is the most general purpose of its functioning. It should be visionary, that is, far-reaching, and it may contain a declaration of the fundamental values of the organization, in particular, the determination of the attitude toward stakeholders (Lewicka-Strzałecka, 1999). In addition to introductions or preface, the code is divided into chapters, subchapters, etc., which are devoted to specific issues or are ordered by types of stakeholders, or built to accommodate a mixed structure (Gasparski, 2002).

In principle, the code of ethics is not formulated in an imperative form, but in a way, informing about the course of action (Tomczyk–Tołkacz, 1994). The best code is one considered to be a combination of a code of values, a code of conduct, and a code of standards to be followed (Gasparski et al., 2002). A concurrent feature of the code is the declaration of legalism, i.e., legal compliance in all circumstances. A common element of the code is the obligation for the organization, the company, to fulfill its moral obligations to all stakeholders (Lewicka–Strzałecka, 1999). The code of ethics constructed in such a manner shows a specific philosophy of ethical operation of the organization, while simultaneously providing the employees themselves with the possibility to refer to it in doubtful situations for solutions. Compliance of all employees with the code of ethics should bring specific effects in the form of the improvement of both the organizational culture and the trust in the company (Kryk, 2001).

In the case of the Big Data code of ethics, it is created by a set of best practices that will guide practitioners through the processes of considering ethical issues at every stage of product development, service delivery as well as each data (knowledge) supply chain.

6.6 Balancing Digital Security with the Innovation Risk in Evidence-Based Management Using Big Data

In the literature on innovation in organizations, some approaches assume data-based management as well as information-based and knowledge-based. Yet another management concept believes that management is based on evidence (evidence-based management). At the same time, the notions of data, information, or knowledge, as well as evidence, are neither unambiguous nor disjoint. Hence, the notions: data-based, information-based, knowledge-based, and evidence-based management, as well as data management, information management, knowledge management, are interrelated. Each of them accepts the great significance of accessing valuable data. The question that arises is: in what manner can issues of digital security and trust in data, as well as ethical or unethical actions associated with data, enable or prevent innovation and their development at the pace required by the company? How to build trust in data and share them in innovation processes without increasing organizational risk?

The concern for data and knowledge security and the increased protection is, in some sense, contrary to the processes of the full availability of Big Data and knowledge dissemination, which is one of the basic knowledge management processes. Such a limitation may significantly limit the company's innovativeness. Organizations have to struggle with such a contrary. This is one of the paradoxes of modern organizations. Therefore, data ethics creates a natural climate for the increase of trust, conditioning the organization's innovation. It is slightly different in the sphere of product innovations as well as in the sphere of organizational services and processes (service and organizational innovations).

There are additional privacy and security challenges that have become more important day by day since the emergence of large data sets. Data privacy conflict, privatization of data, or the reverse phenomenon – resignation from data privacy and their wide sharing – set the limits of security for both organizations and individuals. Many people protest against analytics associated with Big Data as they are convinced that it is unethical due to the violation of people's privacy. Privacy protection advocates believe that engineers can develop new data analysis techniques that will minimize costs for privacy. Undoubtedly, ethical conduct in the process of collecting and processing Big Data can lead to innovative solutions without violating the rights of individuals and other organizations. However, where there is an opportunity to make a profit by creating a new solution that the competition does not possess, there is also the risk of taking unethical action. Violations of ethical principles of Big Data use in business processes, including the creation of new business process patterns, as mentioned before, is one of the digital risks. Detection of privacy violations or other unethical activities exposes organizations to serious losses. This encourages organizations to undertake innovations in the sphere of digital security, which, in turn, causes another wave of increased supervision and the control of employees as well as the associates of the organization.

Organizations that are striving to balance risk and innovation face many challenges, an essential component of which are the ethical, and not just technological, aspects. It is necessary to analyze the company's goals, strategies, and activities in this context. It is also necessary to consider whether there is a real need to change the way the company operates, in which case, many changes will have to be made throughout the organization. Besides, what types of digital risks and at what level is the organization willing to accept? The development of risk profiles facilitates a better understanding of which kinds of innovative activities will be prioritized and implemented as business activities. They may also be used to set expectations on how to balance innovation and risk across an enterprise. The willingness to take risks does not mean that an adequate level of safety is not being provided. In fact, it often informs about various security requirements. To balance the tension between the level of organizational risk and the level of innovation created in the organization (balancing risk and innovation), the actions mentioned above introducing ethical order in the organization, covering the entire cycle of creating Big Data, are necessary. Of course, this does not sufficiently reduce the risk because it only affects the area of data that the organization can influence through regulatory activities and the impact on the culture of the organization. Thus, these do not apply to people and, therefore, do not guarantee the determinism of the regulated activities.

6.7 Conclusion

Ensuring digital business security is not easy. Not only new facilities in running a business but also threats appeared along with Big Data. It is important to update technology constantly, but it is worth remembering that the weakest link in the data supply chain is the human being, and cultural changes in the organization take time. Nowadays, organizations also need to consider the risks resulting from the lack of ethical data management practices and processing algorithms throughout the data lifecycle.

The above remark indicates an increasing demand for information regarding the anticipated digital threats associated with the creation and use of Big Data. Even if digital security can be obtained in 99% of cases, it is enough for cybercriminals or dishonest suppliers and users of digital content using the remaining 1% to be able to cause serious damage to the organization or its stakeholders. These crimes lead, among others, to the creation of Big Data containing false information. The social media are full of such content used, for example, to analyze sentiment to products, people, and organizations, as well as to analyze reputation.

It is clear that the innovations, risk, and digital security of the organization and its members are not insurmountable in conflict. This is not a competition but an inevitable coopetition. Technology and cultural changes, including ethical principles and attitudes, must cooperate in an organization. This forces a change in the way of thinking about risk and digital security and its practice, also in relation to Big Data. The need to apply data ethics in relation to Big Data requires new knowledge from many practitioners and is a specific activity in the portfolio of activities carried out by organizations. Trust is the foundation for any relationship. However, it must have solid rational foundations. This also applies to the relationship between organizations and Big Data, both those created within the organization and those created outside of it and used in the organization's management processes.

References

Banajski, R. (2001). Treści aksjologiczne kodeksów etycznych regulujących sferę życia gospodarczego [Axiological content of codes of ethics regulating the economic life]. In: Gasparski, W., Dietl, J. (eds.), *Etyka biznesu w działaniu – doświadczenia i perspektywy* [*Business Ethics in Practice - Experiences and Perspectives*]. Warszawa: PWN.

Crane, A., McWilliams, A., Matten, D., Moon, J., Siegel, D.S. (2008). *The Oxford Handbook of Corporate Social Responsibility*. Oxford: Oxford University Press.

Dahl, R.J. (2009). Responsibility, ethics and legitimacy of corporations. *Society and Business Review*, 4(3), 266–268.

Davis, K., Patterson, D. (2012). *Ethics of Big Data: Balancing Risk and Innovation*. Cambridge: O'Reilly Media.

Gasparski, W. (2002). Kodeksy etyczne: ich struktura i treść [Codes of ethics: Their structure and content]. *Annales. Etyka w życiu gospodarczym*, 5, 227–239.

Gasparski, W. (2001). Programy etyczne firm i ich projektowanie [Design of companies' ethical programs]. *Annales. Etyka w życiu gospodarczym*, 4, 173–178.

Gasparski, W., Lewicka-Strzałecka, A., Rok, B., Szulczewski, G. (2002). Rola i znaczenie programów i kodeksów etycznych [Role and importance of programs and codes of ethics]. In: Gasparski, W., Lewicka-Strzałecka, A., Rok, B., Szulczewski, G., *Etyka biznesu w zastosowaniach praktycznych – inicjatywy, programy, kodeksy [Business ethics in practical applications - initiatives, programs, codes]*. Warszawa: CIM.

Herschel, R., Miori, V. (2017). Ethics and big data. *Technology in Society*, 49, 31–36.

Klimczak, B. (2013). *Etyka gospodarcza [Ethics in the Economy]*. Wrocław: Wyd. Akademii Ekonomicznej we Wrocławiu.

Kryk, B. (2001). *Czy kodeks przedsiębiorstwa może stanowić rozwiązanie problemów firmy [Can the Code of Conduct Be a Solution to the Company's Problems]*. In: Gasparski, W., Dietl, J. (eds.), *Etyka biznesu w działaniu [Business ethics in practice]*. Warszawa: PWN.

Lewicka-Strzałecka, A. (1999). *Etyczne standardy firm i pracowników [Ethical Standards for Companies and Employees]*. Warszawa: IFiS PAN.

Mayer-Schonberger, V., Cukier, K. (2013). *Big Data: A Revolution that Will Transform How We Live, Work, and Think*. Boston, MA: Houghton Mifflin Harcourt.

Pietrzkiewicz, T. (1997). *Systemy wartości i kodeksy etyczne w gospodarce [Systems of Values and Codes of Ethics in the Economy]*. Warszawa: Wyd. Instytutu Organizacji i Zarządzania w Przemyśle "Orgmasz".

Szulczewski, G. (2003). Programy etyczne firm i ich wykorzystanie w działalności Public Relations [Companies' ethical programs and their use in public relations]. In: Ślusarczyk, S., Świda, J., Tworzydło, D. (eds.), *Public relations w kształtowaniu pozycji konkurencyjnej organizacji [Public Relations in Shaping the Competitive Position of an Organization]*. Wrocław: Wyd. Wyższej Szkoły Informatyki i Zarządzania.

Tomczyk-Tołkacz, J. (1994). *Etyka biznesu – wybrane problemy [Business Ethics - Selected Problems]*. Wrocław: Wyd. Akademii Ekonomicznej we Wrocławiu.

Walkowiak, J. (1998). *Misja firmy a etyka biznesu [Mission of the Company and Business Ethics]*. Warszawa: Centrum Informacji Menadżera.

Zbiegień-Maciąg, L. (1996). *Etyka w zarządzaniu [Ethics in Management]*. Warszawa: Centrum Informacji Menadżera.

Zwitter, A. (2014). Big data ethics. *Big Data and Society*, July–December 1–6. doi: 10.1177/2053951714559253.

BIG DATA IN MANAGEMENT: APPLICATIONS, PROSPECTS, AND CHALLENGES

Chapter 7

Big Data in Modern Farm Management

Monika Gębska
Warsaw University of Life Sciences—SGGW

Contents

7.1 Introduction

Farm management is becoming more and more complicated, and yet its effects are of fundamental importance for food production. Farms are getting bigger, more modern, strongly connected with the market which is strongly regulated and unstable. In addition, the effects of agricultural production depend to a large extent on its adaptation to natural conditions, especially soil quality and climate. Farmers will face many challenges in this respect due to adverse climate changes—weather variability, rainfall irregularity, more frequent droughts (Food and Agriculture Organization, 2017). FAO (2017) also draws attention to the fact that agricultural production will hinder the spread of plant and livestock diseases in the future as a result of increased cross-border human mobility.

Meanwhile, agriculture's job is to feed a growing world population. According to United Nations forecasts, by 2050 the population will increase by 2 billion people, which will require an increase in agricultural production by up to 60% over the next 30 years (United Nations, 2019). This will not be easy due to the limited resources, especially agricultural land and manual workforce.

In this context, researchers and practitioners are increasingly paying attention to the need to produce food in a more sustainable way (Kemp, Girdwood, Parton and Charry, 2004), taking into account current conditions and future needs. Therefore, agricultural activities are increasingly subject to legal regulations in the field of environmental protection (Krol, 2015), animal welfare (Vapnek and Chapman, 2010), or bio-insurance (Dutta, Mueller, Smith, Das and Aryal, 2015). Society expects food to be safe, available, cheap (Piližota, 2012), and produced to many standards, including ethics (Food Standards Agency, 2016; Piližota, 2012) while protecting landscape and biodiversity (Berry, Delgado, Pierce and Khosla, 2004; McConnell and Burger, 2018). Meanwhile, farmers must take into account the profitability of production and the achievement of income, and yet the economic effects of agricultural activities are very variable (Beckman and Schimmelpfennig, 2015) and depend on numerous decisions taken during a long, complicated production cycle.

Because of the number of variables, a farmer must take into account when making decisions, farm management is more difficult than for most enterprises (Kemp, Girdwood, Parton and Charry, 2004). Advanced information technologies such as Big Data, which have already been successfully implemented in other sectors of the economy, can help farmers in managing the farm (Lokers, Knapen, Janssen, van Randen and Jansen, 2016). According to the definition of De Mauro, Greco and Grimaldi (2016, p. 131), "Big Data is the Information asset characterized by such a High Volume, Velocity and Variety to require specific Technology and Analytical Methods for its transformation into Value".

Big Data, thanks to extensive analytical models, gives the opportunity to carry out a detailed analysis of agricultural activities and facilitate making the right decisions in time. As a result, they can make agricultural production more efficient, profitable, and also friendly to society, the environment, animals and, as a result, more sustainable (Waga and Rabah, 2014).

In this context, an essential question is how farmers will be able to manage farms and meet the multiple challenges such as food security, climate change, responsibly water and soil management, biodiversity, animal welfare while improving productivity, lowering at the same time its environmental footprint resulting from greenhouse gas emissions (Sayer and Cassman, 2013).

For the farmers to meet all their expectations, they will need to focus on increasing production in sustainable ways. This is a big challenge and only farmers who manage their farms in reasonably effective way will be successful. Probably many farmers having small farms will leave farming as the costs of production are higher than the net returns making it unprofitable (Sawant, Urkude and Jawale, 2016). Studies conducted by many researchers suggest that efficient data management and processing can be a good solution to problems faced by farmers. It helps decision makers to make appropriate choices, plan agricultural activities, and take preventive and curative measures as needed (Sawant, Urkude and Jawale, 2016).

The aim of this chapter is to present ways of using Big Data in modern farm management based on a critical literature review and to propose future research in the area. Research question used in this study is: Why we need Big Data in agriculture and how Big Data may help manage the farm in a modern way?

The bibliographic analysis in the area under study was performed. First, a keyword-based search was carried out from the Google Scholar. As search keywords, following query was applied: "Big Data" AND "Management" AND ["Precision Agriculture "OR" Smart Farming "OR" Agriculture "OR" Animal Production "OR" Milk production "OR" Pigs "OR" Cows "OR Broiler "OR" Poultry "OR" Meat production"]. From this effort, abstracts of 485 initially identified papers published in English in the years 2010–2019 were checked in terms of content and relationship with the topic of the article. Finally, only 84 were used and fully analyzed.

In the first part of this chapter, its data sources are presented, and next, the use of Big Data in crop and animal production is described. Further, advantages and disadvantages of Big Data adaptation in farm management are presented. Farmers' opinions in these regards are presented. Finally, conclusions and future research directions are proposed.

7.2 Farm Management before the Era of Big Data

Farm management is defined as the "process by which resources and situations are manipulated by the farm manager in trying, with less than complete information, to achieve his goals" (Dillon, 2008). It means making and implementing all the decisions made by organizing and operating a farm for maximum production and profit.

As in the past and today in traditional farming, many decisions are made based on historical data, experience, and intuition (Nuthall and Old, 2018). These decisions determine the use of means of production, including fertilizers, pesticides, feed, as well as the dates of agrotechnical convergences, irrigation, and veterinary treatments. However, as early as the 1990s, the need to develop methods to support farmers' decision making and predicting their results was noticed. Activities in this direction began with modeling of plant growth and crop size (Basso, Ritchie, Pierce, Braga and Jones, 2001). Most of the models used were based on linear regression analysis and multiple linear regression analysis (Kravchenko and Bullock, 2000) and were used to make decisions at the operational level.

In the last 30 years, there has been rapid technical and technological progress resulting mainly from the construction and miniaturization of computers and the invention of the Internet. New devices and systems have also been created that are also applicable in agriculture. The creation of the Global Position System (GPS) (Shanwad, Patil, Dasog, Mansur and Shashidhar, 2002) and radio-frequency identification (RFID) technology using radio waves to identify people and objects at a distance (Luvisi, 2016) was particularly important. Since the method of combining the use of RFID with the Internet has been invented, it has been possible for computers to collect precise data in real time, 24 hours a day without the participation of people and processing them into useful information (Ibarra-Esquer, González-Navarro, Flores-Rios, Burtseva and Astorga-Vargas, 2017).

Such a dynamic network of physical objects, systems, platforms, and applications that are able to communicate and share intelligence among themselves, the external environment, and people is called the Internet of Things (IoT) (Madushanki, Halgamuge, Wirasagoda and Syed, 2019). In contrast, agriculture using IoT solutions is referred to as precision agriculture or smart farming. The management of the farm has changed significantly due to the application of advanced technologies in precision farming. Decisions have become more accurate and are made faster (Madushanki et al., 2019), and their implementation more effective than before. And yet the possibilities of data collection are still growing thanks to more and more modern drones, robots, cameras, sensors located in soil, fields, plants, farm buildings, and even on animals (Delgado, Short, Roberts and Vandenberg, 2019). In addition, many manufacturers of agricultural machinery and equipment install sensors in them to provide farmers with the data they need (Bronson and Knezevic, 2016).

The information obtained is invaluable and helpful in more conscious, modern farm management. Collecting them is, however, only the beginning of the process of transforming observations and measurements into information useful for management. Thanks to IoT, huge amounts of digital data are available, which allows creating models better describing reality than previously used linear models. Thanks to this, the calculation results are useful for making strategic decisions.

It is important to note that precision agriculture and Big Data are not synonymous (Sonka, 2015). What distinguishes precision agriculture from Big Data according to Sonka (2015) is the use of smaller units of management information, e.g., regarding one field, while Big Data requires observation (data) from many fields, many years, and many technologies used. Big Data also assumes the integration of this data with data from other sources and concerning, e.g., temperature, humidity, precipitation, wind power and direction, market data (prices of raw materials and products, demand, supply), and many others (Sonka, 2015). Thanks to such extensive analysis, Big Data allows more versatile than in the case of precision production to determine whether there are any trends or relationships between data.

The creation and development of Big Data concerned mainly plant production, but from around 2010 the situation began to change.

7.3 Big Data in Animal Production Management

Big Data has big potential to transform animal production methods and farm management. Since 2013, the number of articles has been growing and they concern mainly dairy cattle (Lokhorst, Mol and Kamphuis, 2019). The main areas where Big Data can be used are feeding, e.g., forecasting daily intake of cows (Steeneveld and Hogeveen, 2015) and predicting cow's health and fertility (Harty and Healy, 2016) as well as individual and whole herd performance (Yan, Chen, Akcan, Lim and Yang, 2015). White, Amrine and Larson (2018) presented interesting possibilities for the use of Big Data in cattle breeding (2018), who described the possibility of detecting oestrus and bovine diseases based on movement patterns (distance, pace, and movement method). Tracks the position of each animal at short intervals and compares the results with patterns helping to determine whether or not the movements follow the correct pattern (White, Amrine and Larson, 2018; Fernández-Carrión et al., 2017). Quality, visualization, and interpretation of data (Hermans et al., 2017, 2018) were also dealing with reproduction of cows. A farmer quickly received information about heat in one of the females in the herd increases the chances of successful insemination. Green et al. (2016) indicate the possibility of using Big Data to control mastitis in cows. The authors point out the possibility of forecasting which cows are at risk of disease, which they think is their main advantage. Preventing disease or treating it early reduces the amount of medication used and, importantly, improves animal welfare.

Big Data can also be used to assess the performance of fattening cattle as described by Hewitt, Green and Hudson (2018) to monitor the behavior and growth of pigs (Piñeiro et al., 2019) or to achieve rapid genetic progress through genome analysis (Morota, Ventura, Silva, Koyama, and Fernando 2018).

These are just a few examples of the use of Big Data in animal production management, and soon there will be more and more of them because the equipment necessary for precision production is cheaper, and IT technologies and computers are becoming more user-friendly. Table 7.1 shows the main aspects of using Big Data in agriculture.

7.4 Advantages of Big Data in Farm Management

A review of the literature indicates many benefits that can be gained by using Big Data in farm management. Table 7.2 presents the most important of them. The use of Big Data helps farmers better control the production process (Subramanian, Chen and Redd, 2018). They can identify existing problems faster and receive a warning before they occur (Sonka, 2016).

Using Big Data significantly increases production effects (Australian Farm Institute, 2018; Chandra Sekhar, Udaykumar, Kumar and Sekhar, 2018) and

Table 7.1 Effects of Big Data Use in Crop and Animal Production Management

Crop Production	Source	Animal Production	Source
Improved forecasting of yields	Ribarics (2016)	Improved forecasting of animal production	Faverjon et al. (2019)
Real-time decisions and alerts based on data from fields and equipment	Piñeiro et al. (2019)	Real-time decisions and alerts based on data from animals and equipment	Ribarics (2016)
Optimal timing of shipping crops to the market	Ribarics (2016)	Optimal timing of shipping livestock to the market	Ribarics (2016)
Better optimized use of seeds/fertilizers/pesticides	Poppe and Renwick (2015); Ribarics (2016)	Better veterinary management and inspection of herds	White, Amrine and Larson (2018)
Implementation of new methods improving yields, e.g., weed protection	Piñeiro et al. (2019)	Implementation of new methods improving animal production	Faverjon et al. (2019)
Better supply management, cheaper (seeds, fertilizers, pesticides) and lower costs of storage	Wolfert, Verdouw and Bogaard (2017); Lokhorst, Mol and Kamphuis (2019)	Better supply management, cheaper feed for animals, lower costs of storage	Wolfert, Verdouw and Bogaard (2017); Lokhorst, Mol and Kamphuis (2019)
Identify weeds	Bronson and Knezevic (2016)	Optimal climate in buildings where animals are kept	Ribarics (2016)

(Continued)

Table 7.1 (Continued)   Effects of Big Data Use in Crop and Animal Production Management

Crop Production	Source	Animal Production	Source
Higher yields	Wolfert, Verdouw and Bogaard (2017)	Better health and animal performance	Faverjon et al. (2019)
Optimal irrigation of fields	Ribarics (2016)	Better control of water usage at buildings for animals	Australian Farm Institute (2018)
Precise and effective genome editing for plant breeding	Tantalaki, Souravlas and Roumeliotis (2019)	Precise and effective genome editing for animal breeding	Australian Farm Institute (2018)
Improved forecasting of weather	Ribarics (2016)	Improving sustainability	Faverjon et al. (2019)
Spoilage reduction (crops, seeds, fertilizers, etc.)	Waga and Rabah (2014)	Higher animal welfare	White, Amrine and Larson, (2018); Faverjon et al. (2019)

Source: Own elaboration.

Table 7.2 Advantages of Using Big Data in Farm Management

Specifications	Source
Supply data sets for improved decision making and improve analysis and models	Wolfert, Verdouw and Bogaard (2017); Coble, Mishra, Ferrell and Griffin (2018)
Higher accuracy, robustness, flexibility, and generalization performance of Big Data processing techniques	Tantalaki, Souravlas and Roumeliotis (2019)
Better control of the production processes	Wolfert, Verdouw and Bogaard (2017)
Better personalized on-farm management practices	Tantalaki, Souravlas and Roumeliotis (2019)
Real-time decisions and data-driven decisions	Poppe and Renwick (2015); Wolfert, Verdouw and Bogaard (2017); Tantalaki, Souravlas and Roumeliotis (2019)
Integration of production and business performance	Ribarics (2016)
Increase of farm productivity	Henry (2015); Griepentrog, Uppenkamp and Hörner (2017); Coble, Mishra, Ferrell and Griffin (2018)
Increase labor productivity	Poppe and Renwick (2015)
Improving economic gain and profitability	Sonka (2016); Wolfert, Verdouw and Bogaard (2017)
Improving efficiency	Faulkner et al. (2014); Wolfert, Verdouw and Bogaard (2017)
Reduction of support costs	Wolfert, Verdouw and Bogaard (2017)
Reduction of energy and water use	Ribarics (2016)
Reduction of environmental impact	Sonka (2016); Coble, Mishra, Ferrell and Griffin (2018)
Better forecasting crops, demand for seeds, fertilizers, animal feed	Ribarics (2016); Sykuta (2016)
Better forecasting prices and market demand	Ribarics (2016); Shekhar, Schnable, LeBauer, Baylis and VanderWaal (2017)
Tighter relationships between farmer suppliers and buyers	Ribarics (2016); Griepentrog, Uppenkamp and Hörner (2017)

(Continued)

Table 7.2 (*Continued*)   Advantages of Using Big Data in Farm Management

Specifications	Source
Improve food security	Tong, Hong and JingHua (2015); Wolfert, Verdouw and Bogaard (2017)
Better risk management	Wolfert, Verdouw and Bogaard (2017); Kamilaris, Kartakoullis and Prenafeta-Bold (2017); Ferrell and Griffin (2018)
Access to individual data anytime and from anywhere	Wolfert, Verdouw and Bogaard (2017)
Benchmarking	Wolfert, Verdouw and Bogaard (2017)
Automation of agricultural procedures	Tantalaki, Souravlas and Roumeliotis (2019)
Boost innovations	Henry (2015)
More timely scheduling maintaining of equipment	Ribarics (2016)

Source: Own elaboration based on the literature.

economic effects such as improving profitability and efficiency, reducing operating costs (Delgado, Short, Roberts and Vandenberg, 2019).

The possibilities offered by Big Data are huge. In addition to forecasting crop yields and animal performance (Lima et al., 2018), they help you decide what and where to grow, when to sow and plant, how to feed individual animals, when and what to do with their breeding, and even when, what, and where to sell.

The use of Big Data improves risk management (Allepuz, Martín-Valls, Casal and Mateu, 2018). Farmers can, thanks to Big Data, assess the likelihood of precipitation, frost, crop failure, pest infestation, or pathogens (Bauriegel, Giebel, Geyer, Schmidt and Herppich, 2011; Bendre, Thool and Thool, 2016; Astill, Fraser, Dara and Sharif, 2018; Fernandez, 2018). The use of Big Data increases food security (Ahearn, Armbrusterb and Young, 2016).

Wireless data transfer technology permits farmers to access to individual data from anywhere (Wolfert, Verdouw and Bogaard, 2017).

7.5 Disadvantages of Big Data in Farm Management

The literature also mentions many inconveniences and problems associated with the use of Big Data in agriculture (Table 7.3).

The huge amount of data, on the one hand, is an advantage, and on the other hand, an inconvenience. Large data sets are necessary to properly predict the

Table 7.3 Disadvantages of Using Big Data in Farm Management

Specifications	Source
System need a lot of data which are highly dimensional	Tantalaki, Souravlas and Roumeliotis (2019)
High costs and investments	Wolfert, Verdouw and Bogaard (2017)
Cybersecurity issue	Tantalaki, Souravlas and Roumeliotis (2019)
Problems with data ownership	Carbonell (2016); Sykuta (2016); Coble, Mishra, Ferrell and Griffin (2018); Faverjon et al. (2019)
Need of wireless infrastructure for connectivity	Mark, Griffin and Whitacre (2016); Barone, Williams and Micklos (2017)
Data storage issue	Tantalaki, Souravlas and Roumeliotis (2019); Barone, Williams and Micklos (2017)
Information asymmetry between farmers and large agribusiness software companies	Ribarics (2016); Carbonell (2016)
Threatened autonomy of farmers	Wolfert, Verdouw and Bogaard (2017)
Big Data will enable farmers to be replaced by autonomous machines	Henry (2015)
Changing the way farmers are operating	Drucker (2014); Poppe and Renwick (2015)
Farmers' knowledge is about to be replaced by algorithms	Wolfert, Verdouw and Bogaard (2017)
Changes the farm organization	Poppe and Renwick (2015)
Complexity to use, requires considerable technical skills to handle analysis methods	Tantalaki, Souravlas and Roumeliotis (2019); Barone, Williams and Micklos (2017)

Source: Own elaboration based on the literature.

consequences of events and give correct recommendations, unfortunately, some information is difficult to obtain, especially when it concerns a long production cycle. In the case of cereal production, e.g., for data on sowing or plant growth, you have to wait until the next growing season, i.e. you can only get it once a year. For this reason, the preparation time needed to forecast the data set is long. According to Mark, Griffin and Whitacre (2016), sending large amounts of data requires appropriate infrastructure, the construction of which is extremely expensive and only a few operators can afford such an investment. The asymmetry of information that Ribarics (2016) mentions raises concerns. Farmers, in order to have access to modern technologies, reveal a lot of private information without full knowledge by whom and how it will be used. Meanwhile, software providers can aggregate large amounts of private data and develop new products by combining their privileged position with unique access to highly detailed, private data (Ribarics, 2016). Therefore, issues regarding the method and place of data storage become important. It seems that ethical issues, data ownership, and security will be a problem that needs to be solved for a long time (Carbonell, 2016; Sykuta, 2016; Tantalaki, Souravlas and Roumeliotis, 2019).

Another disadvantage is still the low knowledge of advanced technologies among farmers around the world (Sharma and Kaushik, 2019). And yet using Big Data requires considerable skills (Tantalaki, Souravlas and Roumeliotis, 2019). It is comforting that the research of Sharma and Kaushik (2019) shows that young farmers belonging to the new generation are positive about the use of advanced technologies in farm management and more often use it in practice.

Farmers should also consider the need for investment. Purchase of equipment for data collection, license fees can be a significant barrier to the use of advanced technologies in agriculture, especially on small farms (Long, Blok and Coninx, 2016; Sharma and Kaushik, 2019).

Wolfert, Verdouw and Bogaard (2017) underline that the use of Big Data may threaten the autonomy of farmers and change the way they are operating (Drucker, 2014). What is more, farmers' expertise and knowledge, is about to be replaced by algorithms (Wolfert, Verdouw and Bogaard, 2017). Following the suggestion of Henry (2015), one day farmers themselves will be replaced by an artificial intelligence and autonomous machines.

7.6 Farmers' Perception of Big Data

There are few publications in the literature about farmers' opinions on Big Data. Therefore, this section presents farmers' views on the use of various IT technologies in agriculture.

Adrian, Norwood and Mask (2005) reported that producers with higher confidence levels, greater farm size, and more education intend to adopt precision agriculture technologies more than producers with lower levels of each of these variables.

Henry (2015) stated that the most important motivator for the use of precision production was the desire to increase yields. On a scale of 0–10 points, farmers assigned an average of 7.8 points to this factor. The next places were cost reduction (5.5 points), increased profitability (5.4 points), risk reduction (4.6 points), and simplification of activities (4.4 points). On the other hand, the desire to expand business (3.9 points), the desire to use the latest technology (2.3 points), and the desire to improve the environment, to which farmers assigned an average of 2.0 points out of 10 possible (Henry, 2015).

The publication of Jithin, Shubham and Kaushik (2019) shows that the main barriers to the adaptation of smart farming technologies were small farm size, initial investment, complexity to use, not sure about the value, technology inappropriate for farm, data sharing, age (older do not want to change habits), and no proper communication regarding this technology.

Knierima, Borges, Lee Kernecke, Kraus and Wurbs (2018) reported that one of the most important factors inhibiting the use of digital solutions on farms was the low level of education. According to this study, the additional factor was ignoring such solutions by small farm owners. Knierima et al. (2018) pointed out another factor influencing this situation. He blames the lack of proper agricultural advisory service in Europe which is not engaged in creating awareness of such technologies among farmers. Llewellyn and Ouzman (2014) also emphasized the important role of agricultural consulting in this area.

7.7 Conclusions and Proposition for Future Research

Management of farms has always been critically important for food production. Nowadays, farmers face many new challenges, and they need bigger data sets to make responsible and successful decisions. The data are too large or too complex for traditional data processing software. One of the solutions is Big Data technology which helps farmers to manage the farm. It helps to analyze land, soil, and health of crops and animals and save time during making decisions. The Big Data analysis advises farmers in many areas, e.g., what to produce in each season, which crops will give the best yield, and which seeds, fertilizers, pesticides, or feeds for animals should be used. Big Data can assist farmers by giving relevant advice and recommendations to their specific farm-related problems; therefore, the use of Big Data in farm management can reduce uncertainty and bring answers to many farmers' questions. It may be concluded that the use of Big Data will lead to radical changes in farm management.

By using artificial intelligence platforms, one can gather a large amount of data from government and public websites or real-time monitoring of various data, which is also possible by using IoT and then it can be analyzed with accuracy to enable the farmers to address all the uncertain issues faced by farmers in the agriculture sector.

A review of the literature presented in this chapter shows that the Big Data era has begun in the agriculture, like in the other sectors of the economy. Information technologies have appeared earlier in plant production and therefore have become more widespread than in animal production. Despite this, most of the studies analyzed were theoretical. There was less empirical research. Most annoying is the lack of research describing the implementation of, e.g., the IoT system, precision production, or Big Data. Future research should focus on analyzing the costs and benefits of implementing different system options to provide farmers with answers to what extent and at what time investments in advanced technologies will pay off. It may be interesting to compare the effects of digitization on farms with different directions and production systems as well as of different sizes. An important area of research should also be the assessment of the effects of the use of advanced information technologies on the environment and the level of farm sustainability. In addition, it is interesting whether the use of advanced technologies supporting management somehow changes users, and if so how do they react to these changes, how do they assess them, and which skills are absolutely necessary to be able to take maximum advantage of the application's capabilities?

References

Adrian, A., Norwood, S., Mask, P. (2005). Producers' perceptions and attitudes toward precision agriculture technologies. *Computers and Electronics in Agriculture, 48*(3), 256–271.

Ahearn, M. C., Armbrusterb, W., Young R. (2016). Big data's potential to improve food supply chain environmental sustainability and food safety. *International Food and Agribusiness Management Review, Special Issue, 19*(A), 155–172.

Allepuz, A., Martín-Valls, G. E., Casal, J., Mateu, E. (2018). Development of a risk assessment tool for improving biosecurity on pig farms. *Preventive Veterinary Medicine, 1*(153), 56–63.

Astill, J., Fraser, E., Dara, R., Sharif, S. (2018). Detecting and predicting emerging disease in poultry with the implementation of new technologies and big data: A focus on Avian influenza virus. *Frontiers in Veterinary Science, 5*, 263.

Australian Farm Institute. (2018) Research Report. The implications of digital agriculture and big data for Australian agriculture. Retrieved from https://www.crdc.com.au/sites/default/files/pdf/Big_Data_Report_web.pdf.

Barone, L., Williams, J., Micklos. D. (2017). Unmet needs for analyzing biological big data: A survey of 704 NSF principal investigators. *PLoS Computational Biology*, 13, e1005755.

Basso, B., Ritchie, J., Pierce, F., Braga, R., Jones, J. (2001). Spatial validation of crop models for precision agriculture. *Agricultural Systems. 68*(2), 97–112.

Bauriegel, E., Giebel, A., Geyer, M., Schmidt, U., Herppich, W. B. (2011) Early detection of Fusarium infection in wheat using hyper-spectral imaging, *Computers and Electronics in Agriculture, 75*(2), 304–312.

Beckman, J., Schimmelpfennig, D. (2015). Determinants of farm income. *Agricultural Finance Review, 75*(3), 385–402.

Bendre, M. R., Thool, R. C., Thool, V. (2016). Big Data in Precision Agriculture Through ICT: Rainfall Prediction Using Neural Network Approach, in *Proceedings of the International Congress on Information and Communication Technology*, 165–175.

Berry, J. K., Delgado, J. A., Pierce, F. J., Khosla, R. (2005). Applying spatial analysis for precision conservation across the landscape. *Journal of Soil and Water Conservation 60*, 363–370.

Bronson, K., Knezevic, I. (2016). Big Data in food and agriculture. *Big Data and Society, 3*(1).

Carbonell, I. (2016). The ethics of big data in big agriculture. *Internet Policy Review, 5*(1), 1–13.

Chandra Sekhar, C., Udaykumar, J., Kumar, B., Sekhar, Ch. (2018). Effective use of big data analytics in crop planning to increase agriculture production in India. *International Journal of Advanced Science and Technology, 113*, 31–40.

Coble, K. H., Mishra, A. K., Ferrell, S., Griffin, T. (2018). Big data in agriculture: A challenge for the future, *Applied Economic Perspectives and Policy, 40*(1), 79–96.

De Mauro, A. Greco, M., Grimaldi, M. (2016). A formal definition of big data based on its essential features. *Library Review, 65*(3), 122–135.

Delgado, J. A., Short Jr. J. M., Roberts, D. P., Vandenberg, B. (2019, July 16). Big data analysis for sustainable agriculture on a geospatial cloud framework front. Sustain. *Food System, 3*, 1–13. doi: 10.3389/fsufs.2019.00054.

Dillon, J. (2008). The definition of farm management. *Journal of Agricultural Economics, 31*(2), 257–258.

Drucker, P. (2014). Agriculture Springs into the Digital Age. *Fund Strategy.* Retrieved from https://www.fundstrategy.co.uk/issues/fund-strategy-sept-2014/agriculture-springs-into-the-digital-age/.

Dutta, R., Mueller, H., Smith, D., Das, A., Aryal, J. (2015). Interactive visual big data analytics for large area farm biosecurity monitoring: i-EKbase system. In W. Fan, A. Bifet, Q. Yang, and P. S. Yu (eds.), *Proceedings of the 4th International Conference on Big Data, Streams and Heterogeneous Source Mining: Algorithms, Systems, Programming Models and Applications*, PMLR, *41*, 9–18. Retrieved from http://proceedings.mlr.press/v41/dutta15.pdf

Faulkner, A. Cebul, K. (2014). Agriculture Gets Smart: The Rise of Data and Robotics, Cleantech Agriculture Report. Retrieved from https://www.cleantech.com/wp-content/uploads/2014/07/Agriculture-Gets-Smart-Report.pdf.

Faverjon, C., Bernstein, A., Grütter, R., Nathues, C., Nathues, H., Sarasua, C., Sterchi, M., Vargas, M.-E., Berezowski, J. (2019). A transdisciplinary approach supporting the implementation of a big data project in Livestock production: An example from the Swiss Pig production industry. *Frontiers Veterinary Science, 6*, 215.

Fernandez, P. (2018). Spread Model: A Forecasting and Managing Tool in Microbiological Safety. Data Value Chain in the Dairy Production: Opportunities and Challenges in Big Data in the Food Chain: The Un(der)explored Goldmine? *14th Symposium of the Scientific Committee of the Federal Agency for the Safety of the Food Chain*, 57–63.

Fernández-Carrión, E., Martínez-Avilés, M., Ivorra, B., Martínez-López, B., Ramos, Á. M., Sánchez-Vizcaíno, J. M. (2017). Motion-based video monitoring for early detection of livestock diseases: The case of African swine fever. *PLoS ONE, 12*(9): e0183793.

Ferrell, S. L., Griffin, T. W. (2018). Managing Farm Risk Using Big Data A Guide to Understanding the Opportunities and Challenges of Agricultural Data for Your Farm. Retrieved from http://agecon.okstate.edu/farmdata/files/Managing%20Farm%20Risk%20Using%20Big%20Data.pdf.

Food and Agriculture Organization. (2017). The Future of Food and Agriculture. Trends and Challenges. Retrieved from http://www.fao.org/3/a-i6583e.pdf.

Food Standards Agency. (2016, February). Our Food Future. Full report. Retrieved from https://www.food.gov.uk/sites/default/files/media/document/our-food-future-full-report.pdf.

Green, M. J., Archer, S. C., Breen, J. E., Davies, P. L., Down, P. M., Emes, R. D., Green, L. E., Hudson, C. D., Huxley, J. N., Leigh, J.L. Bradley, A. J. (2016). Predictive Biology: The Future for Mastitis Control? In *Proceedings of the World Buiatrics Congress*, 69–71.

Griepentrog, H.W., Uppenkamp, N., Hörner, R. (2017). Digital Agriculture - Opportunities. Risks. Acceptance. A DLG position paper. Retrieved from https://www.dlg.org/en/agriculture/topics/a-dlg-position-paper/

Harty, E., Healy, J. (2016). Using big data and advanced analytics top optimise health and fertility. In C. Kamphuis and W. Steeneveld (eds.), *Precision Dairy Farming 2016*. Wageningen, The Netherlands: Wageningen Academic Publishers. 219–222.Henry, M. (2015). Big data and the future farming. *Australian Farm Institute's Quarterly Newsletter, 12*(4), 1–5.

Hermans K., Opsomer, G., Wageman, W., Moerman, S., De Koster, J., Van Eetevelde, M., Van Ranst, B., Hostens, M. (2018) Interpretation and visualization of data in dairy herds. *In Practice, 40*, 195.

Hermans, K., Waegeman, W., Opsomer, G., Ranst, B. V., Koster, J. D., Eetvelde, M. V. Hostens, M. (2017). Novel approaches to assess the quality of fertility data stored in dairy herd management software. *Journal of Dairy Science, 100*, 4078–4089.

Hewitt, S., Green, M. J., Hudson, C.D. (2018). Evaluation of key performance indicators to monitor performance in beef herds. *Livestock*, doi: 10.12968/live.2018.23.2.72.

Ibarra-Esquer, J. E., González-Navarro, F. F., Flores-Rios, B. L., Burtseva, L., Astorga-Vargas, M. A. (2017). Tracking the evolution of the internet of things concept across different application domains. *Sensors, 17*, 1379.

Jithin, V., Shubham, S., Kaushik, A. (2019). Views of Irish farmers on smart farming technologies: An observational study. *AgriEngineering, 1*, 164–187. https://10.3390/agriengineering1020013

Kamilaris, A., Kartakoullis, A., Prenafeta-Bold, F. X. (2017). A review on the practice of big data analysis in agriculture. *Computers and Electronics in Agriculture, 143*, 23–33. doi: 10.1016/j.compag.2017.09.037

Kemp, D. R., Girdwood, J., Parton, K. A., Charry, A. A. (2004). Farm management: Rethinking directions? *AFBM Journal, 1*(1), 36–44.

Knierima, A., Borgesb, F., Lee Kerneckerb, M., Krausb, T., Wurbsb, A. (2018). What Drives Adoption of Smart Farming Technologies? Evidence From a Cross-Country Study. *13th European IFSA Symposium*, 1–5 July 2018, Chania, Greece, 1–14.

Kravchenko, A., Bullock, D. (2000). Correlation of corn and soybean grain yield with topography and soil properties. *Agronomy Journal, 92*(1), 75–83.

Krol, A. (2015). Legal framework of environmental law for agricultural production in Poland. *Polityki Europejskie. Finanase i Marketing, 13*(62), 86–106. Retrieved from http://sj.wne.sggw.pl/article-PEFIM_2015_n62_s86/

Lima, E., Hopkins, T., Gurney, E., Shortall, O., Lovatt, F., Davies, P., Williamson, G., Kaler, J. (2018). Drivers for precision livestock technology adoption: A study of factors associated with adoption of electronic identification technology by commercial sheep farmers in England and Wales. PLoS One, 13(1), 1–17. doi: 10.1371/journal.pone.0190489

Llewellyn, R. S., Ouzman, J. (2014). Adoption of Precision Agriculture-Related Practices: Status, Opportunities and the Role of Farm Advisers. In: *CSIRO Report Published by GRDC*, Retrieved from https://grdc.com.au/__data/assets/pdf_file/0024/208653/adoption-of-precision-agricultural-related-practices-status-opportunities-and-the-role-of-farm-advisers-2014.pdf.pdf.

Lokers, R., Knapen, R., Janssen, S., van Randen, Y., Jansen, J. (2016). Analysis of big data technologies for use in agro-environmental science. *Environmental Modelling & Software, 84*, 494–504.

Lokhorst, C., de Mol, R., Kamphuis, C. (2019). Invited review: Big data in precision dairy farming animal. *The International Journal of Animal Biosciences, 13*(7), 1–10.

Long, T. B., Blok, V., Coninx, I. (2016). Barriers to the adoption and diffusion of technological innovations for climate-smart agriculture in Europe: Evidence from the Netherlands, France, Switzerland and Italy. *Journal of Cleaner Production, 112*, 9–21.

Luvisi, A. (2016). Electronic identification technology for agriculture, plant, and food. A review. *Agronomy for Sustainable Development, Springer Verlag/EDP Sciences/INRA*, 36(1), 13.

Madushanki, A., Halgamuge, M., Wirasagoda, H., Syed, A. (2019). Adoption of the internet of things (IoT) in agriculture and smart farming towards urban greening: A review. *International Journal of Advanced Computer Science and Applications, 10*(10), 11–28.

Mark, T. B., Griffin, T. W., Whitacre, B. E. (2016). The role of wireless broadband connectivity on 'Big Data' and the agricultural industry in the United States and Australia. *International Food and Agribusiness Management Review, 19*(A), 43–56.

McConnell, M. D., Burger, L. W. Jr. (2018). Precision conservation to enhance wildlife benefits in agricultural landscapes. In J. Delgado, G. Sassenrath, T. Mueller (eds.), *Precision Conservation: Geospatial Techniques for Agricultural and Natural Resources Conservation. Agronomy Monograph 59*, Madison, WI: ASA, CSSA, and SSSA, 285–312.

Morota, G., Ventura, R. V., Silva, F. F., Koyama, M., Fernando, S. C. (2018). Big data analytics and precision animal agriculture symposium: Machine learning and data mining advance predictive big data analysis in precision animal agriculture. *Journal of Animal Science, 96*(4), 1540–1550.

Nuthall, P. L., Old, K. M. (2018). Intuition, the farmers' primary decision process. A review and analysis. *Journal of Rural Studies, 58,* 28–38.

Piližota, V. (2012). Consumer Needs for Affordable Food of Good Quality. Serving Consumer Demands. UDK 664 Pregledni članak Prihvaćeno za tisak: 12. Svibnja 2012. Retrieved from https://hrcak.srce.hr/94430.

Piñeiro, C., Morales, J., Rodríguez, M, Aparicio, M., Manzanilla, E-G., Koketsu, Y. (2019). Big (pig) data and the Internet of the swine things: A new paradigm in the industry. *Animal Frontiers,* 9(2), 6–15.

Poppe, K. J., Renwick, A. (2015). A European perspective on the economics of Big data. *Farm Policy Journal, 12*(1), 11–19.

Ribarics, P. (2016). Big data and its impact on agriculture. *Ecocycles, 2*, 33–34.

Sawant, M., Urkude, R., Jawale, S. (2016). Organized data and information for efficacious agriculture using PRIDE model *International Food Agribusiness Management Review,* Special Issue *19*(A), 115–130.

Sayer, J., Cassman, K. (2013). Agricultural innovation to protect the environment. *Proceedings of the National Academy of Sciences of the United States of America, 110*(21), 8345–8348.

Shanwad, U. K., Patil, V. C., Dasog, G., Mansur, C. P., Shashidhar, K. C. (2002). Global Positioning System (GPS) in Precision Agriculture. *Proceedings of Asian GPS conference*. Retrieved from https://www.researchgate.net/publication/261035926_Global_Positioning_System_GPS_in_Precision_Agriculture/citation/download.

Sharma, V. J. S, Kaushik, A. (2019). Views of Irish farmers on smart farming technologies: An observational study, *AgriEngineering, 1*(2), 164–187.

Shekhar, S., Schnable, P. S., LeBauer, D., Baylis, K. R., VanderWaal, K. (2017). Agriculture Big Data (AgBD). Challenges and Opportunities from Farm to Table: A Midwest Big Data Hub Community † Whitepaper. Retrieved from https://pdfs.semanticscholar.org/c815/75e059a826f39b47367fceaac67a8f55fb07. pdf?_ga=2.171973029.709639680.1569509918–13514251.1568646822.

Sonka, S., Cheng, Y. T. (2015). Precision agriculture: Not the same as big data but…. *Farmdoc Daily, 5,* 206–217.

Sonka, S. T. (2016). Big data: Fueling the next evolution of agricultural innovation. *Journal of Innovation Management, 4*(1), 114–136.

Steeneveld, W., Hogeveen, H. (2015). Characterization of Dutch dairy farms using sensor systems for cow management. *Journal of Dairy Science, 98*(1), 709–717.

Subramanian, B., Chen, S-S., Redd, K. R. (2018). Emerging Technologies for Agriculture and Environment: Select Proceedings of ITsFEW, 77.

Sykuta, M. E. (2016) Big data in agriculture: Property rights, privacy and competition in Ag data services. *International Food and Agribusiness Management Review Special Issue, 19*(A), 57–74.

Tantalaki, N., Souravlas, S., Roumeliotis, M. (2019). Data-driven decision making in precision agriculture: The rise of big data in agricultural systems. *Journal of Agricultural & Food Information,* 1–37. doi:10.1080/10496505.2019.1638264.

Tong, L., Hong, T., JingHua, Z. (2015). Research on the big data-based government decision and public information service model of food safety and nutrition industry. *Journal of Food Safety and Quality, 6*(1), 366–371.

United Nations. (2019). Probabilistic Population Projections based on the World Population Prospects. Retrieved from https://population.un.org/wpp/Download/Probabilistic/ Population/.

Vapnek, J., Chapman, M. (2010). Legislative and Regulatory Options for Animal Welfare. FAO. Legislative Study 104. Retrieved from http://www.fao.org/3/ i1907e/i1907e00.pdf.

Waga, D., Rabah, K. (2014). Environmental conditions' big data management and cloud computing analytics for sustainable agriculture. *World Journal of Computer Application and Technology, 2*(3), 73–81.

White, B. J., Amrine, D. E., Larson, L. R. (2018). Big data analytics and precision animal agriculture symposium: Data to decisions. *Journal of Animal Sciences, 96,* 1531–1539.

Wolfert, S. G. L., Verdouw, C., Bogaardt, M-J. (2017). Big data in smart farming – A review, *Agricultural Systems, 153,* 69–80.

Yan, W. J., Chen, X., Akcan, O., Lim J., Yang, D. (2015). Big Data Analytics for Empowering Milk Yield Prediction in Dairy Supply Chains, *IEEE International Conference on Big Data (Big Data),* Santa Clara, CA, 2015, 2132–2137.

Chapter 8

Big Data Analytics and Corporate Social Responsibility: An Example of the Agribusiness Sector

Marcin Ratajczak and Ewa Stawicka

Warsaw University of Life Sciences—SGGW

Contents

8.1 Introduction

The concept of corporate social responsibility (CSR) is the most important trend in business, supporting sustainable development (Garriga, Mele, 2004, pp. 51–68). Big Data is also a tool that helps organizations understand their environment and consumers who use their products or services better. The factor that drives social innovation is the emergence of a new model for creating network solutions. Therefore, it is puzzling whether companies will manage to use the collected data in an ethical and useful way. Responsible activities in the agribusiness industry are also gaining importance (Waddock, 2008, pp. 87–107). In the past, the term "food economy" was used in the research in Poland concerning the agribusiness sector. Currently, agribusiness concerns a broad approach such as the generation of means of production and services necessary for agriculture and processing of agricultural raw materials, acquisition, production and processing of agricultural raw materials, storage, sorting, sale, export, and import (Kapusta, 2012).

Agribusiness is essential in terms of food security but also safe food (Luhmann, Theuvsen, 2016, p. 673). The importance is growing in the area of planning: analysis in various branches, organizational: creating management strategies, also in the case of the small and medium-sized enterprise sector. Even analytical: seeking advantage and security in the economic, social, and ecological context (Kapusta, 2000). Companies can now use data analysis to unlock, model, and predict consumer and stakeholder behavior (Dyer, Singh, 1998, p. 660). Analyses of this data are compact and comprehensive due to their diversity and volume. Obtaining reliable data on detailed, sensitive CSR indicators can affect the competitive advantage on the market. These data must be used ethically.

The purpose of this chapter is an attempt to determine the relationship between CSR activities in companies from the agribusiness sector and conducting dialogue and consultation with internal and external stakeholders.

The detailed goals of the conducted research are as follows:

■ Learning the scope of knowledge of agribusiness sector entrepreneurs in Poland about social responsibility
■ Determining the relationship between selected independent variables and conducting dialogue and consultation with stakeholder groups (internal and external)

8.2 Premises for Changes in the Agribusiness Sector

In the context of social responsibility, attention is paid to improving the competitiveness of the agri-food sector, sustainable rural development, sustainable supply chain, enhancing the natural environment, enhancing the quality of life, and diversifying the rural economy. Firlej separated the division of the agribusiness sector into broadly defined departments: agriculture, forestry and hunting, fisheries and inland fishing, purchase of agricultural raw materials, their processing and transport, processing of raw materials and the food industry, production means for agriculture and the food industry, services related to agribusiness, food trade, agritourism, agricultural education, and school system (Firlej, 2005, p. 134).

The concept of stakeholders in the agribusiness sector is also becoming increasingly important. A passive approach to the environmental problems of organizations from the food economy has initiated the stimulation of consumer activity. There is also an aspect of a shared economy, i.e., everyday consumption, shared consumption, sharing, and exchange. This can be perceived as a gap between the rapid development of information and the still slow sector of agribusiness in Poland in this respect. On the other hand, social responsibility and sustainable development goals are the elements driving various types of innovations (Black, 2005, p. 73). As emphasized by Rok, CSR is a process of learning about and incorporating the changing expectations of stakeholders into the management strategy (Rok, 2008, p. 18). It is not without reason that the importance of awareness and building a competitive advantage on authentic CSR activities is emphasized. It also turns out that more or less rapid changes in consumer behavior will stimulate transformations in the field of agribusiness (Stawicka, 2017). With the development of the new economy, knowledge economy, and e-economy, the share of knowledge and information in achieving the economic goal and the pace of information transfer increases. Therefore, the process of creating innovation and ensuring the continuous development of offered services and products is gaining importance (Valor, 2005). Under the influence of new technologies and globalization phenomena that facilitate communication, the behavior or even cultural norms of entire societies change (Płoszajski, 2012).

On the other hand, a business should take even greater responsibility as part of a range of global pathologies. The danger of lack of awareness and education means that people do not worry about the future; they focus only on current problems. To produce more and more physical goods, people, culture, and the environment have been degraded in a way that prevents them from providing the quality satisfaction they once gave. To replace lost values such as peace, communion, beauty, and healthy environment, excessive consumption occurs, and this degrades our environment and culture even more (Pater, Lierop, 2006).

The new approach of the agribusiness sector is the first step in creating a *win-win* strategy and also creating economic value in a way that simultaneously creates social value by meeting the needs and problems of society (Porter, Kramer, 2011, p. 124). Non-financial information is becoming material and may be associated with financial consequences. Loss of reputation by an organization may harm its profit or loss account or its market value (Peloza, 2009).

In practice, the agribusiness sector makes little use of CSR and Big Data mechanisms, and the number of innovations is still small. The concept of social responsibility must evolve in the coming years. Their shape and nature will change depending on the economic situation and the expectations of various stakeholder groups (Ratajczak, 2013).

The subject of implementing the concept of CSR in the agribusiness sector is not as extensive in the literature as general approaches to these issues (Engle, 2007; Kong, 2012, p. 78). In most research, they concern instead of a specific aspect chosen by the authors or the area of social responsibility (Poetz, Haas, Balzarova, 2013;

Helmig, Spraul, Ingenhoff, 2016, p. 76). There is a lack of research that comprehensively presents the issues of applying the CSR concept by micro, small, and medium enterprises in the agribusiness sector. It is a permanent element of the organization's management system.

8.3 Methodology

The research covered 3,501 enterprises conducting business activity in the agribusiness sector. The time range of research is 2011 (the analysis concerned only the Mazowieckie voivodeship) and 2017 (the study concerned all voivodeships in Poland). The surveyed population was dominated by micro-enterprises, which constituted almost 41%, small – 33%, and medium-sized – 26% ones, from rural areas. Over half of the surveyed agribusiness enterprises have been operating on the market for a relatively long time since they were established before 1989 (53%); every third company was established in the years 1990–1999. In the pre-accession period of Poland to the European Union, i.e., in 2000–2004, about 14% of entities were registered, and in 2005–2017, only 4% of the analyzed companies.

Almost 47% of enterprises from the agribusiness sector participating in the research described their market activity range as national. Every fifth company indicated international coverage, i.e., in several selected countries (mainly medium-sized entities). About 16% of respondents considered conducting their activities at the local market (in a given town) and regional market (in a given voivodeship). Only 0.6% of enterprises indicated global reach, i.e., in many countries around the world.

The following methods were used to develop and present the research material: comparison methods, inductive and deductive inference, methods of statistical description, and deduction. In the field of research technique, the electronic survey technique used for self-completion (Google Forms) was used, taking into account its conditions: access to the questionnaire via the Internet and the lack of direct interaction with the entrepreneur completing it (Tourengau, Conrad, Couper, 2013, pp. 60–62). The research tool used in the paper was the author's electronic survey questionnaire prepared in Google software.

For this study, Cramer's V tests (2 on 3 rectangular tables, 4 on 5, etc.) and Phi (2 on 2 square tables) were used—these are symmetrical measures based on the Chi-square test, which report the strength of the relationship between variables in crosstabs. For questions on ordinal scales, Kendall's Tau-b tests (for two ordinal variables with the same number of columns and rows) or Kendall's Tau-c tests (for two ordinal variables with different numbers of columns and rows) were used. The obtained correlation results (Kendall's Tau-b and Kendall's Tau-c), as well as the Phi symmetrical measure, can take negative values, which in this case are interpreted as the inverse relationship/correlation. When the crosstab consisted of a nominal and ordinal scale, the statistics were read at a weaker measurement level (Bedyńska, Brzezicka, 2007).

This chapter uses Polish and foreign literature on CSR, data from the Institute of Agricultural and Food Economics—National Research Institute, Food and Agriculture Organization of the United Nations (FAO), EUROSTAT OECD.

8.4 Research Results

Taking into account all the surveyed agribusiness enterprises, can be stated that 24% definitely know the concept of CSR and almost 19% rather know it. Every third respondent indicated that he has not encountered this concept so far and does not know what it means, taking into account theoretical and practical elements.

The following correlations between independent variables (general information) and the dependent variable, knowledge of the concept of CSR have been determined in terms of statistical analyses (Table 8.1.)

Over 35% of the surveyed agribusiness entrepreneurs indicated that they are trying to conduct regular dialogue with all groups of stakeholders. Every fifth respondent stated that he performs the conversation regularly. Still, only with

Table 8.1   Correlations between Knowledge of the Concept of CSR and Selected Independent Variables

Company size	It was determined that there is a very weak, statistically significant correlation. This informs that together with a smaller category of agribusiness enterprise; the respondents less often know the concept of corporate social responsibility—$p < 0.001$, Kendall's Tau-c = −0.09.
Commune type	A weak statistically significant correlation informs that along with a lower degree of urbanization of the enterprise location, the respondents are less likely to know the concept of responsible business—$p < 0.001$, Kendall's Tau-c = 0.12. It is worth emphasizing at this point that over 68% of respondents from urban–rural communes indicated knowledge of the above concept. Almost 40% of companies from rural communes did not hear about this concept at all.
Agribusiness department	The dependency coefficient showed a weak statistically significant relationship. This informs that the respondents who provide services in agritourism and the generation of means of production for agriculture and the food industry state to a greater extent than others that they know the concept of CSR—$p < 0.001$, Cramer's V = 0.25, Chi-square = 906.68 ($df = 24$).

(Continued)

Table 8.1 (*Continued*)   Correlations between Knowledge of the Concept of CSR and Selected Independent Variables

Legal form	The dependency ratio showed a weak, statistically significant relationship, which informs that the respondents representing limited partnerships know the concept of CSR to a lesser extent than the others—$p < 0.001$, Cramer's V = 0.15, Chi-square = 315.30 (df = 20). It should be emphasized that almost 60% of entrepreneurs registered as civil law partnerships and natural persons conducting business activity indicated full knowledge of the concept in question.
Year of establishment	There is a very weak statistically significant correlation, which informs that the older the enterprise (in the aspect of the year of establishment), the respondents are less likely to know the concept of social responsibility—$p < 0.001$, Kendall's Tau-c = −0.09. However, over 70% of companies established in 2005–2017 know the idea of CSR very well.
Range of market activity	There is also a very weak, statistically significant correlation. This says that with a smaller reach of the company, respondents are less likely to know the concept of CSR—$p = 0.002$, Kendall's Tau-b = −0.05. It is very characteristic that all respondents pointing to the global reach stated that they see the idea of responsible business.
Life cycle phase in terms of the market situation	The dependency coefficient showed a weak, statistically significant relationship, which informs that the respondents who believe that their company is in the phase of thorough reconstruction are less likely to say that they know the concept of CSR—$p < 0.001$, Cramer's V = 0.17, Chi-square = 423.45 (df = 20). It is worth noting that almost 43% of respondents indicating the phase of entering the market and expansion showed an explicit knowledge of the concept of CSR.

Source: Own elaboration based on surveys.

selected groups of stakeholders (probably only those keys for the company), about 16% of companies took actions, but informally and irregularly, only at the time of such need. Over 30% of respondents did not enter into dialogue or consultation with their stakeholders at all.

Based on statistical analyses, correlations between independent variables (general information) and the dependent variable, dialogue or consultation with internal stakeholders (employees) were determined.

There was a weak, statistically significant correlation. This means that together with a smaller category of enterprise, the respondents less often indicated that the company conducts a documented dialogue/consultation with internal stakeholders—$p < 0.001$, Kendall's Tau-c = −0.15. Also, in the case of the lower degree of urbanization of the company's location, the respondents less often indicated that the company had a documented dialogue/consultation with internal stakeholders—$p < 0.001$, Kendall's Tau-c = 0.17.

The dependency ratio showed a weak, statistically significant relationship. This relationship informs that respondents providing services in agritourism, wholesale and retail trade in food, as well as the processing of agricultural raw materials and food industry to a greater extent, conducted a dialogue with internal stakeholders. Less often, this type of consultation was conducted in agricultural companies—$p < 0.001$, Cramer's V = 0.16, Chi-square = 244.52 ($df = 18$). The analysis did not show diversification of statistically significant answers given about the year of establishment of the company and dialogue with internal stakeholders.

There was a very weak statistically significant correlation that, along with the smaller range of the company's operations, the respondents less often indicated that the company conducts a documented dialogue/consultation with internal stakeholders—$p < 0.001$, Kendall's Tau-c = 0.08. It is worth emphasizing that all companies with global reach indicated dialogue with their groups of external and internal stakeholders. The analysis did not show the diversification of statistically significant answers given concerning gender and dialogue with internal stakeholders.

There was a weak statistically significant correlation that older respondents were less frequently of the opinion that the company regularly conducts documented dialogue/consultation with internal stakeholders—$p < 0.001$, Kendall's Tau-b = 0.13.

There was a weak statistically significant correlation, which informed that better-educated managers less often confirmed that the company conducts regular documented dialogue/consultation with internal stakeholders—$p < 0.001$, Kendall's Tau-c = 0.15.

Also, correlations between independent variables (general information) and the dependent variable, i.e., conducting a dialogue or consulting with external stakeholders (clients, contractors, suppliers) were calculated (Table 8.2).

Table 8.2 Correlations between Conducting Dialogue or Consulting with External Stakeholders (Clients, Contractors, Suppliers) and Selected Independent Variables

Company size	There is a moderate statistically significant correlation, which informs that together with a smaller category of enterprise, the respondents less often indicate that the company conducts a documented dialogue/consultation with external stakeholders—$p < 0.001$, Kendall's Tau-c = −0.31.
Commune type	There is an almost moderate statistically significant correlation, which informs that along with a lower degree of urbanization of the enterprise location, the respondents less often indicate that the company conducts a documented dialogue/consultation with external stakeholders—$p < 0.001$, Kendall's Tau-c = 0.28.
Agribusiness department	The dependency ratio showed a moderate statistically significant relationship, which informs that respondents providing services in agritourism, wholesale and retail trade in food and processing of agricultural raw materials and the food industry are conducting more documented dialogue with external stakeholders. Less often, this type of consultation is conducted in agricultural companies—$p < 0.001$, Cramer's V = 0.34, Chi-square = 243.52 ($df = 18$).
Legal form	The dependency ratio showed an almost moderate statistically significant relationship, which informs that the respondents representing the partner company and limited partnership less often indicate that the company conducts in any documented way a dialogue/consultation with external stakeholders—$p < 0.001$, Cramer's V = 0.27, Chi-square = 258.06 ($df = 15$).
Year of establishment	The analysis did not show the diversification of statistically significant answers given due to the year of establishing the company and conducting a dialogue with external stakeholders.
Range of market activity	There is a weak statistically significant correlation that informs that along with the smaller scale of the enterprise, the respondents less often indicate that the company conducts a documented dialogue/consultation with external stakeholders—$p < 0.001$, Kendall's Tau-c = 0.16. It is worth noting that all global companies indicated that they were conducting a dialogue with their groups of external stakeholders.

(Continued)

Table 8.2 (*Continued*) Correlations between Conducting Dialogue or Consulting with External Stakeholders (Clients, Contractors, Suppliers) and Selected Independent Variables

Life cycle phase in terms of the market situation	The dependency ratio showed a weak, statistically significant relationship which informs that the respondents who believe that the company is in the declining phase and under thorough reconstruction are less likely than the others to think that the company conducts regular dialogue with external stakeholders—$p < 0.001$, Cramer's V = 0.22, Chi-square = 43.472 (df = 15).

Source: Own elaboration based on surveys.

8.5 Conclusion

Understanding the behaviors of modern external and internal stakeholders is becoming the key to success in the contemporary world. Implementation of new business models in connection with social responsibility and sustainable development becomes a necessity. Knowledge and information about social responsibility and creating social innovations are gaining importance. The organization is also dependent on the environment and stakeholders. Enterprises have to face not only the growing number of stakeholders but also the increasing number of interactions between them. The importance of strategies for stakeholders is emphasized, or at least the dialogue and consultation.

In the agribusiness enterprises in Poland, there were no significant differences in the approach to the level of knowledge of agribusiness sector entrepreneurs about social responsibility. The level of understanding of the issue and awareness of the concept of responsible business is still unsatisfactory (about 24% of respondents in 2018 knew the concept compared to 16% of respondents in 2011). Entrepreneurs from the agribusiness industry with a production and trade profile demonstrated knowledge of the issue. Most often, they were large enterprises, founded in 1990–1999. It is worth emphasizing that global companies most often led CSR activities and solutions in connection with conducting dialogues and consultations with stakeholder groups, practically not at all in organizations operating on the local and regional markets.

The problem is the lack of mapping of stakeholders and the lack of dialogue with them. In Poland, it is difficult to analyze algorithms for Big Data sets in the small and medium enterprises (SME) sector in agribusiness. It is suggested that entrepreneurs acquired knowledge not only about CSR but focused on Big Data and portable computers, by creating a data analysis center and developing strategies in line with their goals and technological maturity.

It is also recommended that entrepreneurs in the SME sector engage in dialogue and cooperate with partners in the implementation of large data set technologies. Stakeholders can help them create platforms for data collection, solve data security problems, and facilitate the use of external and internal integration applications.

In the final analysis, we are in favor of redesigning the collection of data on the agribusiness SME sector so as to achieve the greatest synergy thanks to the integration of private data, government data programs, and detailed data collection studies that are to complement other available tools. Big Data and algorithms are also used for promoting and enforcing sustainable development based on rigorous data management leading to the predictive identification of likely unsustainable event.

The limitations of the study include the selection of meters for the research tool. Due to the multidimensional nature of social responsibility, there is no unified tool. There is a wide variety of measurement methods, research techniques, and indicators used to analyze and evaluate the concept of CSR. Agribusiness, as an object of trust, is not subjective. This chapter is a contribution to determining the scale of importance of conducting dialogue and consultation with groups of stakeholders (internal and external) in the aspect of customer management. There is no measurement of the effects (effects) of activities carried out in the scope of identifying the needs of stakeholders on determining competitive advantages on the market. Hence, it is recommended to conduct further studies to validate the findings of this study by including articles from other databases.

References

Bedyńska, S., Brzezicka A. (2007). *Statystyczny drogowskaz* [Statistical Signpost]. Warszawa, PL: Wydawnictwo Szkoły Wyższej Psychologii Społecznej.

Black, S. (2005). *Public Relations*. Kraków, PL: Oficyna Ekonomiczna.

Dyer, J. H., Singh, H. (1998). The relational view: Cooperative strategy and sources of inter-organizational competitive advantage. *Strategic Management Journal, 23*(4), 660–679.

Engle, R. L. (2007). Corporate social responsibility in host countries: A perspective from American managers. *Corporate Social Responsibility and Environmental Management, 14*(1), 17–27.

Firlej, K. (2005). Analiza perspektywy sektora agrobiznesu w aspekcie rozwoju obszarów wiejskich [Analysis of the perspective of the agribusiness sector in the aspect of rural development]. *Roczniki Naukowe Stowarzyszenia Ekonomistów Rolnictwa i Agrobiznesu, Zeszyt, 7*(4), 117–123.

Garriga, E., Mele, D. (2004). Corporate social responsibility theories – mapping the territory. *Journal of Business Ethics, 53,* 51–71.

Helmig, B., Spraul, K., Ingenhoff, D. (2016). Under positive pressure: How stakeholder pressure affects corporate social responsibility implementation. *Business and Society, 55.* 151–187.

Kapusta F. (2000). Agrobiznes i uwarunkowania jego rozwoju w Polsce [Agribusiness and conditions for its development in Poland]. *Prace Naukowe Akademii Ekonomicznej we Wrocławiu, 865.*

Kapusta F. (2012). *Agrobiznes [Agribusiness]*. Warszawa: Wydawnictwo Difin.

Kong, D. (2012). Does corporate social responsibility matter in the food industry? Evidence from a nature experiment in China. *Food Policy, 37*(3), 323–324.

Luhmann, H., Theuvsen, L. (2016). Corporate social responsibility in agribusiness: Literature review and future research directions. *Journal of Agricultural and Environmental Ethics, 29*(4), 673–696.

Pater, A., Lierop, K. (2006). Sense and sensitivity: The roles of organization and stakeholders in managing corporate social responsibility. *Business Ethics, European Review, 15*(4), 339–351.

Peloza, J. (2009). The challenge of measuring financial impacts from investments in corporate social performance. *Journal of Management, 35*(6), 1518–1541.

Płoszajski, P. (2012). Ruchomy cel: o konieczności redefinicji teorii i praktyki społecznej odpowiedzialności przedsiębiorstw w warunkach nowej gospodarki [A moving target: The need to redefine the theory and practice of corporate social responsibility in the new economy] In P. Płoszajski (ed.), *Społeczna odpowiedzialność biznesu w nowej gospodarce, [Corporate Social Responsibility in the New Economy]*. Warszawa: Wydawnictwo SGH.

Poetz, K., Haas, R., Balzarova, M. (2013). CSR schemes in agribusiness: Opening the black box. *British Food Journal, 115*(1), 47–74.

Porter, M. E., Kramer, M. R. (2011). Tworzenie wartości dla biznes i społeczeństwa, [Creating Value for Business and Society]. *Harvard Business Review Polska, 99*. Available at: https://www.hbrp.pl/a/tworzenie-wartosci-dla-biznesu-i-spoleczenstwa/VOxyDLJV. [accessed 01.02.2020].

Ratajczak, M. (2013). Działania CSR wobec pracowników na przykładzie przedsiębiorstw agrobiznesu z Warmii i Mazur [CSR activities towards employees on the example of agribusiness enterprises from Warmia and Mazury]. *Przegląd Organizacji, 12*, 14–19.

Rok, B. (2008). Biznes społecznie odpowiedzialny – teoria i praktyka, [Socially responsible business - theory and practice]. In Hausner J. (ed.) Ekonomia społeczna a rozwój [Social Economy and Development]. Kraków: MSAP.

Stawicka, E. (2017). Sustainable development and the business context of CSR benefits on the Polish market. *Acta Scientiarum Polonorum. Oeconomia, 16*(3), 73–81.

Tourengau, R., Conrad, F. G., Couper M. P. (2013). *The Science of Web Surveys*. Oxford: University Press.

Valor, C. (2005). Corporate social responsibility and corporate citizenship: Towards corporate accountability. *Business & Society Review, 110*(2), 191–212.

Waddock, S. (2008). Building a new institutional infrastructure for corporate social responsibility. *Academy of Management Perspectives, 22*(3), 87–108.

Chapter 9

Big Data Analytics in Tourism: Overview and Trends

Katarzyna Łukasiewicz

Warsaw University of Life Sciences—SGGW

Contents

9.1 Introduction

The progressive technological development that we have been observing for many years affects all areas of our everyday life. Constant access to information, even on a smartphone, results in the continuous generation of data that characterizes consumer preferences. In Poland, currently, 69% of adults use the Internet at least once a week (this is slightly more than last year, 66%—an increase of 3% points). It is 100% among the respondents aged 18–24, and 99% for those aged 25–34, and finally 90% for the 35–44 age range and 26% for people over 65. The most active group of people declare that they are online all the time—as much as 57% of people aged 18–24. These numbers show that young people of working age are always up to date with information, obtain it, and respond to it via the Internet (CBOS, 2019).

Huge, very often unstructured data sets, referred to in the Polish literature as the "Big Data" (BD), are identified with data sources that are from the Internet (this can be data from social networking sites or discussion forums). We deal with BD when the size of the data sets and their diversity exceed the standard capabilities of companies in need to collect and process them. These include Internet data (from social networking sites and discussion forums), organizational data (e.g., information on typical customer behavior), so-called automatic data (e.g., geolocation data generated when the user uses mobile applications, data from ATMs), and unstructured data (e.g., quoted client statements collected during contacts with the company's call center) (Kachniewska, 2014a).

The data collected and referred to as BD is characterized by considerable size, variability, and diversity. Their processing and analysis create added value.

Many authors write about the use of BD in commercial activities, for example, in trade, services or promotion, and advertising (Kachniewska, 2014a, b; Płoszajski, 2013; Schmarzo, 2013; Chluski and Ziora, 2015) and in decision-making processes in enterprises and institutions (Liebowitz, 2013; Provost and Fawcett, 2013).

The purpose of this chapter is to present the conditions for using databases in the tourism industry. The presented chapter is an attempt to answer the following question: is the tourist industry able to effectively use data from the Internet (social media, extensive databases) to make decisions at various levels, especially in the strategic dimension, which would contribute to the development of tourism. The first part of the study presents a review of the literature in the field of BD. The conditions of using database analysis in the tourism industry were also presented. Particular attention was paid to the importance of Internet access and the use of information from portals and social media. The final part of this chapter presents the conclusions and future perspectives related to the use of BD in the tourism industry.

9.2 Conditions for Using Big Data Analysis in the Tourism Industry

The tourism sector plays a big role in the global economy. In the light of research carried out by the World Travel and Tourism Council (WTTC) since 2010, this sector is still growing and at a much faster rate than the entire global economy in global terms. Currently, it directly or indirectly generates 10.3% of global GDP and thus provides over 300 million jobs. In addition, this sector accounts for 20% of new jobs. The tourist sector covers 6.5% of global exports and almost 30% of services exports; however, almost 3/4 of tourism revenue comes from domestic markets. According to *Report on World Tourism Economy Trends 2018* (Report, 2018), in 2017, 77% of all travel expenses were spent on recreational travel (a total of USD

4.2 trillion), and 23% on business trips. The Polish tourism sector generates over 5% of GDP.

The very fast development of new technologies and various possibilities of their application cause that the world around us is changing—societies, human behavior, and preferences are changing. We colloquially say that the world is shrinking because we are becoming more mobile. We are able to travel even over long distances in a much shorter time, thanks to greater price and transport availability, we travel more often, and at the same time, we are increasingly using the opportunities offered by electronic mobile devices. The demand for travel is constantly growing because more and more people travel in connection with their work, study abroad, visits to family or friends (The Travel, 2017). In line with the general trends in tourism, the demand for trips and more and more personalized offers, taking into account the preferences and capabilities of a given client (Digital, 2016), is increasing. It is also worth noting that the skill of self-preparation of the trip is growing among travelers (Kachniewska, 2014a). Having access to many information, a tourist wants to prepare a travel plan and then implement it consistently (Dejnaka, 2019).

Increased complexity of the structure of the tourism product and the distance between supply and demand caused that the development of tourism and its dynamics depend on the specificity and level of development of intermediary and organizational services. When making a decision about the direction of a tourist trip, one of the basic factors is the availability and information visualization method (graphics, sound). Its attractiveness affects the formation of the idea of future travel because it is not possible to check it at the booking stage. In this situation, the more the information, the better the decision. The availability of information means that the process of distribution of tourist services can be subject to complete computerization. Another factor affecting the need for changes in this area is the fact that the tourist profile is largely the profile of a person using the Internet and mobile applications (Kachniewska, 2014b).

All social networking sites are focused on collecting data almost about every aspect of our lives and every action taken. Virtual tourist communities (e.g., TripAdvisor) function in a similar way, which, thanks to visits from millions of Internet users and the opinions they leave, can, without a doubt, formulate and verify emerging trends in consumer behavior both within tourism, leisure activities, or business trips (Kachniewska, 2014a). The amount of all unused data on tourists (both actual and potential) results from the frequency of online transactions, frequent Internet searches, using available price comparison websites, and presence on social networks. Each visit leaving a trace in the form of an air or hotel reservation or even car rental is a digital trace, which, analyzed along with the entire data set, creates information on the basis of which one can formulate specific conclusions and make decisions in the area of management (Davenport et al., 2012). The significance of BD is determined not only by the size of these large collections but also by their diversity and flow rate: any comments, "likes", or sharing on social media and blogs, filing complaints or discussions on Internet forums using the brand name, region tourist facilities or tourist attractions create a data stream that, when analyzed, can definitely strengthen the relationship of the entity with buyers and contribute to the creation of unique experiences which form the basis of competitive advantage (Kachniewska, 2014a).

Most of the research that deals with the use of information and communication technologies (ICT), in connection with growing consumer expectations and rapid fashion changes, contribute to extraordinary pressure toward the technologization and computerization of the tourism industry, which often seems incomprehensible to small entrepreneurs who perceive their business in a traditional way. The same problem affects the necessary change in the ways of distribution and promotion of the tourist offer, namely the wide application of online sales channels, the use of new media, or the phenomenon of sales personalization (Bloch and Segev, 1996; Collins et al., 2003; Kachniewska, 2014a).

The number of transactions that are concluded via the Internet is constantly growing, which significantly facilitates the acquisition and then the use of information on the preferences of tourist service buyers.

The possibilities arising from the analysis of BD Analytics in tourism relate to five main dimensions of data, namely all data relating to the customer, product, time, location (geo-spatial), and channels. For example, hotels can use predictive analytics to track and send personalized messages by testing tourist behavior (Kachniewska, 2019).

Using data from various sources enables customer profiling in such a way that sales activities can be directed to a strictly selected target group. The tourist service provider is able to narrow down the customer group on the grounds of demographic data and his decisions, all on a real-time basis.

Research presented in 25 Polish hotels marked with 4- and 5-stars indicates that 67% of guests are not interested in the availability of TV, but only access to the Internet is important for them—especially Video on Demand (VoD) and information platforms. Data were collected not on the basis of surveys or reviews—but only via the Internet. When it comes to reservations, most online reservations are made using stationary devices: 20%–50% of reservations are made from mobile devices (Travolution, 2018). As many as 90% of travelers share photos and travel experiences in social networks. Millions of travel-related reviews are made available online every day. The so-called "sentimental analysis" allows estimating the polarization of these bars in milliseconds (Global Report, 2018). Hidden patterns exposed by the process allow predicting what tourists buy depending on the time of the month or what other items they can buy. The use of BD can help to understand user behavior based on (Kachniewska, 2019):

- Early warning (to quickly detect irregularities in the use of electronic devices and services and solve the problem as soon as possible)
- Real-time monitoring (monitoring current user behavior, emotions, and preferences)
- Real-time feedback (obtaining current feedback from users)

9.3 The Use of Big Data in Tourism

Forecasting tourist behavior in the future must be based on a personalized approach to the customer. For example, people running a business can go whenever they want, parents with school-aged children will look for trips during summer and winter holidays, single people will look for trips in the company of young people to places that seniors certainly would not go. For each of these groups of people, one can accurately adjust the offer and reach with information when it is needed. Therefore, the right marketing creation is formed for a specific group of recipients. This approach forms the basic assumptions of predictive marketing. There are several examples of the application using components of predictive analysis (Amadeus, 2018).

Systems recommending tourist products (flights, hotels):

- Voice, voice and image recognition systems
- Optimization of clicks and conversions of tourist products
- Social media analysis
- Alarming and monitoring
- More dynamic tourist product offers
- Thoughtful segmentation and grouping of passengers
- The ability to detect fraud
- Enhancement of passenger data
- Forecasting

Considering at least one of the elements that is the analysis and use of social media in tourism, we can distinguish content generated by social media users, i.e., User-Generated Content (Kaplan and Haenlein, 2010) or Consumer-Generated Content (Muniz and Schau, 2011), which can be used to make inferences regarding the observation of these users as customers.

Currently, the organization's success on the market may depend on the ability to obtain and process data in order to use them to make important economic decisions. The trick is to use the right data in the right way. The advantage of social media is that after sending information, one has the chance to get immediate feedback (Minkwitz, 2018). The powerful development of BD and social media has also brought positive aspects for tourism. Through the social networks specializing in a narrow area (e.g., TripAdvisor—travels, Booking—hotels, Kayak—flights, Zomato—restaurants), one can get wide access to information. These portals are constantly growing to meet the expectations of customers. In the case of Booking, it changed its place in the world ranking from 101 in 2017 to 60 in 2019, TripAdvisor from 269 to 232 (Alexa, 2019).

Google search engine is still in the first place, Facebook is in third place. Google collects user reviews but also has its own importance in tourism. Typing in the search engine, e.g., monuments in a given city, a list of hints immediately appears to us. In 2019, Facebook had 2.3 billion users who like 4.1 million posts in just 60 seconds. However, as far as Twitter users are concerned, the number of tweets per minute increased from 456,000 in 2017 to 473,400 in 2018. Twitter is one of the big companies that use large data sets as well as artificial intelligence (preventing inappropriate content) (Statystyki, 2019).

The volume of data collected is a huge challenge in BD analysis. The fast increase in the amount of data is a big problem. According to VCloudNews, in 1992, 100 GB of data was generated per day; in 1997, 100 GB of data per hour; in 2002, 100 GB of data per second; in 2013, 28,875 GB of data per second; and in 2018, 50,000 GB of data per second (Everyday Big Data, 2019).

There are 4.1 billion Internet users in 2019. According to the 2017 Global Web Index Report, Internet users spent 6.5 hours a day online. So, if each of the 4.1 billion Internet users spent about 6.5 hours online on a daily basis, in 2018 alone 2.8 million years online were spent (Statystyki, 2019). Every minute, 206,000 posts are published on the Instagram.com website, 204,000,000 emails are sent, and YouTube users watch 4,146,600 videos (Everyday Big Data, 2019).

Nowadays, it is very important to respond quickly to emerging trends that can be a problem with such rapid data growth. This speed will refer to the pace of increasing the resource volume of the created database with new updates but also to the addition of new sources, which appear literally every second. Systematic, continuous observation of events is of great importance here (Minkwitz, 2018).

9.4 Trends in the Use of Big Data in Tourism

BD refers to huge data sets collected from many sources. These data sets cannot be collected, stored, or processed using any of the existing standard statistical tools. These actions are limited by the amount and complexity of data. It is estimated that the market for analyzing large data sets will reach USD 103 billion by 2023 and will increase by 20% (Statystyki, 2019).

According to the New Vantage report, 97.2% of organizations invest in BD and artificial intelligence. Research has been conducted among executives from companies such as Motorola and American Express. As many as 62.5% of respondents said that their organization appointed a Data Director (a fivefold increase since 2012—then 12%). The highest percentage of organizations (60.3%) invested below USD 50 million. About one-third of respondents (27%) said their companies' combined investments in large data sets and artificial intelligence were in the range from $ 50 million to $ 550 million. Only 12.7% of respondents said that their companies had invested over $ 500 million. This data illustrates how much attention is paid to the analysis of data sets (Statystyki, 2019).

In tourism, in addition to the importance of proper exploitation of the potential of regions in the world, great attention is also paid to geopolitics and security. Geopolitical events in some parts of the world affect travel. Terrorist threats and political tensions can lead to travel restrictions. In many situations, increased security or border control and a lot of administrative burden for the traveler are introduced that have a negative impact on traveling (Global Report, 2017).

Cybersecurity is another issue. Tourist enterprises are investing huge amounts in the acquisition and use of systems that are to ensure the protection of information processing space and interactions in ICT networks. This is a priority area.

Because we operate in the world of 3G and 4G smartphones technology, we have the ability to react to certain things immediately on the go (for example, change of booking). Using a smartphone gives us continuous connectivity and network activity. Therefore, a connected, active traveler is also a current trend. Uninterrupted connectivity facilitated by mobile Internet and smartphones means that in the event of travel disruptions, plan changes can be made during locomoting.

Personalization is also one of the key issues related to the use of BD. The tourist industry is investing a lot of money to offer a lot of tailor-made and contextual offers for travelers (car rental, next flight). They enable the latest innovations in front-end technologies.

The sharing economy is another area that should be highlighted. As far as tourism is concerned, leisure traveling is of great significance, but it can be linked to various other aspects. Travel agencies or hotels add to their offers, for example, renting a house. Car sharing may raise interest.

In the era of many economic changes, more attention is paid to data protection and privacy. The General Data Protection Regulation in the European Union, in force since May 2018, is intended to protect the privacy of the data of all EU citizens. BD can also be used here.

Another issue worth noting is the use of cloud computing. It includes better utilization of resource infrastructure and allows for economies of scale, flexibility, and agility, to which customers pay special attention.

It is worth mentioning about the messaging platforms. Chat availability is now a gigantic quick opportunity to respond to events and exchange information and is far better than sending text messages. There is a trend from chatting with people to chatting with chatbots (intelligent conversation platforms).

The Internet of Things and connected devices (actuators, sensors, controllers) are another area of interest in the future. With the help of these devices, one can, for example, track luggage. According to the Amadeus report, the future of travel looks extremely bright: innovation, cooperation, and sustainable business practices. And thanks to this the company will provide better, more satisfying traveling conditions in the future (Global Report, 2018).

9.5 Conclusion

In the tourism industry, the opportunity to observe the potential behavior patterns of tourists gives great opportunities. The complete development of the tourist offer should be based on the use of all available data, often varied and extensive.

Therefore, it is necessary and reasonable to use BD. Currently, it is used on the market by the largest companies that have the capital to invest in the latest technologies. Creating a system that integrates all levels requires the cooperation of many entities involved in the provision of tourist services. Then, there is a chance to undertake joint actions and multi-faceted analysis of available information, which can undoubtedly contribute to improving the competitiveness of tourism enterprises.

This chapter mainly focuses on the possibilities and broad conditions of applying BD in tourism, to use the data in an optimal way to achieve the basic goal of a satisfied customer. These data are obtained from many sources: from users of services and from those offering services in order to extract the most desirable shape of the offer on this basis. The effective use of BD in business requires the fulfillment of many conditions: from highly qualified personnel to the right hardware and software. BD is a new business-building model in which the ability to properly segregate data and use them effectively in the business decision-making process is essential. The analysis of the use of BD in the tourism industry has some limitations associated with the accurate, very precise identification of all analyzed factors, related to the update of the customer's individualized needs. Information (the ability to obtain it) is becoming a new basis for business, a new factor of production and the economic equivalent of capital and labor (Tuziak, 2017).

Future research directions:

- BD analysis can be used as a tool for predictive analysis and personalization of tourism activities, which requires human capital equipped with vast knowledge, various skills, and qualifications.
- The Internet or social media can be used to formulate complex marketing activities on a large scale (use of data on specific groups of people, mutual friends to adapt or optimize the offer, so-called meeting expectations), which is very important in the tourism industry (using information about interests or needs arising from visiting some websites on the Internet).
- Proper use of BD will also allow companies to optimize revenue management, which can determine success in gaining a competitive advantage.
- Thanks to databases, a contextual analysis can be conducted, in which by using data stream analysis, a package of services that will provide benefits to both the service provider and the buyer can be created, what in the future can result in establishing a long-term, profitable relationship.

References

Alexa. (2019). Retrieved from www.alexa.com Available [12.10.2019].

Bloch, M., Segev, A. (1996). *The Impact of Electronic Commerce on the Travel Industry. An Analysis Methodology and Case Study.* Retrieved from http://195.130.87.21:8080/dspace/bitstream/123456789/748/1/Impact%20of%20electronic%20commerce%20in%20the%20travel%20industry.mht Available [12.10.2019].

CBOS. (2019). *Public Opinion Research Center. Current Problems and Events.* Retrieved from https://www.cbos.pl/SPISKOM.POL/2019/K_095_19.PDF Available [20.10.2019].

Chluski, L., Ziora, A. (2015). The role of big data solutions in the management of orgaizations. Review of select practical examples. *Procedia Computer Science, 65*, 1006–1012.

Collins, C., Buhalis, D., Peters, M. (2003). Enhancing SMTE's business performance through the Internet and e-learning platforms. *Education and Training, 45*(8–9), 483–494.

Davenport, T. H., Barth, P., Bean, R. (2012). How big data is different. *MIT Sloan Management Review, 54*(1), 43–46.

Dejnaka, A. (2019). *Mobile marketing,* Warszawa: Difin Publishing House.

Digital. (2016). *We Are Social's Compendium of Global Digital, Social and Mobile Data, Trends and Statistics.* Retrieved from https://www.slideshare.net/wearesocialsg/digital-in-2016 Available [12.10.2019].

Gobal Report. (2017). *Amadeus.* Retrieved from http://www.amadeus.com/msite/global-report/2017/en/home/ Available [20.10.2019].

Global Report. (2018). *Amadeus.* Retrieved from http://www.amadeus.com/msite/global-report/2018/en/home/ Available [20.10.2019].

Everyday Big Data. (2019). *Every Day Big Data Statistics – 2.5 Quintillion Bytes of Data Created Daily.* Retrieved from http://www.vcloudnews.com/every-day-big-data-statistics-2-5-quintillion-bytes-of-data-created-daily/ Available [20.10.2019].

Kachniewska, M. (2014a). Big data analysis as a source of competitive advantage of enterprises and tourist regions. *Folia Turistica, 32*, 2014, 35–54.

Kachniewska, M. (2014b). Impact of digitization of distribution channels on the structure of the market of tourist intermediation services. *E-Mentor, 1*(53), 86–91.

Kachniewska, M. (2019). Big data analysis as a tool for predictive intelligence and experience personalization in tourism. *Entrepreneurship and Management, 20*(2), 39–52.

Kaplan, A., Haenlein, M. (2010). Users of the world, unite! The challenges and opportunities of social media. *Business Horizons, 53*(1), 60.

Liebowitz, J. (2013). *Big Data and Business Analytics.* Boca Raton, FL: CRC Press, Taylor & Francis Group.

Minkwitz, A. (2018). Social networking as a big data source for tourism. In: Z. Młynarczyk, A. Zajadacz (eds.), *Conditions and Plans for Tourism Development. Nature Tourism and Its Development Conditions.* Tourism and Recreation - Studies and Work, 20, (pp. 83–91), Poznań, PL: Bogucki Wydawnictwo Naukowe.

Muniz, A., Schau, H. (2011). How to inspire value-laden collaborative consumer-generated content. *Business Horizons, 54*(3), 209–217.

Płoszajski, P. (2013). The big data. A new source of companies' advantages and growth. *E-Mentor, 3*(50), 5–10.

Provost, F., Fawcett, T. (2013). Data science and its relationship to big data and data-driven decision making. *Big Data, 1*(1), 51–59.

Report. (2018). *Report on World Tourism Economy Trends.* Retrieved from: https://www.wtcf.org.cn/uploadfile/2017/1114/20171114051111772.pdf Available [12.10.2019].

Schmarzo, B. (2013). *Big Data: Ununderstanding How Data Powers Big Business.* Indianapolis, IN: John Wiley&Sons.

Statystyki. (2019). *Big Data Statistics 2020.* Retrieved from https://techjury.net/stats-about/big-data-statistics/ Available [12.10.2019].

The Travel. (2017). *The Travel & Tourism Competitiveness, Report 2017.* Retrieved from https://www.weforum.org/reports/the-travel-tourism-competitiveness-report-2017 Available [12.10.2019].

Travolution. (2018). *Research Identifies Four Key Holiday Booking Trends.* Retrieved from https://bit.ly/2zEAhWB Available [10.10.2019].

Tuziak, R. (2017). Big Data w kontekście kapitału ludzkiego [Big data in the context of human capital]. *Nierównosci Społeczne a Wzrost Gospodarczy, 52*(4), 302–314.

Chapter 10

Use of Big Data for Assessment of Environmental Pressures from Agricultural Production

Adam Wąs, Piotr Sulewski,
Edward Majewski, and Paweł Kobus
Warsaw University of Life Sciences—SGGW

Contents

10.1 Introduction

The issue of Big Data in the field of agriculture has appeared relatively recently and is usually cited in the context of discussions about the concept of Smart Farming (Wolfert, Verdouw, & Bogaardt, 2017; Schönfeld, Heil, & Bittner, 2018), which underlines the use of information technology in farm management and agricultural production. Modern information technologies have been used in agriculture as early as in the 1980s in Precision Agriculture (Delgado, Short, Roberts, & Vandenberg, 2019; Schönfeld et al., 2018). Generally, these applications were focused on controlling cultivation operations in plant production based on detailed measurements made with the use of sensors installed on harvesting machines and data on physicochemical properties of soils from satellite images, appropriately processed using global positioning techniques (GPS) and mapping with the Geographic Information System (GIS).

Other examples of Big Data applications in the agri-food sector (Bronson & Knezevic 2016; Fleming, Jakku, Lim-Camacho, Taylor, & Thorburn, 2018) can be found in the literature. However, at the current stage of development, the practical use of Big Data in agriculture is relatively small, to some extent because it is poorly regulated by Law in many countries (Schönfeld et al., 2018). In the discussion on the usefulness of Big Data analyses in the agricultural sector, it is worth emphasizing that this concept is quite broad and there is no satisfactory, uniformed definition provided.

In an agricultural context, Big Data "generally emphasize extremely large data sets (…), analyzed with state-of-the-art computer power to reveal patterns, trends, and associations of value for a variety of decision making purposes" (Ahearn, Armbruster, & Young, 2016, p. 158). Coble et al. (2016) suggest that Big Data refers to "large, diverse, complex, longitudinal, and/or distributed data sets generated from click streams, email, instruments, Internet transactions, satellites, sensors, video, and/or all other digital sources available today and in the future." According to the Big Data classification presented by the McKinsey Global Institute, Big Data also has a large proportion of "open data" and "open government data" (Manyika et al., 2013). However, these categories of data are not completely separate, which leads to the distinction of six data subtypes such as (Ramaswamy, 2015): (1) non-public data for marketing, business, analysis, and national security; (2) citizen engagement programs not based on data (e.g., petition websites); (3) large datasets from scientific research, social media, or other non-government sources; (4) public data from state, local, and federal government; (5) business reporting, other business data (e.g., consumer complaints); and (6) large public government datasets (e.g., weather, GPS, census, and health care), local or federal government (e.g., budget data).

The use of Big Data in agriculture has been raised by many authors (Ribarics, 2016; Boehlje, 2016; Bronson & Knezevic, 2016; Mishra & Singh, 2016, Kumar et al., 2018). They pointed out that the use of Big Data in the decision-making process can bring many benefits, including such benefits as the reduction in fertilizers, cost savings, yield optimization, streamlining of food supply and more. The use of Big Data in the area of agriculture is to support decision-making processes not only by agricultural producers but also by consumers as well as policymakers, at the end enhancing improvement of market efficiency. Today, it is emphasized that the key challenge facing agriculture is not only the improvement of technical efficiency but above all the reconciliation of the need to increase food production, due to the increase in the world's population (Alexandratos & Bruinsma 2012), with the need to limit the negative impact of agricultural production on the environment in conditions of progressing climate change (United Nations [UN], 2018). This requires a change in approaches to farm management in such a way as to enable to maintain productivity level and increase the sustainability of agricultural systems (Delgado et al., 2019; Tilman, Balzer, Hill, & Befort, 2011; Spiegal et al., 2018).

Agricultural production affects the environment in many ways (Organization for Economic Co-operation and Development [OECD], 2004; Pingali, 2012). As stated in the OECD study, "agricultural multi-air pollutants have contributed to multi-environmental effects through acidification, eutrophication, ozone depletion, and climate change, as well as affecting the health of human populations" (OECD, 2008, p. 32). GHG emissions can be considered one of the synthetic measures of these negative impacts. On a global scale, agriculture accounts for around 14% of emissions (The Intergovernmental Panel on Climate Change [IPCC], 2014, p. 88). The environmental performance of agriculture is becoming a more and more important subject of policy regulations that create a greater need for monitoring the environmental effects of the policy instruments.

Assessing trends and environmental effects of technology and policy changes is a challenging task, mainly due to the lack of data sufficiently reflecting the complexity of the relationship between agricultural production and the environment in the large scale. The Big Data approach seems to be particularly useful in bridging the existing gap.

The main objective of this chapter is to demonstrate the potential in using FADN data for estimation of environmental pressures resulting from climate change and identification of key factors having an impact on the environmental performance of farms in Poland. FADN (Farm Accountancy Data Network) has the characteristics of "large datasets from scientific research" and "large public government datasets" according to the aforementioned classification (Ramaswamy, 2015). So, FADN can be considered a particular example of Big Data.

10.1.1 Farm Accountancy Data Network (FADN)

FADN is a system of collecting farm data through annual surveys carried out by the Member States of the EU from a sample of agricultural holdings in all European Union countries. Derived from national surveys, the FADN is the source of harmonized microeconomic data from the sample of farms representative along three dimensions: region, economic size, and type of production. Currently, the annual sample counts approximately 80,000 holdings, which represent a population of about 5,000,000 farms in the EU. This population covers approximately 90% of the total utilized agricultural area (UAA) and accounts for about 90% of the total agricultural production. The information collected from a single farm is a set of approximately 1,000 variables. They provide different types of physical and structural data, such as location, area of crops grown and livestock numbers, labor force, and also the value of production from all commodities, stocks, sales and purchases, production costs, assets, liabilities, and subsidies that are required to assess economic and financial performance. The amount of FADN data is limited; however, the development of electronic transactions and automation of collecting financial information (records of invoices, bank transfers, subsidies, parcel information, taxes, and medicine use (Vrolijk & Poppe 2016)) may facilitate gathering more data in the future. As a result, traditional forms of data acquisition may increasingly play a complementary role in the FADN system. As indicated above, the FADN is intended to serve policymakers in shaping agricultural policy, but large amounts of data collected can be used for other purposes.

10.1.2 GHG Emissions: Challenge for the Farming Sector

The emission of greenhouse gases (GHGs) may be estimated as amounts of specific GHGs, but the carbon footprint is the commonly used measure that presents emissions as an equivalent of CO_2 per unit of the product. Calculation of carbon footprint is usually based on the Life Cycle Assessment (LCA) methodologies within defined system boundaries (International Dairy Federation [IDF], 2010). For specific products, it can be the whole distribution chain (cradle to grave) or production processes (cradle to gate) (Kulczycka & Wernicka, 2015). The latter applied to the farming sector can be converted into "field to farm gate", a simplified or partial version of the LCA (Belflower et al., 2012). GHGs, as it is believed, are responsible for climate change and that is why they deserve special attention from environmentalists and policymakers. It is estimated that globally agriculture-related up-stream activities (e.g., fertilizer manufacturing) and land-use change are responsible for about one-third of the total human-induced warming effect (Paustian, Antle, Sheehan, & Paul, 2006; Audsley et al., 2009).

Several studies attempt to measure agricultural emissions and demonstrate the impacts of different technologies and farming systems. Many publications focus on the carbon footprint of milk and beef production since cattle are considered the main source of GHG emissions from agriculture. LCA methods were applied to compare carbon footprints of milk from confinement and grass-based dairy farms (Belflower et al., 2012; O'Brien, Capper, Garnsworthy, Grainger, & Shalloo, 2014). Crosson et al. (2011) modeled whole-farm systems of GHG emissions from pastoral suckler beef cow production systems. Zehetmeier, Baudracco, Hoffmann, and Heißenhuber (2011) modeled cattle farms with two scenarios considering different ratios of milk to beef production. GHG emissions from beef and dairy cattle production systems were measured by Crosson et al. (2011), who indicated the importance of improvements in animal productivity, which goes along with an intensification of production. Capper, Cady, and Bauman (2009) compared modern and historical beef production systems in the United States in the years 1977 and 2007. There were also studies comparing organic and non-organic farming systems (Williams, Audsley, & Sandars, 2006; Werf, Kanyarushoki, & Corson, 2009). Comparison of GHG emissions for the Irish, UK, and US dairy systems which were calculated with the use of dairy farm GHG model that uses "cradle-to-gate" LCA approach to quantify all on- and off-farm GHG sources (e.g., fertilizer, pesticide, and fuel manufacture) associated with milk production up to the farm gate (O'Brien et al., 2014).

The examples of estimation of GHG emissions presented above relate to individual farms or comparison of production systems for selected production activities. This is how the LCA methodology is most often used for agriculture. There are also estimates of GHG emissions for the entire agricultural sector based on macro data. They indicate the share of agriculture in global GHG emissions, but their analytical usefulness is limited. Our approach with the use of FADN data, which over time could be supplemented with Big Data obtained from other sources, allows conducting in-depth analyses at the level of farm types and production systems on a regional and national scale. It also allows a detailed assessment of the impacts of various factors on the volume of emissions.

10.2 Methodology

Emission of GHGs in CO_2 equivalent [kg CO_2e/ha] was estimated with the "field to farm-gate" approach using the sample of over 12,000 representative farms registered in the Polish FADN database in the year 2012. Based on these estimates, the main determinants of the emissions were identified with the use of the linear regression model.

In the estimation of GHG emissions, the following sources have been taken into account: production and application of fertilizers, fossil fuels (diesel oil, gasoline, coal), electricity, and farm animals (livestock).

The FADN dataset consists mainly of financial data, but not all information on amounts of physical inputs is directly available. Because of this limitation, a specific procedure was applied to convert farm expenditures on energy into physical inputs based on average prices of electricity, fuel, and heating (conversion into amounts of coal).

In the next step, volumes of physical inputs have been converted into GHG emissions with the use of respective coefficients as indicated in Table 10.1. Fertilizers-related GHG emissions have been calculated both for the fertilizers' production stage and after their applications to the fields. Normative coefficients were used to estimate GHG emissions from fossil fuels including electricity. Emissions of GHG

Table 10.1 Normative Coefficients Used for the Estimation of GHG Emissions

Source of Emission	Physical Units	Conversion Ratio to kg of CO_2e
Fertilizers[a]		
Urea	kg	5.15
Nitro-chalk	kg	2.4
Potassium chloride	kg	0.25
Superphosphate	kg	0.27
Source of Emission	Physical Units	Conversion Ratio to kg of CO_2e
Livestock[b]		
Dairy cattle	head	4,854
Beef cattle	head	1,705
Horses	head	470
Sheep and goats	head	183
Swine	head	364
Poultry	head	2.1
Source of Emission	Physical Units	Conversion Ratio to kg of CO_2e
Fuels and energy[c]		
Coal	t	2,143.74
Diesel	l	2.62
Electricity	kWh	0.831

Source: Own elaboration based on sources listed in the table.

[a] Fertilizer Europe (2015).
[b] Liu (2015).
[c] 22.63 GJ/t coal*94.73 kg CO_2/GJ Kobize (2014); Fleetnews.uk (2015); Kulczycka and Werenicka (2015).

from livestock have been estimated based on the number of livestock and an average emission per animal (Liu, 2015).

To compare GHG emissions from different types of farms, carbon footprint values have been calculated per hectare of agricultural land. For revealing key drivers of GHG emissions in different farm types and different production systems, several multiple regression models have been built.

Four categories of factors, most crucial for characterizing farm businesses, were taken into account: soil quality, the scale of farm business operations, production system, and intensity of production. There are several indicators available in the FADN dataset to measure specific factors within each category. A set of four independent variables that provide the best fit of the model have been chosen: for soil quality—soil quality index 0.05–1.95 (the higher value, the better), for scale of farm business operations—agricultural land area in hectares, for production system—organic versus non-organic and for intensity of production—volume of production expressed in the number of German Grain Equivalents[1] (GGE) per hectare of agricultural land. The models have been estimated for each of the eight farm production types according to the FADN TF8 typology.[2]

The general formula of the multiple regression model for each of the models is as follows:

$$Y_i = b_0 + b_1 X_{1i} + b_2 X_{2i} + b_3 X_{3i} + b_4 X_{4i} + e_i$$

where Y—GHG emission (kg CO_2e/ha), X_1—soil quality index, X_2—agricultural land (ha), X_3—organic production system (0/1), X_4—intensity of production (GGE/ha), ε_i—error term, β_0—intercept, and $\beta_1,..., \beta_4$—respective regression coefficients.

Due to stratified sampling used in the FADN system, each of the farms in the sample represents the different number of farms in the general population. To reflect those differences, weighted least squares Horvitz–Thomson estimators were used (1952).

10.3 Results

Simple descriptive statistics (Table 10.2) show differences between farm types. Animal farms (cattle and pigs) have much higher GHG emissions per hectare of arable land compared to average levels. Field crop farms, which are specialized in typical field crops like cereals, proteins, oilseeds, and root crops are located on the

---

[1] German grain equivalents (Woermann, 1944) are reflecting nutritional value of the farm product [1 unit is equal of nutritional value 100 kg of barley].

[2] Field crop, mixed crops, cattle, pigs, mixed animals, mixed. Horticultural farms and wine yards were not analyzed.

Table 10.2 Weighted Mean Values of the Model Variables

Type of Farming	GHG Emission (kg CO₂e/ha)	Soil Quality Index	Agricultural Land (ha)	Share of Organic Farms (%)	Intensity of Production (GGE/ha)	Number of Farms in the Sample	Number of Represented Farms
Field crop	1,623	0.99	29.2	4.8	46.8	3,135	132,373
Mixed crops	2,165	0.89	12.8	18.2	34.2	208	17,111
Cattle	4,574	0.6	18.8	11.7	75.1	2,468	86,684
Pigs	4,591	0.81	22.7	0.3	113.3	752	21,750
Mixed animals	3,438	0.64	13.4	3.9	69.5	955	121,570
Mixed	2272	0.78	15.3	5.0	54.7	2,751	311,567

Source: Own research.

best soils, have the biggest average area and are characterized by a relatively low intensity of production. In contrast, mixed crop farms are usually less specialized, grow a high number of very different crops, and have the smallest size. Even though they are located on relatively good soil, this cluster of farms is characterized by the lowest intensity of production.

This might be due to a high share of organic farms in this group (18.2%). Pig farms are relatively big (22.7 ha), with the highest intensity of production measured in the number of GGE per hectare of arable land. There are no organic farms in the pig farms cluster. Cattle farms are characterized by the lowest quality of soils, they achieve, however, relatively high production from a hectare of agricultural land (>75 GGE/ha—produce a high amount of food per hectare of land). In this cluster, the share of farms using organic production systems is 10%.

Determinants of emissions were estimated at first for the pooled sample representing all farms in the FADN population (Table 10.3—1st row). Results show that GHG emissions can be explained to a large extent by the selected drivers ($R^2 \sim 0.6$). In the case of GHG, the main drivers decreasing emissions per hectare of agricultural land are better quality of soils and greater size of farms. The first might be explained by a high share of crop farms (with relatively low GHG emissions) on good soil. However, the high share of good soils is not decreasing emissions itself but enables running farm even without animal production, what contributes finally to lower emissions. What is quite obvious the greater the size of the farm the lower are emissions of GHG per hectare, as some "fixed" emissions (e.g., heating of buildings, electricity, etc.) are distributed on the larger area of agricultural land. On the opposite, increasing intensity of production, which is usually related to higher usage of all inputs (fertilizers, feedstuff, fuel, etc.), results in higher GHG emission per hectare.

Table 10.3 also presents the result of the models explaining GHG emissions in farm types considered. It could be noticed that the most explanatory power has the models for farm types with animal production (R^2 0.45–0.95), while on the opposite, drivers considered are hardly explaining the variability on GHG emissions in farms specialized in crop production (R^2 0.044–0.125). It suggests the necessity of additional research on GHG emissions drivers in the case of crop farms. The most promising direction seems to be the effectivity of inputs depending on the weather conditions.

The pig farms can be considered most intensive in terms of GGE/ha. However, the increase in production intensity on cattle farms generates much greater growth of GHG emissions.

Increasing area of the farm tends to decrease the GHG emission per hectare of land, especially in farms with cattle (farm types: "cattle" and "mixed animals") what could be explained by the distribution of "fixed" emissions (e.g., heating of buildings, electricity, part of fuel) on a larger area of agricultural land.

In most of the farm types, the GHG emission per hectare is lower on better soil. However, this relation is significant only in farms specialized in animal production.

Table 10.3 Weighted Multiple Regression for GHG Emission (kg CO_2e/ha)

Type of Farming	Soil Quality Index	Agricultural Land	Organic Production	Intensity of Production (GGE/ha)	Adjusted R^2
All types	−634.211***	−6.746***	−107.19	53.666***	0.593
Field crop	82.671	−0.621.	−694.844***	14.537***	0.125
Mixed crops	−20.963	−17.231*	−1043.101**	43.923***	0.044
Cattle	−506.938***	−16.901***	−295.645*	70.232***	0.767
Pigs	−726.272***	−2.048	82.476	45.766***	0.947
Mixed animals	−119.94	−18.553***	−547.741***	56.88***	0.687
Mixed	−278.049***	−6.466***	−81.349	43.031***	0.45

Source: Own research.

GGE, German Grain Equivalent has been proposed by Woermann (1944) as an equivalent of nutritional value of 100 kg of barley.

Significance codes: "***" p-value < 0.001; "**" < 0.01; "*" < 0.05; "." < 0.1.

This might be, at least to some extent, explained by a negative correlation between soil quality and stocking density rates.

The reduction of GHG emissions due to the introduction of the organic production system is greater in the crop than in livestock farms. This is due to strongly limited and restricted mineral fertilizers use in organic farms, which are the main source of GHG emissions in conventional crop farming. There is no such effect in livestock organic production systems (cattle and pig farms) because livestock is the main source of environmental pollution. Since GHG emission is generated by animals, the volume of total emission is similar irrespective of the farming system, however, in the case when calculated by the unit of production emissions may increase in organic farms, due to lower productivity of organic animals. In all organic farm types, increase of production intensity by one GGE per hectare of arable land leads to higher emissions than in conventional. As was already mentioned, the highest increase could be observed in cattle farms, followed by mixed animal farms (usually keeping both pigs and cattle). The lowest increase in emission due to intensification of production could be observed in field crop farms. It might be expected that an increase in the intensity of production, resulting in more food produced per hectare of land, is not only a result of a greater amount of inputs but at least partly an outcome of more efficient use of resources.

The last two models have been estimated to determine differences between main drivers of environmental pressures in conventional and organic farms (Table 10.4). Organic farms show potential for reducing GHG emissions, however, what could be expected, model estimates are statistically significant only for farm types with a noticeable share of organic farms. Looking at the differences between conventional and organic farms in GHG emissions, it might be observed that the model for organic farms is better fitted, although the soil quality index is not statistically significant.

In both production systems, increasing the size of the farm leads to lower emissions; however in the case of conventional farms, the marginal decrease is slightly higher. Estimates for the intensity of production seem to be more interesting.

Table 10.4 Weighted Multiple Regression—Conventional vs. Organic

Production System	Soil Quality Index	Agricultural Land	Intensity of Production	Adjusted R^2
GHG emission (kg CO_2e/ha)				
Conventional	−674.029***	−7.435***	54.346***	0.559
Organic	−401.921.	−6.018***	70.547***	0.709

Source: Own research.

Significance codes: "***" *p*-value < 0.001; "**" < 0.01; "*" < 0.05; "." < 0.1.

Although the organic production system may be perceived as relatively more environmentally friendly, any increase of its intensity leads to much higher emissions than in the case of conventional systems.

10.4 Discussion and Conclusions

In the study, we indicated a possible, specific way of utilizing the European FADN data that goes beyond the original purpose of collecting FADN data. It is the largest microeconomic database on farms in the EU with some of the characteristics of Big Data collections. Observing the progressing automation of the data collection process, it can be assumed that in the future FADN will probably meet all key assumptions of the Big Data definition. Currently, the data stored in the FADN database are used primarily by the European Commission to shape agricultural policy and by scientists for research in the field of agricultural economics. In our example, we have indicated that under certain assumptions, this can also be a useful source of information for estimating the environmental pressure of farms expressed in the form of GHG emissions and more in-depth analyses related to this phenomenon. The development of an effective and easy mechanism to assess the environmental pressure of farms is an important element in environmentally friendly farm management.

The models estimated for particular farm types of the Polish FADN sample show that environmental pressures and their drivers vary depending on the farm production orientation and farming systems. This is in line with the results of many studies. It has been noticed by De Cara, Houzé, and Jayet (2005) that a large part of heterogeneity in emissions can be attributed to farm size, crop yields, number of animal numbers, or use of inputs. The difference in the level of GHG emissions and the polluting potential of nutrients related to farm characteristics were found by many others (e.g. Belflower et al., 2012; O'Brien et al., 2014).

The results of our study reveal that pig farms created the highest environmental pressure in GHG emission, but cattle farms are at a similar level. In all types of livestock farms, GHG emissions depend strongly on stocking rates. This observation was made also by Olesen et al. (2006).

Crop farms affect the environment much less in terms of GHG emissions. In crop farms, differently than in livestock farms, dependent variables explain a relatively small part of environmental pressures.

Models estimated for organic farming systems, that are perceived more environmentally friendly, show that any attempt to intensify production may result in higher marginal emissions of GHG than in farms with the conventional production system. It raises the question, whether expanding the size of the organic agriculture sector, as it is desired by supporters of this farming system, would mitigate GHG emissions. It is doubtful since a growing global demand for food and industrial crops would reinforce intensification of production increasing environmental pressures.

It might be concluded that there are different possibilities for reducing environmental pressures caused by agriculture. The results of all models show that the increase in farm size leads to a decrease in GHG emissions per hectare. This is an effect of dispersion of a relatively fixed volume of GHG emissions over a larger area. Unlike the size of farms, the increase of the production intensity results in a higher environmental load per hectare of land in most farm types. That indicates the importance of improving the productivity of land allowing to mitigate the emissions per unit of production, as calculated in most of the models based on the LCA methodologies. This is in line with the conclusion made by Crosson et al. (2011) that improvements in animal productivity and fertility can reduce GHG emissions per kg product. Moreover, intensification of production measured by the volume of output/ha can reduce emissions/kg product provided inputs of feed and fertilizers are not excessive.

To satisfy the demand for food for a growing population of the world, an increase in the global-scale food supply is needed. However, responsibility for the well-being of future generations requires compliance with the Sustainable Development paradigm, and lessening environmental pressures is a must.

That is why studies on GHG emission mitigation should be expanded in the search for more environmentally friendly and economically viable production systems. There is also a need for the development or finessing methods of assessment of the environmental pressures caused by the agricultural sector. For estimating GHG emissions, the LCA farm models *from cradle to farm gate* allowing measuring carbon footprint are most commonly used. Estimates presented in this chapter based on the FADN data proved to provide results comparable with the results of more in-depth analyses. Despite shortcomings of the FADN database, mainly unavailability of physical inputs parameters, and thus the need to make several simplifying assumptions, possibility of analyzing large, heterogeneous samples of farms may be considered as an advantage of this approach. Thus, aptitude of the FADN database as an example of Big Data for assessing environmental pressures of agriculture was positively verified.

References

Ahearn, M.C., Armbruster, W., & Young, R. (2016). Big data's potential to improve food supply chain environmental sustainability and food safety. *International Food and Agribusiness Management Review, Special Issue 19*(A), 155–171.

Alexandratos, N. & Bruinsma, J. (2012). *World Agriculture Towards 2030/2050. The 2012 Revision*. Rome: FAO.

Audsley, E., Brander, M., Chatterton, J., Murphy-Bokern, D., Webster, C., & Williams, A. (2009). How low can we go? *An Assessment of Greenhouse Gas Emissions from the UK Food System and the Scope for Reduction by 2050*, Report for the World Wildlife Fund (WWF) and Food Climate Research Network (FCRN), UK, 1–80.

Belflower, J.B., Bernard, J.K., Gattie, D.K., Hancock, D.W., Risse, L.M., & Rotz, C.A. (2012). A case study of the potential environmental impacts of different dairy production systems in Georgia. *Agricultural System, 108*, 84–93.

Boehlje, M. (2016). How might big data impact industry structure and enhance margins? *International Food and Agribusiness Management Review* Special Issue *19*(A), 13–16.

Bronson, K. & Knezevic, I. (2016). Big data in food and agriculture. *Big Data & Society*, *3*(1), 1–5.

Capper, J.L., Cady, R.A., & Bauman, D.E. (2009). The environmental impact of dairy production: 1944 compared with 2007. *Journal of Animal Science, 87,* 2160–2167.

Coble, K., Griffin, T.W., Ahearn, M., Ferrell, S., McFadden, J., Sonka, S., & Fulton, J. (2016). *Advancing U.S. Agricultural Competitiveness with Big Data and Agricultural Economic Market Information, Analysis, and Research* (No. 249847). Washington, DC: Council on Food, Agricultural, and Resource Economics.

Crosson, P., Shalloo, L., O'Brien, D., Lanigan, G. J., Foley, P.A., Boland, T. M., & Kenny, D. A. (2011). A review of whole farm systems models of greenhouse gas emissions from beef and dairy cattle production systems. *Animal Feed Science and Technology, 166–167,* 29–45.

De Cara, S., Houzé, M., & Jayet, P.A. (2005). Methane and nitrous oxide emissions from agriculture in the EU: A spatial assessment of sources and abatement costs. *Environmental & Resource Economics, 32,* 551–583.

Delgado, J.A., Short, N.M. Jr., Roberts, D.P., & Vandenberg, B. (2019). Big data analysis for sustainable agriculture on a geospatial cloud framework. *Front Sustain Food Systems*, 16 July, 1–13.

Fleetnews.uk. (n.d.) *Vehicle CO_2 Emissions Footprint Calculator.* Retrieved June, 2016 from http://www.fleetnews.co.uk/costs/carbon-footprint-calculator/.

Fleming, A., Jakku, E., Lim-Camacho, L., Taylor, B., & Thorburn, P. (2018). Is big data for big farming or for everyone? Perceptions in the Australian grains industry. *Agronomy for Sustainable Development*, *38*(3), 24.

Horvitz, D.G. & Thompson, D.J. (1952). A generalization of sampling without replacement from a finite universe. *Journal of the American Statistical Association, 47,* 663–685.

IDF. (2010). A common carbon footprint approach for dairy. The IDF guide to standard life cycle assessment methodology for dairy sector. *Bulletin of the International Dairy Federation 445*, Brussels, Belgium, 1–46.

IPCC. (2014). Climate change 2014: Synthesis report. In: R.K. Pachauri and L.A. Meyer (eds.), *Contribution of Working Groups I, II and III to the Fifth Assessment Report of the Intergovernmental Panel on Climate Change [Core Writing Team.* Geneva: IPCC, 151.

KOBiZE. (2014). *Wartości opałowe i wskaźniki emisji w roku 2012 do raportowania w ramach Wspólnotowego Systemu Handlu Uprawnieniami do Emisji za rok 2015* (ang. Calorific values and emission indices for year 2012 for reporting in European Union Emission Trading System – EU ETS in 2015).

Kulczycka, J. & Wernicka, M. (2015). Metody i wyniki obliczania śladu węglowego działalności wybranych podmiotów branży energetycznej i wydobywczej. *Zeszyty Naukowe Instytutu Gospodarki Surowcami Mineralnymi i Energią Polskiej Akademii Nauk, 80,* 133–142.

Kumar, P., Kumar, A., Panwar, S., Dash, S., Sinha, K., Chaudhary, V.K., & Ray, M. (2018). Role of big data in agriculture- a statistical perspective. *Agricultural Research New Series, 39*(2), 210–215.

Liu, Z. (2015). Carbon footprint of livestock production. *Biological and Agricultural Engineering, 2,* 1–14.

Manyika, J., Chui, M., Farrell, D., Van Kuiken, S., Groves, P., & Doshi, E.A. (2013). *Open Data: Unlocking Innovation and Performance With Liquid Information.* New York City, NY: McKinsey Global Institute.

Mishra, N., & Singh, A., (2016). Use of twitter data for waste minimisation in beef supply chain. *Annals of Operations Research, 270,* 337–359.

O'Brien, D., Capper, J.L., Garnsworthy, P.C., Grainger, C., & Shalloo, L. (2014). A case study of the carbon footprint of milk from high-performing confinement and grass-based dairy farms. *Journal of Dairy Science, 97*(3), 1835–1851.

OECD. (2004). *Agriculture and the Environment: Lessons Learned from a Decade of OECD Work.* Paris: OECD Publishing.

OECD. (2008). *Environmental Performance of Agriculture in OECD Countries Since 1990.* Paris: OECD Publishing, 1–577.

Olesen, J.E., Schelde, K., Weiske, A., Weisbjerg, M.R., Asman, W.A.H., & Djurhuus, J. (2006). Modelling greenhouse gas emissions from European conventional and organic dairy farms. *Agriculture, Ecosystems & Environment, 112,* 207–220.

Paustian, K., Antle, J.M., Sheehan, J., & Paul, E.A. (2006). Agriculture's Role in Greenhouse Gas Mitigation. *Pew Center on Global Climate Change.* Arlington, VA, 1–87.

Pingali, P.L. (2012). Green revolution: Impacts, limits, and the path ahead. *PNAS, 109*(31), 12302–12308.

Ramaswamy, S. (2015). *Big Data and the Future of Agriculture.* Soil, Big Data, and Future of Agriculture Conference held on June 25, 2015 in Canberra, Australia. Retrieved June 2019 from https://nifa.usda.gov/sites/default/files/resource/Big_Data_Agriculture_Future.pdf.

Ribarics, P. (2016). Big data and its impact on agriculture. *Ecocycles, 2*(1), 33–34.

Schönfeld, M., Heil, R., & Bittner, L. (2018). Big data on a farm—smart farming. In: T. Hoeren, B. Kolany-Raiser (eds.), *Big Data in Context.* Springer Briefs in Law. Cham: Springer.

Spiegal, S., Bestelmeyer, B.T., Archer, D.W., Augustine, D.J., Boughton, E.H., Boughton, R.K., & Duncan, E.W. (2018). Evaluating strategies for sustainable intensification of US agriculture through the long-term agroecosystem research network. *Environmental Research Letters, 13*(3), 034031.

Tilman, D., Balzer, C., Hill, J., Befort, B.L. (2011). Global food demand and the sustainable intensification of agriculture. *Proceedings of the National Academy of Sciences, 108,* 20260–20264.

United Nations. (2018). *Statement by the Secretary-General on the IPCC Special Report Global Warming of 1.5°C.* Retrieved 01 July, 2019 from https://www.un.org/sg/en/content/sg/statement/2018-10-08/statement-secretary- general-ipcc-special-report-global-warming-15-%C2%BAc.

Vrolijk, H.C.J. & Poppe, K.J. (2016). *Structural Change in Dutch Agriculture; Impact on Farm Level Statistics.* Seventh International Conference on Agricultural Statistics. ICASVII, Rome 26–28 October.

Werf van der, H.M.G., Kanyarushoki, C., & Corson, M.S. (2009). An operational method for the evaluation of resource use and environmental impacts of dairy farms by life cycle assessment. *Journal of Environmental Management, 90,* 3643–3652.

Williams, A. G., Audsley, E., & Sandars, D. L. (2006). *Determining the Environmental Burdens and Resource Use in the Production of Agricultural and Horticultural Commodities.* Main report. *Defra Research Project IS0205.* Cranfield University and Defra, Bedford, UK, 1–97.

Woermann, E. (1944). Ernahrungswirtschaftliche Leistungsmasstabe, *Mitteldungen fur die Landwirtschaft, 59*(36), 787–792.

Wolfert, S., Ge, L., Verdouw, C., & Bogaardt, M.-J. (2017). Data in smart farming –a review. *Agricultural Systems, 153*, 69–80.

Zehetmeier, M., Baudracco, J., Hoffmann, H., & Heißenhuber, A. (2012). Does increasing milk yield per cow reduce greenhouse gas emissions? A system approach, *Animal, 6*, 154–166.

Chapter 11

Big Data as a Key Aspect of Customer Relationship Management: An Example of the Restaurant Industry

Agnieszka Werenowska

Warsaw University of Life Sciences—SGGW

Contents

11.1 Introduction

Food is a basic commodity in every economy. It is a special kind of social and cultural heritage, necessary for human health and life, much more than products of other industries, which is the quintessence of why it has such huge significance (Morgan and Sonnino, 2010). Food and gastronomy are increasingly recognized as potential determinants of balanced economic, social, and environmental development at local and global levels. The European Parliament's Committee on Culture and Education approved in 2014 the proposal of the European Parliament resolution on the "European gastronomic heritage: cultural and educational aspects", which recognized the importance of food and gastronomy as an artistic and cultural expression and as the fundamental pillars of family and social relations (European Parliament, 2019).

Gastronomy is a specific platform for understanding the mechanisms of food consumption. Its essence is to identify factors affecting food consumption. Food is a basic good and fundamentally determines human well-being and health.

Nowadays, digital technologies open new, previously unknown, and inaccessible opportunities to learn about and meet the needs of consumers. The analysis of large data sets through guest reviews on companies in aggregators of opinions such as TripAdvisor, Google, Facebook, Pyszne, and Uber, which are also available to users in the form of mobile applications, has particular potential. World statistics clearly point to the huge development and interest in mobile applications. In 2017, the number of downloads of mobile applications increased by 60% compared to 2015, to 175 billion downloads. Consumer spending on applications also increased by as much as 105% and amounted to 86 billion dollars. The time spent by users in applications increased by 30% throughout the year. Everyday consumers spent about 3 hours in them, and most on developing markets, in countries such as Indonesia, Mexico, and Brazil (Mobile trends, 2017). These trends also apply to broadly understood gastronomy. On September 11, 2019, at 4.532.270.430 (2002) Internet users were recorded, 4,140,600 cell phones were sold worldwide (World meters, 2019).

The approach to analyzing consumers' behavior is changing. The mobile channel is becoming the main source of information about their interests and preferences. Big Data is one of the most promising research trends of the decade, which attracts the attention of all market and society segments. Properly profiled data allow implementing an advertising campaign of the restaurant to a precisely defined group of consumers interested in specific products or services. The target group can be specified not only because of gender, location, or language but also by the interests and needs of users. Full use of the Big Data capabilities is possible when this issue is treated comprehensively (Tabakow, Korczak and Franczyk, 2014).

The aim of the research was to present digitization as an element of creating a personalized offer and the possibility of using it in the process of customer relationship management in the catering industry. The research methods used are analysis of the subject literature and source materials, and case study. The first part of the study brings forward the Customer Relationship Management (CRM) system presenting its main assumptions. The next section characterizes the gastronomy market in Poland and the structure of expenses, using data from the Central Statistical Office (CSO) in Poland. The second part of this chapter is devoted to the characteristics of the examined object and the analysis of processes related to Big Data. This chapter presents digitization and use of data on consumer behavior in creating a personalized offer and research on consumer behavior in creating strategies for influencing purchasing decisions. The study was crowned with conclusions.

11.2 Customer Relationship Management

One of the most important values for every enterprise, in particular, the gastronomic one, is customer satisfaction, and the goal is to meet their needs. Achieving it is a process accompanied by sales and marketing support. CRM philosophy also implies the involvement of all employees as an important source of information, remembering that this is a company's strategy, not just technology. It focuses on the client, not the organization itself. A partnership approach to the client and creating links with the company with the support of new technologies becomes the most important factor. The philosophy is based on the systematic collection of information about clients, their environment, needs, and expectations, the fulfillment of which is the company's goal.

There are many benefits to using the CRM system. They can be grouped according to three areas: cost reduction, revenue growth, and strategic benefits. The use of this system can increase the efficiency of sellers by 10%–15%, revenues (10% per annum), the number of successful transactions (increase of the index by 5% per year), it is also possible to increase the level of customer satisfaction by 3% per year (Wróblewska, 2013). Increasing the level of sales is possible thanks to acquiring new customers, creating customer databases taking into account their preferences. In the whole process of creating relationships with clients, it is extremely important to be able to keep in touch, e.g., via e-mail, newsletter, or text messages. One should not forget about improving the internal communication system between individual departments in the organization. Using the CRM system, it is necessary to constantly update the data, to filter, and add parameters.

11.3 Analysis of the Gastronomy Market in Poland

Poland is one of the fastest-growing European economies. These changes concern the services sector including catering. In 2017, there were over 71,000 gastronomic establishments in Poland, mostly private (98.3%), including 20,086 restaurants, 20,172 bars, 4,383 canteens, and 26,415 gastronomic outlets. In the structure of establishments, restaurants, bars, and gastronomic outlets constituted about 30%, and canteens—6.2%. The total number of catering establishments increased by 1.0% compared to 2016, the number of gastronomic outlets increased by 7.6% and restaurants by 2.4% while the number of bars decreased by 7.2% and canteens by 3.1% (GUS, 2017).

The increase in consumer demand for the use of gastronomic services is conditioned, among others, by the change in Poles' lifestyles and the development of the gastronomic offer. The effect of the growth in demand for catering services is an increase in consumer groups' expenditure on catering outside the home. Poland's membership in the European Union has also contributed to the creation of foreign gastronomy enterprises, mainly fast-food chains and cafes (Kowalczuk, 2012). Growing competition leads companies to implement new offers, in line with customer expectations and new ways of communication.

According to the nomenclature of the Polish CSO, four basic types of gastronomic establishments (GUS, 2017) are distinguished: restaurants, bars, canteens, and gastronomic outlets. According to the CSO terminology, restaurants are catering establishments available to all consumers, with full waiter service, offering a wide and varied range of dishes and drinks, served to consumers by a menu card. According to the CSO data on the number of restaurants, the demand for catering establishments is still growing in Poland.

Data on revenues from catering activities indicate an increase in the value of the gastronomy market. Total sales generated by all catering outlets in 2017 reached almost PLN 39.92 billion. Revenues from gastronomic production in 2017 were higher than in the previous year by PLN 2,690 million (GUS, 2017). An apparent increase in the value of sales applies to all segments of the gastronomy market; however, the greatest dynamics concerns restaurants, bars, and cafes.

In addition to quality and taste, the key elements of consumers' purchasing decisions today are experiences such as the need to relax (the desire to spend time in a pleasant and friendly atmosphere), the desire to try new and diverse flavors, and the need to develop contacts with other people. On the other hand, there are growing concerns arising from uncertainty about the quality of the ingredients of dishes eaten out.

11.4 Structure of Consumer Spending

The development of the Polish gastronomy market confirms the increase in the share of various groups of buyers. In 2017, 56% of Poles used gastronomy out in town. According to CSO data, the amount of disposable income of households in Poland is growing, which is also associated with the increase in expenditure on gastronomy. The most visited gastronomic outlets among consumers are restaurants (26%), pizzerias (25%), fast food restaurants (21%), bars and pubs (14%), and cafes (10%) (GUS, 2017).

In Poland, there are significant disproportions in the expenditure on food in catering establishments, depending on the number of people in the household.

The highest was recorded in single-person household budgets. With the increase in the number of people in the household, spending on eating out is also decreasing.

It is worth noting that the largest number of catering establishments is located in the Masovian Voivodeship. It is in the Masovian Voivodship that the average expenditure per person is PLN 1,370.71, including PLN 72.17 for gastronomy (Small Statistical Yearbook of Poland 2016, Central Statistical Office, Warsaw, 2016).

The data from the consumer climate indicators of Poles (TNS Consumer Index[1]) are also important. They indicate a long-term increase in consumer optimism in Poland for the last 22 years, and since 2016, they have been positive. A high level of consumer optimism characterizes groups with high purchasing potential on the market.

The consumer climate index in November 2018 was seven points and has been positive for over a year and a half. In November, the value of the index increased—by 1.6% points compared to October of the year in question (TNS Polska, November 2018).

Constant improvement in the material situation of households in Poland was observed, which results in higher and higher incomes and an increase in expenditure on consumption. In the structure of the monthly expenditure of Polish consumers in 2016, expenditure per one person for food and non-alcoholic beverages was PLN 273, for restaurants and hotels PLN 49 (4.32% on monthly expenses—PLN 1132/person). The largest expenses (PLN 72.17) were incurred by residents of the Mazowieckie voivodship—over 5% (GUS, 2016). Therefore, Warsaw can be a good representative of catering services in Poland.

Warsaw is an important center of gastronomy development, represented by various types of gastronomic establishments. This is due to a large number of residents and tourists arriving. In 2017, Warsaw was visited by 25,750,000 tourists, of whom 27% were foreign tourists (Warsaw Tour, 2019). This is one of the reasons why in Warsaw the number of gastronomic establishments outside the center of the city has increased in the last decade. Most of them operate in the following districts: Śródmieście, where most hotels, administrative facilities, and tourist attractions are located (19.2%), and Mokotów (12.2%). These locations are spatially developed, and they bring together many jobs and are located in the middle of a system of various types of communication (Derek et al., 2013).

11.5 Characteristics of the Pizzeria "L'Olivo"

The Italian restaurant and pizzeria "L'Olivo" (L'Olivo Limited Liability Company) specializes in the sale of Italian specialties: pizza and pasta. Food products are purchased from certified suppliers who can document the fact of meeting all required

---

[1] Indicator informing about the current assessment and forecast of the economic situation of the country and households. It can take values from −100 to 100.

legal standards, Polish and those of the EU. The offer of the restaurant is a proposition of real Italian cuisine and selected wines at available prices.

The main source of the company's revenues is catering, which is characterized by systematic growth on an annual basis. Revenues of the restaurant are characterized by seasonality, which depends, among others, on weather changes and the associated variable number of tables and fewer sales days in the winter months. The highest revenues are achieved in the third quarter and the lowest in the first quarter of the year. When analyzing the cost aspect, attention should be paid to a significant improvement in the restaurant's work efficiency in recent quarters. The efficiency improvement was influenced by:

- Price policy. The company has successfully introduced changes in price management. The previous owners introduced the price offer regardless of the perception of the location and groups of consumers using the services of the restaurant. The new management has adapted the offer to various customer segments and thus achieved the appropriate sales volume while maintaining the assumed sales profit.
- Reduction of other costs. Other costs include telecommunications services, marketing costs, costs of website creation, repairs, and the like. This whole group of costs in relation to revenues is around 15%. In recent quarters, the company has carried out many activities aimed at limiting this cost category, such as renegotiating contracts; rationalizing the costs associated with playing music in the premises; and creating a new website for the restaurant based on a ready WordPress template with further supplementing the content and adapting it to the template layout, choosing photos, and configuring the appropriate layout.

Market position, the current perception of the company by contractors, and the company's current activities allow the company to acquire more customers, build loyalty in relation to the ability to introduce new products, and maintain the high quality of services.

The SWOT analysis concept used (see Table 11.1) was to identify the strengths and weaknesses of the surveyed company and to identify opportunities and threats in its environment. The current situation and future forecast were analyzed. According to the own study, based on IQS data, the biggest competitors are local pizzerias. The company has taken measures to eliminate weaknesses. The main barrier to the dynamic development of the premises is the high costs of running a restaurant, and in the event of breaking the barriers to growth, additional marketing and management costs are needed.

The financial situation of the company has improved significantly, but the perspective of the next years requires further intensive work on business development. The perception of the restaurant in the near future will be influenced by understanding and acceptance of the strategy aimed at safe development, improvement of

Table 11.1 SWOT Analysis of "L'Olivo" Restaurant

	Positive Factors	*Negative Factors*
	Strengths	Weaknesses
Internal factors	1. Location of the restaurant for eight years in the same place. 2. Company results enabling further development. 3. High customer loyalty. 4. High customer satisfaction with the service received. 5. A continuous increase in the ratings of customers visiting the restaurant. 6. Efficient management of the offer for clients. 7. Italian products, management, and chef. 8. Favorable conditions negotiated with suppliers of goods from Italy (90% of the offer of the restaurant). 9. Maintaining the right quality of ingredients and dishes. 10. The high commitment of the management in the work of the restaurant.	1. Three times the change of the owner of the restaurant, which makes building the brand difficult. 2. Errors made by previous owners. 3. Waiters rotation. 4. The premises rented for the restaurant, no own premises. 5. Location of the premises, site not visible. 6. The sensitivity of the Polish consumer to prices. 7. Lack of active promotion of the restaurant on social media profiles. 8. Lack of developed marketing plan. 9. Lack of loyalty programs—until now.
	Opportunities	Threats
External factors	1. Dynamic residential and office development. 2. Growing customer purchasing power. 3. Growing demand for good-quality services. 4. Change in clients' eating habits and an increase in the frequency of visits to restaurants. 5. Decrease in unemployment. 6. Growing consumer optimism. 7. Strengthening of the national currency (PLN).	1. Unfavorable tax changes. 2. Increase in competition in the segment. 3. The growing interest in cooking at home and cheap fast food offers. 4. Increase in rental prices and real estate prices. 5. Increase in loan costs.

Source: Own calculations based on L'Olivo company.

the company's results and balance, growth rate and quality, effects of promotional activities on social profiles, and implementation of forecasts.

The following research methods and techniques were used in the study: in the theoretical part methods of analysis, synthesis, and deduction, whereas, in the empirical part, the methods of statistical, comparative, and economic analysis as well as heuristic techniques. The revealed phenomena and results were presented in a descriptive and graphic form.

11.6 Digitization and Use of Data on Consumer Behavior in Creating a Personalized Offer

A modern Internet user develops and functions in various areas thanks to data obtained using modern technologies. In a sense, as a species, he has evolved into becoming homo informaticus (EY, 2015). The existence of a situation in which recipients have access to almost countless sources of information makes it necessary to develop and improve the skills of selecting and filtering information. The dynamic development of information and communication technologies has significantly influenced changes in the gastronomy sector. Acquiring customers and their favor, positive feedback becomes an important element of promotion. Especially in the group of clients of generation Y, who are extremely demanding, among others, to adapt to their needs and lifestyle. This generation actively uses various communities. On Facebook, people aged 15–30 constitute over 60% of all Polish users of this website (Emplo, 2018). Deloitte's analysis shows that by the end of 2023 in developed countries, over 90% of adults will use SM, the standard of equipment will be elements of artificial intelligence (Doloitte, 2019). This is a clear signal for many brands and industries how to organize communication with this unique generation.

In creating a personalized offer in the studied restaurant, Facebook social networking statistics were used. They concerned the observation of changes in the behavior of portal users during the advertising campaign from May 12, 2019, in order to like the page.

When launching the advertising campaign using Facebook digital technology, the group of recipients, their location (city of Warsaw), and interests were precisely defined. This is extremely important information for any campaign, without which it would not really matter.

Data obtained from Facebook statistics allow tracking user behavior and their location. They also give the opportunity to study the number of recipients of an advertising campaign. In the discussed case, within 14 days, it amounted to 1,963 people, including 66 people who liked the site. From the point of view of creating customer relationships and customizing the offer, other data that can be obtained from Facebook statistics are also important. These include, apart from demographic data, the number of ad displays and devices used by the followers.

Big Data is nowadays a natural resource for organizations, a digital inventory, as well as a detailed look at the past (Conway and Klabjan, 2013).

Digitization allows to examine the behavior of a selected group of recipients, including socio-demographic variables; optimize the offer and the final product; and create individualized offers.

11.7 Research on Consumer Behavior in Creating Strategies for Influencing Purchasing Decisions

Modern consumers, especially representatives of generation Y, are very mindful. Once a consumer, the so-called homo oeconomicus (Latin for economic man), was compared to an efficiently counting calculator making rational and selfish decisions. However, this concept was quickly questioned by the lack of rationality in making purchasing decisions. The mechanisms that increase the customers' willingness to buy were analyzed. An analysis of the determinants of consumer assessment of the studied restaurant was carried out. All examined variables have shown that clients of the examined object and consumers nationwide identify quality mainly by the taste characteristics of the product.

To check consumer behavior, a series of studies were conducted. As follows from the observation of a person participating directly in the surveyed place, the main determinants of L'Olivo consumers' loyalty are primarily the quality of dishes, which is the main factor determining a return to L'Olivo, customer service, and the atmosphere prevailing in the restaurant. Digital technologies and statistics of opinions aggregators on enterprises in the catering industry allow to more effectively examine the behavior of a selected group of recipients, including socio-demographic variables, optimize the offer and final product, and create individualized offers.

Analyzing the collected data, it becomes legitimate to state that the main determinant of the impact on purchasing decisions of the customers of the studied restaurant is, above all, maintaining a constant level of quality, including maintaining or improving the organoleptic characteristics of the dishes served, the level of service, and decor of the place.

Based on a comparative analysis of quality measures offered by the examined restaurant and perceived by consumers, it is justified to state that one of the main tasks in creating a strategy to influence consumer purchasing decisions is to disseminate information on the quality of ingredients for served dishes and the highest quality products presented in the offer. These are products with European quality labels DOC (designation of confirmed origin), DOCG (designation of controlled and guaranteed origin, a higher category of wine classification in the card), DOP (protected designation of origin), which constitute the majority of L'Olivo's offer.

A study of consumer behavior of a selected gastronomic establishment allows defining main determinants of impact on purchasing decisions and enables the creation of strategies to increase consumer confidence in the restaurant, consequently contributing to increased sales. Understanding which data ensure the achievement of business goals, improving customer service can be time-consuming and requires specialized knowledge on statistical correlations. It should be remembered that Big Data are data that are not subject to so-called sampling. They are completely related to the creation of databases thanks to electronic sources. Importantly, their main goal is not a statistical inference (Horrigan, 2013). Big Data without proper development is not worth much. They gain value only after processing and careful analysis carried out by specialists.

Figures from Big Data analyses can have a very high material value, especially when combined with other data both from inside the organization and from outside (Trajman, 2013). According to many analysts, the value of the global Big Data market is constantly increasing. In 2014, it was about USD 18 billion. Forecasts for 2026 indicate that it will rise to around $ 92 billion (Connick, 2017).

This phenomenon is becoming more and more worrying for businesses, especially because consumers are increasingly aware of the value of their personal data. That is why building relationships with clients and searching for ways to optimize services using analytical tools is becoming increasingly important.

11.8 Conclusion

Acquiring loyal customers becomes a real challenge for a company. In this process, important is the efficient management of customer experience at every stage of cooperation and engaging them in the company's operations (e.g., promotion, development of new products). This cannot be achieved without knowing the client's expectations, needs, and habits (Buchnowska, 2017). Therefore, modern enterprises are almost forced to use systems that support this goal. New technologies and Big Data are helpful in this process. The analysis of large data sets through guest reviews on companies in aggregators of opinions such as TripAdvisor, Google, Facebook, Pyszne, and Uber, which are also available to users in the form of mobile applications, has particular potential. Nowadays, digital technologies open new, previously unknown, and inaccessible opportunities to learn about and meet the needs of consumers. Digital technologies and statistics of opinion aggregators on enterprises in the catering industry allow to more effectively examine the behavior of a selected group of recipients, including socio-demographic variables, optimize the offer and final product, and create individualized offers. They have become an inseparable tool for creating strategies for building positive customer relationships that are particularly important in the catering industry.

Consumers follow a certain sequence of behaviors that are conditioned by various factors. The results obtained are related to the empirical context of the research.

More research is needed, along with variables and possibly other methods of analysis, to increase the effectiveness of these studies. Continuous research on consumer behavior, its changes, and dynamics allows for a better understanding of consumers, adapting to their expectations and needs, which in turn leads to increased sales and profits for the company.

Digital technologies open up new, previously unknown opportunities for gastronomy establishments. Thanks to them, it becomes possible to know and meet the needs of consumers. Analysis of large data sets has particular potential. For this purpose, guest reviews collected in aggregators of opinions about the companies: TripAdvisor, Google, Facebook, Pyszne, and Uber, also available to users in the form of mobile applications, are necessary. The mobile channel has become the main source of information about interests and preferences. Profiled data allow the implementation of an advertising campaign of the restaurant targeted at a very specific group of consumers interested in specific products or services.

Replication studies of clearly diverse consumer groups should be conducted, maintaining main research variables and including changing attitudes and motivations. It should also be mentioned that research restrictions relate to the empirical implementation of research and its consequences for the results.

References

Buchnowska, D. (2017). Systemy CRM w dobie konwergencji nowoczesnych technologii informacyjnych [CRM systems in the era of convergence of modern information technologies]. *Zarządzanie i Finanse Journal of Management and Finance, 15*(4), 225–226.

Connick, H. (2017). *Turning Big Data into Big Insights*. Retrieved from https://www.ama.org/marketing-news/turning-big-data-into-big-insights/.

Conway, D., Klabjan, D. (2013). Innovation Patterns of Big Data. In J. Liebowitz, *Big Data and Business Analytics*, Boca Raton, FL: CRC Press, Taylor & Francis Group, LLC, pp. 131–147.

Derek, M., Duda-Gromada, K., Kosowska, P., Kowalczyk, A., Madurowicz, M. (2013). Problemowe i problematyczne ABC turystyki w Warszawie [Problem and problematic ABC of tourism in Warsaw]. *Prace Geograficzne*, 134–140.

Doloitte. (2019). *Technology, Media, and Telecommunications Predictions 2020*. Retrieved from https://www2.deloitte.com/content/dam/Deloitte/cz/Documents/technology-media-telecommunications/DI_TMT-Prediction-2020.pdf [accessed 20.11.2019].

Emplo. (2018). Retrieved from http://emplo.pl/blog/pokolenie-y-w-social-media/ [accessed 20.11.2019].

European Parliament. (2019). Retrieved from http:www.europarl.europa.eu [accessed 2.12.2019].

EY. (2015). *Homo Informaticus: How Do Digital Consumers Behave Online?* Retrieved from https://www.ey.com/Publication/vwLUAssets/Raport_EY_Homo_informaticus/$FILE/ey_homo_informaticus.pdf [accessed 2.12.2019].

Facebook. (2019). Retrieved from https://www.facebook.com/pizzeriaristorantelolivo.

GUS. (2016, 2017). Statistics Poland. Retrieved from http:www.stat.gov.pl/gus [accessed 20.12.2019].

Horrigan, M. (2013). *Big Data: A Perspective from the BLS*, Amstat News, January 2013 Retrieved from http://magazine.amstat.org/blog/2013/01/01/sci-policy-jan2013/.

Kowalczuk, I. (2012). *Zachowania konsumentów na rynku usług gastronomicznych [Consumer Behaviour on the Catering Market]*. Warszawa, PL: Wydawnictwo SGGW.

Mobile Trends (2017). Retrieved from www.mobiletrends.pl/raport-2017-roku-rynek-aplikacji-mobilnych-mial-sie-swietnie [accessed 10.12.2019].

Morgan, K., Sonnino, R. (2010). The urban foodscape: World cities and the new food equation. *Cambridge Journal of Regions: Economy and Society, 3*(2), 209–210.

Tabakow, M., Korczak, J., Franczyk, B. (2014). Big data – definicje, wyzwania i technologie informatyczne [Big-data-definitions, challenges, and information technologies]. *Business Informatics, 1*(31), 139–141.

Trajman, O. (2013). The intrinsic value of data, in big data and business analytics. In J. Liebowitz, (ed.), Boca Raton, FL: CRC Press, Taylor & Francis Group.

Warsaw Tour. (2019). Retrieved from http://www.warsawtour.pl.

Worldometers. (2019). Retrieved from https://www.worldometers.info.

Wróblewska, W. (2013). Zarządzanie relacjami z klientami jako źródło sukcesu organizacji [Customer relationship management (CRM) as a source of organization success]. *Zeszyty Naukowe Uniwersytetu Przyrodniczo – Humanistycznego w Siedlcach, 97,* 229–239.

Chapter 12

Blockchain and Big Data: Example of Management of Beef Production

Sławomir Jarka

Warsaw University of Life Sciences—SGGW

Contents

12.1 Introduction

The use of blockchain technology is becoming wider in Poland and in the world. New applications are introduced that use the hard rules of mathematics and cryptography, which are the foundation of blockchain. The technology is used in processes of using distributed databases. Blockchain can be defined as a decentralized and distributed operations register (Iansiti & Lakhani, 2017). In the context of managing the beef production process, blockchain is a technology that allows you to create a distributed register of operations and events that took place during the rearing period (Bheemaiah, 2017). Importantly, from the point of view of the transparency of the decreed operations, this register is available on the Internet and all authorized users have access to it.

The main purpose of the study was to present the possibilities of using innovative blockchain technology in improving the functioning of supply chains in the beef market.

The first part of this chapter presents the genesis of blockchain technology as well as its development stages and features. The second part discusses the reasons for using blockchain in the production of high-quality beef in Poland. The last part of this chapter presents the concept of using blockchain technology and discusses limiting factors in beef production in Poland.

12.2 Statement of the Problem

One of the answers to contemporary challenges related to globalization and the growing demands of consumers is the development of 4.0 industry (the fourth industrial revolution). The effect of this development understood as the implementation of new technologies is the use of Internet of Things or Big Data in agriculture and the food industry (Osmólski & Koliński, 2018). European agriculture is undergoing transformations aimed at meeting a strong competitive position both on the domestic market and on the global market. High quality and food safety standards play a strategic role in the development model of European agriculture (European Commission, 2013).

An important element of these changes in the model of European agriculture is the improvement of product quality, obtained by improving the supply chain. In order to exclude faulty processes that do not meet the requirements of good agricultural practice, there is a need to identify, monitor, and manage the supply chain on the food market (Osmólski & Koliński, 2018).

Another problem that occurs in the beef production chain is due to the attitudes of modern consumers. As indicated by the researcher of consumer trends (Vejlgaard, 2008, p. 9), the trend in consumer behavior is understood as a specific direction of change in the lifestyle of consumers, acting objectively, regardless of their will and awareness. In broad terms, it can be said that consumer trends arise as a result of influencing consumer purchasing behavior in the technological, economic, social, legal, political, demographic, and technological dimensions, and as a result affect changes in consumption patterns. Undoubtedly, such a trend that has been observed among modern consumers has become as the result of the use of technology and mobile devices (Nord, Achituv & Paliszkiewicz, 2017). As a result, consumers are increasingly showing adaptation to changes in which goods and services are delivered. The increasing access to information for modern consumers, especially their ability to better understand and transform information into awareness and a rational decision, is a reliable test of the changes and proper consumer behavior which are rational decisions on the innovative market.

Assael (2004) distinguishes four factors that have an impact on the complex purchasing decisions that people make:

■ The nature of the product—complex consumer behavior applies to high-price goods and products referring to the buyer's ego (cosmetics, clothes)
■ No time pressure (having longer time to think when shopping)
■ The availability of sufficient information needed to assess competing brands
■ The buyer's ability to process the information properly (innovative attitude)

On the beef market, one can observe the impact and pressure resulting from the factors presented above (Gutkowska, Czarnecki, Głąbska & Batóg, 2018). What problem results from the analysis of the behavior of food consumers who consciously make market choices and are guided by premises that can be empirically verified during their purchasing decisions? This is undoubtedly the problem of trust, and more precisely the problem of crediting factors shaping individual stages of the market chain, especially on the market of selective products, in this case, high-quality beef. Using the advantages of blockchain technology seems to be a natural, currently available solution. In case in which, even the smallest event is recorded in an inseparable chain, starting from monitoring the place of birth and body temperature of the cattle, and then ending with the signature of the transport company to the store. Solution based on blockchain gives grounds to trust that the process of food supply is transparent.

12.3 The Genesis of Blockchain Technology and Its Development Stages

Speaking of the history of blockchain technology, one should go back to 1991. It was then that the idea of blockchain technology was described when scientists Stuart Haber and W. Scott Stornetta presented a solution to the world that digitally meant documents preventing them from being altered or falsified. The presented system used a cryptographically secured blockchain to store documents bearing so-called time stamps. In 1992, the project was included (the so-called Merkle Trees), increasing its efficiency and enabling the collection of many documents in one block. However, this technology was ultimately not used and used by anyone, and the patent itself expired in 2004. That is, 4 years before Bitcoin was created.

The next step in the history of blockchain technology was RPoW (Reusable Proof of Work). In 2004, the world-famous IT specialist and cryptographer Hal Finney (Harold Thomas Finney II) introduced a system called RPoW. The system was based on receiving invariant and/or indestructible Hashcash, and instead created a token signed by the RSA key, which can then be transferred from person to person.

This solution solved the so-called double spending by maintaining ownership of tokens on a trusted server that was designed to allow users around the world to check their validity and integrity in real time. RPoW can be considered an early prototype and a step forward in the history of cryptocurrencies—on this basis, Bitcoin was built by an unknown creator operating under the pseudonym Satoshi Nakamoto.

Basically speaking, a blockchain is created using distributed register technology contains information grouped into interrelated blocks. Each block is associated with the previous one using a hash, or a link to the previous block, and a time stamp specifying the time when the shortcut was created (Treiblmaier, 2018). In other words, blockchain is a distributed, collective database that enables data collection and communication by registering information through computers that are part of the same network. However, the innovation of blockchain technology relates to the combination of various fields: software engineering, distribution computer science, cryptographic science, and economic game theory (Kisielnicki, 2018).

Thus, blockchain technology essentially creates a digital recording book. Transaction information is stored in chronological order and made available to participating entities. Each transaction placed in this book is verified by system participants. Single block represents a set of transactions that are included within it. Once information or transition is placed to the blockchain it becomes immutable (Steiner, Baker, Wood, & Meiklejohn, 2017). This integrity and immutable system character are accomplished due to the fact that each newly created block has an abbreviation (hash) of the previous block, thus enabling them to work in an inseparable data chain—blockchain (Swan, 2015).

The process of registering and validating transactions takes place without involving both parties and third parties. In most types of blockchain, validating node blocks must find proof of work, that is, to solve the equation whose difficulty is regulated by the adopted algorithm. Thanks to these solutions, blockchain technology ensures the security of data transmission as well as reliability and correctness of data. Each transaction and its value are visible to everyone who has access to the system (Iansiti & Lakhani, 2017).

Blockchain is a distributed, collective database that enables data collection and communication by registering information through computers belonging to the same network. However, the innovation of blockchain technology relates to the combination of various fields: software engineering, distribution computer science, cryptographic science, and economic game theory (Sultan, Ruhi & Lakhani, 2018).

The history of the creation of blockchain technology is inseparably connected with the history of the digital currency known as Bitcoin and its creator, the mysterious Satoshi Nakamoto. The true identity of the inventor of one of the most revolutionary technologies of our time remains unknown, despite the fact that this person (or people) hidden under a pseudonym, actively participated for over 2 years in developing the source code of Bitcoin software (Puczyński & Kosieradzka, 2018).

The event that is considered an announcement of the Bitcoin network was the registration of the bitcoin.org domain on August 18, 2008. However, the key moment in the history of Bitcoin, using blockchain technology, was the publication of the White Paper document by Nakamoto on October 31, 2008 titled: "Bitcoin: A Peer to Peer Electronic Cash System" (Nakamoto, 2008).

According to Crosby, at the beginning the technology was only used to distribute digital cryptocurrency—Bitcoin (first stage). It was aimed at sending, receiving, storing, and trading cryptocurrencies. Initially, the network was based on long records of code lines, but thanks to this, the authors (Crosby et al., 2015) talk about the security of stored and distributed data. However, it was very quickly noticed that this technology could also be useful for greater digitization of individual business entities, institutions, sectors, and, as a consequence, entire economies. This is the second stage in the development of the technology. Therefore, the use of blockchain technology has been developing dynamically for over a decade, causing the effect of a blockchain technology boom.

Finally, another extremely important stage for the development of blockchain technology is a solution dedicated to business and enterprises. In 2015, thanks to the Linux Foundation, Hyperledger was created, built by the largest technological entities such as IBM, Intel, SAP, or Oracle. Hyperledger enabled the introduction of private blockchain technology to sectors such as banking, insurance, and supply chain tracking. It draws attention to supervise the network and preserve privacy, even by verifying its users in the Know Your Customer (KYC) process. Unlike the blockchain used in the world of cryptocurrencies, participants of the Hyperledger Fabric network are not anonymous; therefore, the transaction validation process takes place in a different way, mainly due to the aforementioned business relations. The process is quite more complex and requires the involvement of many nodes, each of which has a corresponding task assigned to it. But once closed, the block is irreversible, and the information stored in it is visible only to authorized parties, and not as in the case of public blockchain for all network users.

The definition of food safety is set out in the National Food Safety and Nutrition Act of August 25, 2006, and it means, "The general conditions that must be fulfilled, in particular: the substances and flavours used, levels of pollutants, pesticide residues, food irradiation conditions, organoleptic characteristics and actions that must be taken at all stages of food production or marketing—to ensure human health and life" (Dz. U. [*Journal of Laws*] from 2015, item. 594). According to Kosior (2018), blockchain solutions and applications take into account most of the problems and needs that arise in managing the flow of agri-food products between individual parts of the chain. These chains are currently extremely developed and complex. This was due to, among others, liberalization of world trade, growing competition between agri-food sector enterprises, product and process innovations. Thus, along with the increase in the level of internationalization of enterprises, the use of blockchain technology increases. As indicated by the Blockchain in

Agriculture Market forecast (2019), the value of blockchain will reach 430 million dollars in the agricultural and food market by 2023. It will be used in supply chains, in the reorganization of decision-making processes of individual organizations, prevention of food-borne epidemics, in the process of reducing the number of frauds in the food industry, reducing the amount of waste, etc. This will be possible thanks to tracking food production processes (in the case of animals, e.g., monitoring their nutritional and health parameters) and transport (Szymczak & Sadowski, 2019).

12.4 The Concept of Using Blockchain Technology and Factors Limiting It in Beef Production in Poland

One of the possible applications of blockchain technology is the beef production process, which by its nature is long-lasting and the effects for the breeder may be achievable even after 2 years from the beginning of the animal fattening. It can be seen that due to the length of the beef production process, the risk to the farmer resulting from the economic calculation is higher. Other stakeholders forming the market chain of beef production are also exposed to this risk, especially financial institutions (banks), which often co-finance the operational activity of farms (Figure 12.1). The problem breeders have to face is monitoring animals using Internet of Things (IoT) technology, to start preventive or early intervention measures for animals at the right time. It is assumed that the use of blockchain technology will contribute to reducing the level of production risk of the breeder but also of other participants in the production chain (Kosior, 2018). This part of the chapter focuses primarily on building blockchain and the responsibility of individual stakeholders in management of beef production. In relations to the criterion of access rights (Atzori, 2015), blockchain solutions are divided into:

■ *Public blockchain*, available to everyone and allowing all entities to read ongoing transactions, as well as to submit transactions to be saved in the network
■ *Private blockchain*, available only to selected participants

It should be noted that the presented concept of the beef production chain concerns the use of the *private blockchain* potential. It is based on a private data register, available only to selected participants who have the right to read transactions or who can submit transactions to place in the block. Thus, approval of participation in the network is required and new users must be invited. In such private networks, there may be a complex security system based, for example, on deciding whether new participants belong to the network of subsequent units. Licenses for participation in a given network may be introduced, and the previously created consortium will be able to make decisions about new entities (Cole et al., 2019).

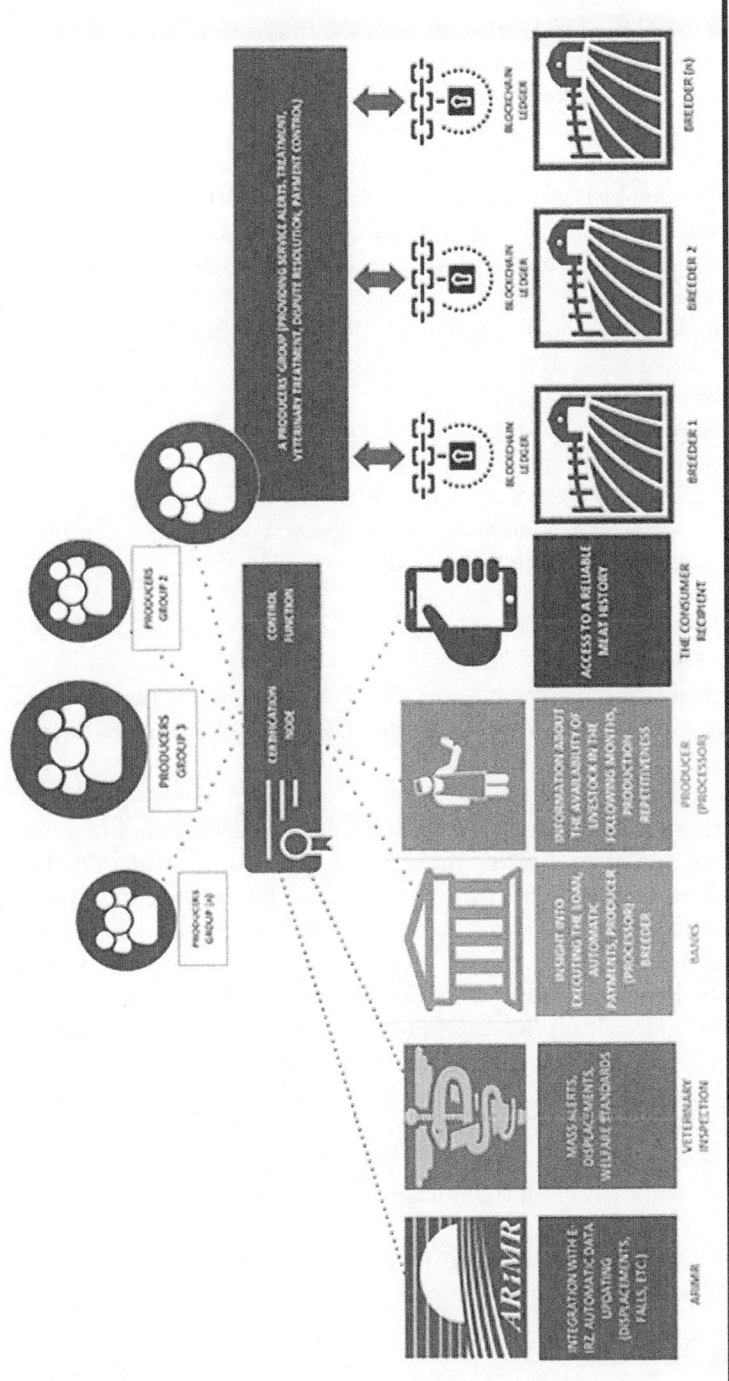

Figure 12.1 The concept of building blockchain on an example, Federation of Groups and Producers Wołowina Polska. (Based on materials prepared by G. Dobiesz and M. Mular, Oracle Polska.)

Actions in this area have been taken, among others, by the author of this chapter in real and practical terms through the initiative of establishing an organization of farmers (beef producers) and organizations supporting this complex process. Manufacturers keep meat breeds such as Charolaise and Limousine, which constitute the largest share in the possession of these animals in Poland. The process of implementing blockchain technology into the beef production chain was preceded by horizontal integration activities. The Federation of Groups and Producers Beef Poland has been registered this year in the National Court Register as a result of the initiative of the leaders of this concept (http://wolowinapolska.com/en).

The federation's stakeholders include the following entities:

- Farmers and beef producers
- Agricultural producer groups
- Meat processing plants

Depending on the strategy adopted, the group of stakeholders using blockchain may also include business environment units such as:

- Banks
- Veterinary inspection
- Units regulating and monitoring the state of animal population, i.e. The Agency for Restructuring and Modernisation of Agriculture (https://www.arimr.gov.pl)

It should be emphasized that the presented concept was the result of a grassroots initiative of a group of farmers and the academic community, who started the process of horizontal integration first. Subsequently, after joining this type of beef processing plant structure, it can be mentioned that the next, important stage of improving the efficiency of farming and improving the level of food safety is being, namely the vertical integration of the beef industry and processing units. An important element of blockchain technology in beef production is planning and access to the appropriate technical infrastructure, which is an integral part of the system besides the relevant software. Attention should be drawn to an innovative solution on a European agriculture scale, which consists in the development and installation of special sensors on animals, continuously and uninterruptedly monitoring devices that focus on such animal parameters as:

- Admission of the animal to register (blockchain) with the opening balance
- Body temperature anomaly or behavioral changes
- Ordered treatment
- Start of the feeding cycle
- Readiness to receive after obtaining adequate technological maturity

Data on the state of animal life parameters forming the Big Data collection are subject to a cryptographic procedure and stored in secured ledgers. Each block contains the end of the previous block (hash), thus enabling them to be combined into a string. All participants (stakeholders) included in a given blockchain have access to information collected in blocks. The advantage of using blockchain technology is the full sharing of information and knowledge among stakeholders of a given chain.

The information on the level of animal health collected in this way practically reflects their behavioral profile. It can be analyzed in the long term, i.e., during the full period of raising the animal, starting from birth and ending with the animal achieving technological maturity. In Polish conditions, this breeding period ranges from 18 to even 24 months, depending on the planned weight of the animal. The system dependencies presented in Figure 12.1 show that beneficiaries interested in information on the behavioral profile of animals may also be individual clients who can obtain it through the QR Code system. The analysis of the behavioral profile of animals in the short term also provides interesting results, that is, during the last 3 months of farming, which are very important in terms of shaping the level of food safety.

12.5 Conclusions, Limitations, and Further Research

In addition to many prospects and opportunities associated with the use of blockchain technology, there are also problems and barriers that may limit the wider use of this technology in agriculture and beef production in Poland (Ge, Brewster, Spek, Smeenk & Top, 2017).

Insufficient resources and funds necessary to undertake the required investments, i.e., among beef cattle farmers, may prove to be a barrier to the implementation of blockchain technology in food safety and quality management processes in the beef production chain. Some farmers may use their computer infrastructure with access to the Internet, which will reduce the level of required investment outlays. However, operating costs include the purchase of sensors that will be installed on animals, which will also be another expense.

In addition to economic and financial restrictions, also behavioral barriers on the part of individual participants in the beef production chain should be taken into account. First of all, the problem may be the lack of appropriate digital competences, especially among less educated beef producers and units that will have to learn the principles of blockchain technology. It should be expected that in the initial period of implementation of this unique technology at farm level, there may be a stage of adaptive changes (Kosior, 2018, p. 28). In terms of shaping the effectiveness of the entire group of agricultural beef producers, cooperation of all stakeholders is a significant problem (Jarka, 2016). The proper operation of the blockchain, which will allow to fully use its potential, requires the cooperation of all entities involved in the beef production chain.

In summary, the factors limiting the use of blockchain technology in beef production in Poland include:

■ Technical, technological, and organizational barriers
■ Economic and financial barriers
■ Barriers resulting from the skeptical attitude of farmers regarding the possibility of cooperation in the group of agricultural producers

Undoubtedly, the role of the group leader will be active organic work to eliminate the abovementioned barriers.

This paper presents the first step in the process of using blockchain technology in beef production in Poland. Further research should concern the effects of blockchain technology implementation on purpose-selected farms with beef production in Poland, based on meat breed animals. An important goal of this research will be to determine the factors affecting the economic calculation of the planned implementation of blockchain technology on farms. As previously indicated, relationships between individual stakeholders that should be based on mutual trust are of great importance in relation to the implementation of blockchain technology in farms with fattening cattle. The final effect of the actions taken in the producer group will depend on the ability to diagnose and solve problems that may affect them. Thereupon, the next stage of the research should be focused on conducting a diagnosis of relationships occurring in the group and indicating activities that can help to build them.

The aim of the study was to present the possibilities of using innovative blockchain technology to improve the functioning of the beef production chain. Research shows that the properties of blockchain make it a technology that can solve many of the problems and shortcomings of the current beef production system and contribute to ensuring food safety and quality. Primarily, the added value resulting from the use of blockchain technology is a significant increase in the transparency of operations among all stakeholders using data and applying practical technology solutions in beef production management.

References

Assael, H. (2004). *Consumer Behavior. A Strategic Approach*. Boston, MA: Houghton Miffein Company.

Atzori, M. (2015). *Blockchain Technology and Decentralized Governance: Is the State Still Necessary?* Rochester, NY: Social Science Research Network.

Bheemaiah, K. (2017). *The Blockchain Alternative, Rethinking Macroeconomics Policy and Economic Theory*. New York: Apress.

Zion Market Research. *Blockchain in Agriculture Market: Global Industry Analysis, Size, Share, Growth, Trends, and Forecast, 2018–2026*. Retrieved from: https://www.zion-marketresearch.com [accessed 19 January 2018].

Crosby, M., Nachiappan, P.P., Verma, S., Kalyanaraman, V. (2015). *Blockhain Technology. Beyond Bitcoin. Sutardja Center for Entrepreneurship & Technology Technical Report.* Berkeley, CA: University of California (6–19).

European Commission. (2013). *EU Food Market Overview. Enterprise and Industry.* Retrieved from: http://ec.europa.eu/enterprise/sectors/food/eumarket/index_en.htm.

Ge, L., Brewster, Ch., Spek, J., Smeenk, A., Top, J. (2017). *Blockchain for Agriculture and Food. Findings from the Pilot Study.* The Hague: Wageningen Economic Research.

Gutkowska, K., Czarnecki, J., Głąbska, D., Batóg, A. (2018). Consumer perception of health properties and of other attributes of beef as determinants of consumption and purchase decisions. *Roczniki Państwowego Zakładu Higieny, 69*(4), 413–419.

Iansiti, M. Lakhani, K. (2017). The thru about Blockchain. *Harvard Business Review, 95*(1), 118–127.

Jarka, S. Ruciński, M. (2016). *High Commitment Management a New Direction in the Management of Staff.* Warszawa, PL: Wydawnictwo SGGW.

Kisielnicki, J. (2018). Blockchain jako technologia przepływu informacji i wiedzy w zarządzaniu projektami [Blockchain as a technology of information and knowledge flow in project management]. *Przegląd Organizacji, 8,* 8–13.

Nakamoto, S. (2008). *Bitcoin: A Peer-to-Peer Electronic Cash System.* Retrieved from: https://bitcoin.org/en/bitcoin-paper [accessed September 2019].

Nord, J.H., Achituv, D.B., Paliszkiewicz, J. (2017). Communication through social technologies: A study of Israeli women. *Journal of International Technology and Information Management, 26*(1), 45–70.

Osmólski, W. Koliński, A. (2018). Wykorzystanie technologii blockchain w obrocie produktami spożywczymi [The use of blockchain technology in the marketing of food products]. *Przemysł Spożywczy, 72,* 64–68.

Puczyński, P., Kosieradzka, A. (2018). Blockchain - koncepcja i potencjał rozwoju w dziesiątą rocznicę powstania [Blockchain - concept and development potential for the tenth anniversary]. *Przegląd Organizacji, 8,* 52–56.

Steiner, J. Baker, J., Wood, G., Meiklejohn, S. (2016). *Blockchain: The Solution for Transparent in Product Supply Chains, A White Paper was Written by Project Provenance Ltd.*

Sultan, K., Ruhi, U., Lakhani, R. (2018). Conceptualizing blockchains: characteristics & applications. *11th IADIS International Conference Information Systems,* 49–57.

Swan, M. (2015). *Blockchain: Blueprint for a New Economy.* Sebastopol, CA: O'Reilly Media.

Szymczak, J. Sadowski, A. (2019). Technologia blockchain jako stymulanta zachowania bezpieczeństwa żywności w łańcuchu dostaw [Blockchain technology as a stimulus for maintaining food safety in the supply chain]. *Zagadnienia Doradztwa Rolniczego, 2*(96), 49–63.

Treiblmaier, H. (2018). The impact of the blockchain on the supply chain: a theory-based research framework and a call for action, *Supply Chain Management, 23*(6), 545–559.

Chapter 13

Big Data Analysis for Management from Solow's Paradox Perspective in Polish Industry

Piotr Jałowiecki

Warsaw University of Life Sciences—SGGW

Contents

13.1 Introduction

Technological progress is most often understood as a process that leads to an increase in productivity because the same volume of production can be produced using smaller inputs of other factors of production or with the same inputs it is possible to increase production. Increases in capital and labor in the modified Solow–Swan model lead only to a time increase, which lasts until the economy reaches a new state of steady-state growth, while permanent growth is ensured only by technological changes (Solow, 1957). With this approach, technological progress in the product of the production function served as the "rest" that aggregates all factors affecting product growth except for capital and labor as an additional factor shaping production growth. It was called "the rest of Solow", but is better known as the Total Productivity Factor (TPF). It is defined as the product of the level of technological progress and the rate of technology growth. It should be emphasized that other ways to take into account technological progress within the production function were also sought, assuming that it can supply capital growth or increase of work.

In 1967, Denison distinguished three main components of TPF: (1) shifts of resources from agriculture to industry; (2) progress in knowledge and technical, organizational, and management skills; and (3) so-called "residual productivity". Also, Solow suggested that technological progress is included only in new investments and that it has an impact primarily on improving the quality of work. Based on empirical studies for the US economy in the first half of the 20th century, he estimated the size of the rest of Solow at around 87%. This meant that the explanation of economic growth to a large extent does not result from the accumulation of capital and labor. The modified Solow–Swan model shows that the development of information and communication technologies (ICT) should lead to increased productivity. First of all, investments and implementation of modern ICT should lead to an increase of technical equipment of work, and thus to increase its efficiency. Secondly, technological progress is transferred, as it were, automatically from the ICT industry to other industries thanks to lower prices of goods, which should lead to lower production costs. Thirdly, ICT is a general-purpose universal technology and, therefore, generates significant non-financial external effects also known as spillover effects.

However, in the '70s and '80s of the last century, the results of empirical research on the state of the economy in the United States showed a decline in productivity despite very significant and growing investments in modern technologies of information processing and transmission. The obtained results did not confirm the existence of a positive relationship between the implementation of modern ICT and the increase in productivity. Also, it turned out that the greatest drop in productivity occurred in the sectors of the economy in which investments in ICT were the largest, and the share in the employment of people serving them was the highest (Brynjolfsson, 1993). Therefore, already in 1987, Robert Solow formulated his famous paradox of productivity, noting that investments in ever more modern ICT solutions being a catalyst for changes in almost all areas of life, do not translate into an increase in productivity both on the micro- and macroeconomic scales.

Since the formulation of the productivity paradox by Solow, many attempts have been made to explain it. They can be divided into two main trends. As part of the first one, not rejecting neoclassical theories of growth, in particular, the modified Solow–Swan model, various factors are being sought that affect the lack of translating investments into ICT solutions into the financial results of enterprises. The second trend is connected with new theories and models of product growth, in which the possibility of eliminating imperfections found in the Solow–Swan model itself is sought. Thus, in the mid-1990s, four main groups of arguments explaining the existence of the productivity paradox were identified: (1) problems resulting from the lack of accuracy in the measurement of enterprises' outlays and results, (2) profit redistribution, (3) adjustment processes that the economy must undergo, and (4) lack or insufficient investment complementary to investment in modern ICT (Milgrom and Roberts, 1995; Jorgenson, 2001) (Brynjolfsson and Saunders, 2010; Cardona et al., 2013).

Research on the occurrence of the Solow productivity paradox in various countries in the 21st century led to the conclusion that it is much more visible in less developed countries, but also that the period of the economy's adaptation to ICT, followed by an increase in productivity is shorter in more developed countries. Also, in the United States and EU, in 1990–2008, three factors that have the strongest influence on these differences were distinguished: faster development of the service sector, faster technological progress, and larger sizes of ICT solutions providers. Only in recent years, the differences in the impact of the use of advanced ICT technologies on the increase in productivity between the US economy and the economies of the leading EU countries have started to decrease significantly (Jorgenson and Vu, 2005; Dedrick et al., 2013; Niebel, 2014).

The purpose of the research, the results of which were presented in the work, was to identify sources and the frequency of using Big Data in Polish enterprises, taking into account their division into employment size groups, PKD sections, and voivodeships. The impact of using Big Data for business management purposes and the generation of PKD in the examined groups of business entities was also examined. Which discusses issues related to the Solow productivity paradox and attempts to explain it so far, this chapter includes a chapter containing the most important information about Big Data, a chapter which briefly describes the objectives and scope of research, source data, and applied research methodology, as well as chapter with research results and the last chapter with conclusions resulting from research. Because data on the use of Big Data in Polish enterprises and economic characteristics of enterprise groups are also available in aggregate form from previous years, further research will be conducted to identify development trends of both the use of Big Data as well as to assess changes in the strength of the relationship between them and selected characteristics economic.

13.2 Big Data

Nowadays, unprecedented progress can be observed in the field of digital technologies, primarily ICT, both in the implementation of ever new solutions and systems in the field of information management, as well as their dynamic development consisting in their rapid dissemination and, consequently, their use in virtually every field of science, economy as well as social and private life.

The dynamics of the increase in computing power of computers are best described by Moore's Law formulated in 1965 and modified by the author 10 years later. According to it, the number of transistors placed in microprocessors doubles every 18 months, and now, after Moore corrected the law in 1975, every 24 months. However, as early as 1999, Moore corrected his law again, predicting that in the recent past the rate of doubling the number of transistors in chips would slow down to every 4–5 years (Sienkiewicz, 2005). Even later Moore's law was slightly reformulated, and instead of the number of transistors, the computing power of computers became an element of doubling. By analogy with the original version of Moore's law, similar rules apply to the amount of RAM, hard disk capacity, bandwidth in computer networks, and above all the ratio of computing power to the cost of obtaining it.

Regardless of how Moore's law is formulated, the inevitable extension of the doubling period of the number of transistors placed in integrated circuits should be expected because its course depends on the technological possibilities in the field of miniaturization of transistors. According to International Technology Roadmap for Semiconductors, in 2009, the average transistor size was 32 nm; in 2012, 22 nm; in 2015, 14 nm; in 2018, 10 nm; in 2019, 7 nm; and in 2020, it will be approx. 5 nm, while in 2022, about 3 nm. However, the further development of this miniaturization trend is under question due to technological limitations.

As a consequence, the focus on the development of ICT has moved to two other areas. The first of them, certainly very promising, are the modern technologies of the future: quantum computers, biocomputers, recording information on crystal media, etc., which does not change the fact that it must probably take a long time before they are brought into a form enabling their production, implementation, and widespread use. The second direction is already successfully implemented and is a derivative of two relatively well-known and widespread technologies: high-speed and ubiquitous Internet and multiprocessor systems. Their widespread use has led to the convergence sociosphere, infosphere, and technosphere, and consequently to the formation of the so-called cyberspace, which Castells (1990) originally referred to as the "Internet Galaxy". Within this cyberspace, different secondary technologies, for example, e-commerce, e-business, e-administration, social media, or just a Big Data are formed and rapidly disseminate.

Nowadays, the understanding of this term has been extended by two additional aspects: variability and complexity. Especially the latter feature is very characteristic for modern Big Data sets, and consequently for their management methods and their analysis. Nowadays, Big Data collections are created in a completely automatic way based on detailed source data from very many, very diverse sources.

There are quite a large number of Big Data classifications, but the most frequently used in practice are classifications based on their origin. The most general Big Data classification covers five categories: (1) public data, (2) private data, (3) data exhaust, (4) community data, and (5) self-quantification data. The source of public data is government and self-governing institutions and organizations. In turn, private data comes from business, non-profit organizations, and individuals. A specific category of Big Data is data exhaust, that is, for those who generate them have no meaning or is it negligible, they are collected almost automatically, and the gain value only in conjunction with other types of data. Community or social data is a category of unstructured data, most often text data from social media, and primarily concerns user preferences. Self-quantification is data collected automatically from various Internet and mobile applications regarding user behavior. They often arise as a result of monitoring, e.g., its location (Kennedy, 2008; George et al., 2014).

Big Data sets are used in many different areas, among others, to prepare management information, i.e., information that can be used directly in decision-making processes. Of course, depending on the specific area of human activity, decision-making processes will be very diverse, as a consequence, the form of management information will be varied, as well as the sources and form of Big Data used to prepare it. Different areas of business activity can be a good example of this. It should be noted that depending on the specific area of different profiles are the source of their origin. Enterprises operating in various areas of the economy and using Big Data sets for business analysis can be a good example. Each area of the economy has a different profile of sources from which Big Data is obtained (see Table 13.1). In this study, the division of primary sources of Big Data were categorized into three most popular main groups: I—sensors and smart AI (Artificial Intelligence) devices, e.g., using communication between devices (M2M machines), digital sensors, radio-frequency identification (RFID) labels, etc.; II—geolocation data obtained from mobile devices, e.g., from mobile devices using telecommunications networks, wireless connections, or GPS; and III—data generated by social media, e.g., social networking sites, blogs, and websites used to exchange multimedia information.

The other primary sources of Big Data were grouped in the last fourth category (IV). Of course, a large number of companies executing Big Data analysis used more than one category of its primary data (see Table 13.1). Another important aspect of using Big Data for business analysis is performing them using the company's resources or outsourcing them to specialized external entities. Also, in this respect, different solutions are preferred in different areas of the economy (see Table 13.1).

The use of Big Data for business analyses partly or in the vast majority automated way is a combination of modern ICT technologies and methods of managing, above all, customer relationship management (CRM) area. Thanks to the use of Big Data, it is possible to personalize the approach to the customer very effectively and virtually fully automated, as well as to adapt the services and products offered to his individual needs and expectations (Romika Yadav and Tarun Kumar, 2015; Anshari et al., 2019). Big Data most often in aggregate form are also used in macroeconomic analyses, enabling overall tracking of preferences, demand trends, and consequently modification of the product basket, effective product basket management, conducting effective marketing policy, as well as the use of business intelligence technology (defining key performance index, creating dashboards, etc.) (Chen et al., 2012; Elgendy and Elragal, 2014; Hu, 2018).

Table 13.1 Percentages of Enterprises Using Big Data for Business Analyses by Employment Size Groups and PKD 2007 Sections

Group	% Big Data	Category I (%)	Category II (%)	Category III (%)	Category IV (%)	More (%)	Own (%)	Outsource (%)
Small	8.9	10.0	50.4	22.8	16.8	71.4	44.8	35.3
Middle	17.4	22.6	39.4	19.3	18.7	69.0	52.1	26.2
Large	44.9	34.5	31.4	17.0	17.2	57.5	51.1	19.7
Section C	8.5	25.7	37.5	18.5	18.3	70.3	54.7	24.9
Section D	24.4	26.4	60.9	6.4	6.3	68.9	50.8	27.7
Section E	25.5	23.4	62.8	7.9	5.9	69.2	49.9	28.7
Section F	7.6	4.3	68.5	14.5	12.6	81.6	42.3	39.6
Section G	10.6	14.6	39.2	26.1	20.1	64.0	43.3	32.5
Section H	18.6	11.2	71.0	9.0	8.8	79.8	45.4	40.1
Section I	9.0	9.6	28.8	48.1	13.5	57.1	39.7	27.3
Section J	37.1	17.0	27.9	28.2	26.9	55.3	48.9	19.9
Section K	15.8	18.3	24.4	26.8	30.5	63.4	49.4	28.7
Section L	6.2	16.1	33.5	17.4	32.9	84.5	52.8	52.2
Section M	13.6	14.0	31.5	29.4	25.0	63.6	46.0	31.0
Section N	13.2	12.5	49.4	28.4	9.7	71.6	47.6	30.5
All	11.4	16.2	45.5	21.1	17.1	69.1	47.3	31.0

Source: Own preparation based on of GUS data.

13.3 Scope, Data Sources, and Methods

The purpose of the research, the results of which were presented in this chapter, was to examine the extent to which Solow's paradox concerns the use of Big Data as the basis for business analyses in various groups of Polish enterprises. To this end, the share of entities using Big Data in all entities in individual groups was compared, above all, with the average financial results achieved by enterprises belonging to these groups.

The research was based on mass statistics data made available by the Polish Central Statistical Polish Statistical Office (polish abbreviation GUS – Główny Urząd Statystyczny). In the studies, the latest available data for 2017 were used. Data are available in two repositories: "ICT in enterprises" and "industry inputs and results". Data on gross domestic product (GDP) were also obtained from the GUS mass statistics data. They are available in the repository "Statistical Yearbook of Voivodeships". The surveyed enterprises were grouped according to the three criteria. The first was an employment size group. According to the GUS nomenclature, it was three categories: small (from 10 to 49 employees), middle (from 50 to 249 employees), and large (250 and more employees). The smallest micro-enterprises were not included because the GUS does not collect or process data on them in this area. The second criterion of enterprise grouping was a branch due to the Polish Classification of Activities in the version from 2007 (PKD 2007). It was decided to research at the PKD 2007 section level. For obvious reasons, not all PKD 2007 sections were taken into account, but only those in which enterprises used mass data for business analyses. Consequently, the research covered 12 sections of PKD 2007: C—industrial processing; D—production and supply of electricity, gas, steam, hot water, and air for air conditioning systems; E—water supply; sewerage, waste management, and remediation activities; F—building industry; G—wholesale and retail trade; repair of motor vehicles, including motorcycles; H—transport and storage; I—activities related to accommodation and catering services; J—information and communication; K—financial and insurance activities; L—activities related to real estate market services; M—professional, scientific and technical activities; and N—administrative and support service activities.

Finally, the third last criterion for grouping the surveyed enterprises was voivodeship. In each of the groups of enterprises defined in this way, profiles of primary data sources used for Big Data acquisition proportions were prepared. At the same time, in each group, a proportion was determined between enterprises that implement Big Data on their own and those that use the services of external companies.

In a nutshell, Solow's productivity paradox lies in the lack of transfer of investments in modern ICT technologies, including in the analysis based on Big Data, on the financial result of the entity implementing such investments. Therefore, to assess the occurrence or not of this paradox in the Polish industrial sector, the analysis of the relationship between the share of enterprises using Big Data analysis and their average gross and net financial results, as well as for comparison purposes with the average amount of income tax paid by them was used. In the studies, both Pearson's linear correlation and Spearman's rank correlation coefficients were used. The reason was the desire to identify the possible linear nature of the relationships studied. Also, the second of the mentioned correlation coefficients is less sensitive to outliers. The value of Spearman's rank correlation coefficient was determined, and their statistical significance was checked by a test based on Student's t-distribution due to the small sample size with significance level $\alpha = 0.05$.

Unfortunately, it was not possible to check the strength of correlation on detailed data on individual enterprises, but only on aggregates of data for individual categories of enterprises (employment size groups, sections of PKD 2007, and voivodeships). For this reason, correlation coefficient values were determined for all three examined business divisions. Thanks to the way it was possible to identify which factor strongly differentiates the incidence of Solow's productivity paradox.

The groups of surveyed enterprises classified according to the PKD 2007 group and the voivodeship were additionally classified according to the division method based on the mean value $(\bar{\bar{x}}_i)$ and standard deviation (s_{x_i}). As a consequence, the groups of surveyed enterprises were divided into four categories due to sharing of enterprises using Big Data for business analysis: I—the lowest share $\left(\min(x_i) \leq x_i \leq \bar{x}_i - s_{x_i}\right)$; II—share below mean $(\bar{x}_i - s_{x_i} < x_i \leq \bar{x}_i)$; III—share above mean $(\bar{x}_i < x_i \leq \bar{x}_i + s_{x_i})$; IV—the highest share $(\bar{x}_i < x_i \leq \max(x_i))$. Categories II and III set the limits of a typical range of variation, which, according to the three sigma rule, over 67% of the value belongs to.

13.4 Results

Of the surveyed enterprises, only 11.4% declared using Big Data for business analysis. Inevitably, the question arises, is it a lot or little in Polish conditions? Undoubtedly, given the common nowadays ICT technologies, such as computers and mobile devices (96.2%), Internet (95.6%), e-invoices (83.3%), and e-government, understood as using the Internet in dealing with public administration (95.1%), this is quite low. Considering Internet technologies, this situation is not so clear. For example, compared to the percentage of enterprises owning a website (66.8%) or providing e-sales to clients (64.3%), the difference is still very large, about six times. Taking into account while making the company an e-purchases (33.6%), the use of social media (33.9%), and online advertising (26.0%), the frequency of their use is only a threefold compared to use Big Data for business analysis. However, in the case of online advertising, the use of tracking user activity (7.7%) or geolocation (7.0%), i.e., technologies also used to obtain Big Data, is lower. Comparison of the frequency of using Big Data in Polish enterprises with other rather new ICT technologies, such as electronic document management (22.9%), the use of open public data (16.4%), or the use of cloud computing (11.5%) the difference is already so big. It is thus seen that the prevalence of relatively young Polish ICT industry is at a similar level.

Considering all surveyed enterprises, almost half of them indicated category II (45.5%) as the main source of Big Data, i.e., geolocation data. 21.1% of enterprises indicate category 3 (social media) as the source of Big Data, 16.2% category I (sensors and smart devices), and 17.7% category IV (other sources). Over 2/3 of enterprises (69.1%) declare using more than one source of Big Data acquisition. Almost half of the enterprises (47.1%) declare using external services while acquiring Big Data, almost 1/3 (31.0%) declare acquiring them on their own, while the remaining ones do not indicate the way they do it.

Considering the size of employment as a criterion for the division of the surveyed enterprises, it is clear that as it increases, the percentage of enterprises using Big Data for business analyses also increases (see Table 13.1). Pearson's linear correlation coefficient between the percentage of enterprises using Big Data for business analysis and the average financial result, taking into account the division of enterprises into employment size groups, was very high ($r_p = 0.985$, $\alpha = 0.05$, $t_{\alpha/2} = 12.706$, $t = 18.108$, p-value $= 0.035$). Also for the average income tax payable by a single enterprise ($r_p = 0.984$, $\alpha = 0.05$, $t_{\alpha/2} = 12.706$, $t = 17.528$, p-value $= 0.036$) and for the average net financial result ($r_p = 0.985$, $\alpha = 0.05$, $t_{\alpha/2} = 12.706$, $t = 18.231$, p-value $= 0.035$) the values of the Pearson linear correlation coefficient were very high. All three correlation coefficients were statistically significant.

Therefore, in the case of the division of the surveyed enterprises into employment size groups, there was no Solow's productivity paradox concerning Big Data because the higher the share of enterprises using such data for business analysis, the better they achieved average financial results (see Tables 13.1 and 13.2). It should be emphasized that the results of previous studies on the occurrence of the Solow productivity paradox in the Polish food industry have just indicated the employment size group as the factor that differentiates this phenomenon most strongly (Jałowiecki, 2018).

On the other hand, assuming the sections of PKD 2007 as the division criterion in which the surveyed enterprises operated, the existence of weak non-linear relationships between the percentage share of enterprises using Big Data for business analyses and the average gross ($r_S = 0.294$, $\alpha = 0.05$, $t_{\alpha/2} = 2.228$, $t = 0.972$, p-value $= 0.354$) and net financial results ($r_S = 0.238$, $\alpha = 0.05$, $t_{\alpha/2} = 2.228$, $t = 1.709$, p-value $= 0.118$) and the average relationship with the average income tax ($r_S = 0.476$, $\alpha = 0.05$, $t_{\alpha/2} = 2.228$, $t = 0.774$, p-value $= 0.457$). The non-linearity of these relationships was confirmed by 2–3 times higher Spearman rank correlation coefficient values than Pearson's linear correlation coefficient values (see Tables 13.1 and 13.2).

Such results indicate the occurrence of the Solow productivity paradox, a good example of which can be section J, i.e., information and communication enterprises, among which the share of entities using Big Data for business analysis was

Table 13.2 Average Financial Results of the Surveyed Enterprises per One Entity (in Millions PLN), by Employment Size Groups and PKD 2007 Sections

Group	% Big Data	Brutto	Tax	Netto
Small	8.9	0.85	0.11	0.74
Middle	17.4	2.69	0.39	2.30
Large	44.9	30.42	5.11	25.31
Section C	8.5	5.02	0.73	4.29
Section D	24.4	44.87	5.34	39.53
Section E	25.5	1.51	0.30	1.21
Section F	7.6	1.55	0.29	1.27
Section G	10.6	2.47	0.42	2.04
Section H	18.6	2.28	0.46	1.83
Section I	9.0	1.34	0.19	1.15
Section J	37.1	4.14	0.67	3.47
Section K	15.8	103.06	7.96	85.95
Section L	6.2	2.20	0.26	1.94
Section M	13.6	2.98	0.31	2.67
Section N	13.2	1.32	0.25	1.07
All	11.4	3.48	0.55	2.93

Source: Own preparation based on GUS data.

by far the highest (37.1%) and the financial results quite average (see Table 13.2). It should also be emphasized that all three correlation coefficients were statistically insignificant, although due to the very small sample, the issue of statistical significance or insignificance should be treated very carefully because it is always determined by the size of the sample (Kośny and Peternek, 2011).

When analyzing the enterprises grouped by voivodeships in which they operate, strong and statistically significant relationships were found between the percentage share of enterprises using Big Data in business analyses and the average gross financial result ($r_p = 0.588$, $\alpha = 0.05$, $t_{\alpha/2} = 2.145$, $t = 2.298$, p-value = 0.037), net ($r_p = 0.565$, $\alpha = 0.05$, $t_{\alpha/2} = 2.145$, $t = 2.165$, p-value = 0.048), and the average value of income tax ($r_p = 0.646$, $\alpha = 0.05$, $t_{\alpha/2} = 2.145$, $t = 2.675$, p-value = 0.018).

Similarly, as in the case of division of surveyed enterprises by employment size group, also in the case of the division by voivodeships, the values of the Pearson linear correlation coefficient were higher than the analogous values of the Spearman rank correlation coefficient. This demonstrates the non-linear nature of the relationships found (see Tables 13.3 and 13.4).

As you can see, using different criteria for dividing the surveyed enterprises into groups, ambiguous results were obtained, which do not allow us to determine whether among Polish enterprises we are dealing with the paradox of Solow's productivity concerning the technology of using Big Data in business analyses.

Given the sections of PKD 2007 as a criterion for the division of enterprises, the typical area of variability in the share of enterprises using Big Data for business analysis was from 7.0% to 24.7%. Then, the PKD 2007 groups of the surveyed enterprises were divided into four categories according to the mean value and standard deviation.

Category 1 (the lowest share of enterprises using Big Data in business analyses) belonged only to section L, i.e., enterprises dealing with real estate services. Category 2 (share below the mean) included the largest number of seven sections of PKD 2007: C (industrial processing), F (building industry), G (wholesale and retail trade; repair of motor vehicles, including motorcycles), I (activities related to housing and catering services), K (financial and insurance activities), M (professional, scientific, and technical activities), and N (administration and supporting activities). Two categories of PKD 2007 belonged to category 3 (share above the mean): D (production and supply of electricity, gas, steam, hot water, and air for air conditioning systems) and H (transport and storage). Whereas, category 4 (the highest share) belonged to two sections of PKD 2007: E (water supply, sewerage, waste management, and remediation activities) and J (information and communication). The last of the mentioned sections of PKD 2007 includes enterprises among which the percentage of those that use Big Data for business analysis is by far the highest and amounts to 37.1%.

Considering voivodeship as the criterion for the division of enterprises, the typical range of variability for the share of entities using Big Data in business analyses was from 7.9% to 12.9%. Therefore, it can be seen that it was significantly narrower than in the case of the PKD 2007 section, which means that voivodeship is a feature significantly less differentiating the surveyed enterprises in terms of using Big Data.

Category 1 (the lowest share of enterprises using Big Data for business analyses) includes three voivodeships: Lubuskie, Świętokrzyskie, and Warmińsko-Mazurskie. Five voivodeships belonged to category 2 (share below average): Lubelskie, Opolskie, Podkarpackie, Pomorskie, and Wielkopolskie. Six voivodeships belonged to category 3 (share above average): Dolnośląskie, Łódzkie, Małopolskie, Podlaskie, Śląskie, and Zachodniopomorskie. Finally, only two voivodeships belonged to category 4 (the highest share): Kujawsko-Pomorskie and Mazowieckie. The last of these voivodeships were characterized by the highest percentage share of enterprises using Big Data (16.6%).

Table 13.3 Percentages of Enterprises Using Big Data for Business Analyses by Voivodeships

Group	% Big Data	Category I (%)	Category II (%)	Category III (%)	Category IV (%)	More (%)	Own (%)	Outsource (%)
Dolnośląskie	11.2	22.5	36.1	17.7	23.7	64.3	49.9	24.1
Kujawsko-Pomorskie	13.5	17.8	50.6	15.7	15.9	63.4	44.8	27.6
Lubelskie	9.3	15.6	53.0	16.4	15.0	72.4	50.3	27.3
Lubuskie	7.4	17.6	63.6	15.0	3.7	81.8	62.0	27.8
Łódzkie	11.3	13.0	47.9	26.7	12.4	78.5	56.2	29.1
Małopolskie	11.9	10.3	46.2	26.2	17.3	70.1	50.6	32.3
Mazowieckie	16.6	16.1	36.5	23.9	23.5	66.8	46.9	32.7
Opolskie	10.2	25.2	50.8	10.6	13.4	65.4	44.9	27.6
Podkarpackie	8.5	17.7	52.2	17.5	12.7	68.4	49.8	31.8
Podlaskie	12.4	15.3	49.5	18.6	16.6	74.6	48.9	33.6
Pomorskie	9.5	18.4	47.8	19.5	14.3	73.2	50.5	33.7
Śląskie	11.0	17.2	52.7	18.4	11.7	69.1	44.3	30.0
Świętokrz.	6.9	8.3	53.8	32.5	5.3	73.4	30.2	48.5
Warmińsko-Mazurskie	6.6	22.9	47.3	19.7	10.1	70.2	40.4	34.0
Wielkopol.	9.3	14.8	50.0	21.4	13.8	71.9	44.9	32.4
Zachodniop.	10.6	15.5	43.8	19.2	21.5	60.0	35.0	31.2
All	11.4	16.2	45.5	21.1	17.1	69.1	47.3	31.0

Source: Own preparation based on GUS data.

Table 13.4 Average Financial Results of the Surveyed Enterprises per One Entity (in Millions PLN) and Percentage of GDP, by Voivodeship

Voivodeship	% Big Data	Brutto	Tax	Netto	% GDP
Dolnośląskie	11.2	3.01	0.57	2.45	8.4
Kujawsko-Pomorskie	13.5	2.16	0.30	1.86	4.4
Lubelskie	9.3	2.58	0.44	2.14	3.8
Lubuskie	7.4	2.01	0.26	1.75	2.2
Łódzkie	11.3	2.74	0.45	2.29	6.0
Małopolskie	11.9	2.92	0.46	2.47	8.0
Mazowieckie	16.6	6.53	1.01	5.52	22.3
Opolskie	10.2	1.93	0.33	1.60	2.1
Podkarpackie	8.5	2.52	0.29	2.23	3.9
Podlaskie	12.4	1.78	0.23	1.55	2.2
Pomorskie	9.5	3.59	0.58	3.01	5.8
Śląskie	11.0	3.09	0.52	2.57	12.3
Świętokrzyskie	6.9	2.54	0.15	2.39	2.3
Warmińsko-Mazurskie	6.6	1.73	0.24	1.49	2.7
Wielkopolskie	9.3	3.44	0.57	2.88	9.9
Zachodniopomorskie	10.6	1.76	0.25	1.50	3.7
All	11.4	3.01	0.57	2.45	100.0

Source: Own preparation based on GUS data.

The relationship between the percentage share of enterprises using Big Data in business analyses in individual voivodeships and the percentage share of these voivodeships in generating GDP was also examined (see Table 13.4). It turned out that there is a statistically significant and quite strong linear relationship between both voivodeship characteristics ($r_P = 0.677$, $\alpha = 0.05$, $t_{\alpha/2} = 2.145$, $t = 3.439$, p-value $= 0.004$). The linear nature of this relationship is demonstrated by the Pearson's linear correlation coefficient more than one and a half times higher than the Spearman's rank correlation coefficient, which is statistically insignificant ($r_S = 0.434$, $\alpha = 0.05$, $t_{\alpha/2} = 2.145$, $t = 1.803$, p-value $= 0.671$). This seems to prove the existence of a translation of the implementation and use of modern ICT solutions and technologies, in this case, Big Data, into the generation of higher income and the wealth of society.

13.5 Conclusion

The most important conclusion resulting from the obtained research results is the ambiguity of Solow's productivity paradox concerning Big Data technology, taking into account the division of the surveyed enterprises into groups according to different criteria. While the industry division of enterprises by PKD 2007 section, the occurrence of the Solow productivity paradox is visible and confirmed by the lack of a linear and non-linear correlation relationship between the frequency of using Big Data for business analysis and financial results of enterprises, taking into account the size of employment as a division criterion of the examined entities, it is practically invisible, which, in turn, is demonstrated by very strong correlation relations between the mentioned characteristics. In turn, taking into account the division of the surveyed enterprises by voivodeships in which they operate, analogous correlation relationships are clear but not very strong. Nevertheless, it seems that in the case of such grouping of the surveyed enterprises, Solow's productivity paradox is not visible. To sum up, this undoubtedly means the need to research individual enterprises, e.g., in a manner analogous to the research of the food sector conducted in recent years by the author (Jałowiecki, 2018).

The second conclusion corresponds to the aforementioned research results indicating the occurrence of a greater intensity of the Solow productivity paradox in developing countries characterized by weaker economies and lower revenues. The obtained research results indicate that a similar situation occurs in the case of the division of enterprises into groups according to the size of employment, and even according to section PKD 2007. This was also confirmed by the correlation study between the share of enterprises using Big Data in individual voivodeships and the share of these voivodeships in GDP. In this case, a fairly strong linear relationship between both characteristics was found.

Finally, the third conclusion is that the factor that most differentiates the occurrence of the Solow productivity paradox in the Polish industry is the size of employment, then membership in the PKD 2007 section and the least differentiating is the voivodeship in which the entity operates.

The main limitation of the conducted research was the lack of access to data for individual enterprises. Unfortunately, the Central Statistical Office (CSO) provides only cross-sectional data in aggregate form, broken down by different characteristics of using Big Data, including employment volume, PKD section or voivodeship. The same limitation applies to the financial characteristics of the surveyed enterprises. Detailed research would have to be based on surveys carried out among a representative sample of enterprises and this is one of the planned future directions. Because data on the use of Big Data in Polish enterprises and economic characteristics of enterprise groups are also available in aggregate form from previous years, further research will be conducted to identify development trends of both the use of Big Data as well as to assess changes in the strength of the relationship between them and selected characteristics economic.

References

Anshari, M., Almunawar, M.N., Lim, S.A., Al-Mudimidh, A. (2019). Customer relationship management and big data enabled: Personalization & customization of services. *Applied Computing and Informatics, 15*(2), 94–101.

Brynjolfsson, E. (1993). The productivity paradox of information technology. *Communications of the ACM, 36*(12), 67–77.

Brynjolfsson, E., Saunders, A. (2010). *Wired for Innovation. How Technology is Reshaping the Economy.* Cambridge, MA: MIT Press.

Cardona, M., Kretschmer, T., Strobel, T. (2013). ICT and productivity: Conclusions from the empirical literature. *Information Economics and Policy, 25*(3), 109–125.

Chen, H., Chiang, R.H.L., Storey, V.C. (2012). Business intelligence and analytics: From big data to big impact. *MIS Quarterly, 36*(4), 1165–1188.

Dedrick, J., Kraemer, K.L., Shih, E. (2013). Information technology and productivity in developed and developing countries. *Journal of Management Information Systems, 30*(1), 97–122.

Denison, E.F. (1967). *Why Growth Rates Differ: Postwar Experience in Nine Western Countries.* Washington, DC: Brookings Institution.

Elgendy, N., Elragal, A. (2014). Big data analytics: A literature review paper. In: P. Perner (ed.), *Advances in Data Mining.* Applications and Theoretical Aspects. St. Petersburg, Russia: 14th Industrial Conference, 214–227.

George, G., Haas, M., Pentland, A. (2014). Big data and management. *The Academy of Management Journal, 57*(2), 321–326.

Hu, Y. (2018). Marketing and business analysis in the era of big data. *American Journal of Industrial and Business Management, 8,* 1747–1756.

Jałowiecki, P. (2018). *Paradoks produktywności Solowa w polskim przemyśle spożywczym.* [*The Solow's Productivity Paradox in Polish Agri-Food Industry*]. Warszawa: Wydawnictwo SGGW w Warszawie, (in Polish).

Jorgenson, D.W. (2001). Information technology and the U. S. economy. *American Economic Review, 91*(1), 1–32.

Jorgenson, D.W., Vu, K. (2005). Information technology and the world economy. *Scandinavian Journal of Economics, 107*(4), 631–650.

Kennedy, M.T. (2008). Getting counted: Markets, media, and reality. *American Sociological Review, 73,* 270–295.

Kośny, M., Peternek, P. (2011). Wielkość próby a istotność wnioskowania statystycznego. [The sample size and the significance of statistical inference]. *Didactics of Mathematics, 8*(12), 71–80 (in Polish).

Milgrom, P., Roberts, J. (1995). Complementarities and fit strategy, structure, and organizational change in Manufacturing. *Journal of Accounting and Economics, 19*(2 3), 179–208.

Moore, G. (1965). Cramming more components onto integrated circuits. *Electronics Magazine, 38*(8), 114–116.

Niebel, T. (2014). *ICT and Economic Growth – Comparing Developing.* Emerging and Developed Countries. Paper prepared for IARIW 33rd General Conference, Rotterdam, Netherlands.

Romika Yadav, M., Tarun Kumar, G. (2015). Usage of big data analytics for customer relationship management. *International Journal of Advanced Research in Computer Science, 6*(2), 1–3.

Sienkiewicz, P. (2005). Ontologia cyberprzestrzeni [Cyberspace ontology]. *Zeszyty Naukowe Warszawskiej Wyższej Szkoły Informatyki, 13*(9), 89–102.

Solow, R.M. (1957). Technical change and the aggregate production function. *Review of Economics and Statistics, 39,* 312–320.

Chapter 14

Big Data on Commuting: Application for Business

Nina Drejerska

Warsaw University of Life Sciences—SGGW

Contents

14.1 Introduction

The theory of location describing agricultural land use surrounding a city, whose precursor was Johann H. von Thünen, is reported as one of the longest histories among theories describing human activities in space. Although this model is often presented as a historical approach, there are also opinions that, along with Thünen's less-known works on the mechanisms of industrial agglomeration, it is a kind of basis for the new economic geography, which refers to these ideas using modern modeling tools (Fujita, 2012). Then the model of central place by Walter Christaller and August Losch develops an explanation of the concentration of economic activity in the center due to economies of scale and transport costs. This concentration of enterprises and employees attracts retail activities and personal services, resulting in a diverse supply of products, skills, and information. This diversification can be seen as a positive external effect of the center and is an incentive to locate new companies and employees there resulting in increasing nature of agglomeration processes. However, centrifugal forces also operate—competition for space and other negative externalities, such as pollution or congestion, push the participants of these processes out of the center (Terulin, 2000). Fujita, Krugman & Venables (1999) list issues determining agglomeration processes among which commuting is indicated as an element of centrifugal forces. In line with the above, the new economic geography started to become rather spatial economy undoubtedly well-grounded in theoretical and empirical consideration of economy.

Certainly, commuting plays a significant role in forming functional urban areas and is often a base for delineation of metropolitan regions (Drejerska & Chrzanowska, 2014). As a result, statistics on individuals' mobilities are applied for public management, for example, regarding planning, organization, and managing of public transport systems within functional regions. This approach is additionally facilitated by using data of public statistics or other administrational sources (i.e., tax registers). However, recent years have brought different sources of Big Data, including also those on commuting. It can be applied for more accurate diagnosis of flows and, for example, for more precise planning of public transport. The public and private sectors have now become more and more aware of the fact that the Big Data availability and new methods of its use may be utilized for gaining benefits (Maciejewski, 2017). From the perspective of private businesses, Big Data started to be perceived as a source of information enabling to offer products and services of greater value for consumers.

Given this background and taking into consideration that very few studies have been carried out in order to understand the role of Big Data on commuting for business, this chapter is intended to outline research results on successful examples of such applications. The aim of the study is to explore business purposes for which Big Data on commuting is reported to be particularly useful in the process of decision-making.

Fulfilling the purpose specified above is related to the hypothesis adopted in this chapter that Big Data on commuting can support design and offer of products and services of increased value for consumers. From the methodological perspective, the study also assumes interdisciplinary approach merging different scientific disciplines (economy, geography, IT, etc.), reflected by the following review of the literature, for better achievement of business outcomes.

This chapter is structured as follows. Sources of information as well as advantages of Big Data on commuting usage for business are reviewed. After methodology is provided, examples of Big Data on commuting application for private companies are presented and analyzed. Discussion of the findings enriches the study with a possible wider range use of Big Data on commuting for the business. In the end, this chapter concludes with final remarks by the author.

14.2 Review of the Literature

Big Data technologies provide large amounts of data (Filipczyk et al., 2018). The review of the state of the art on the Big Data sources in the area of commuting leads to the conclusion on the importance of GPS, Internet data, and mobile telephony data (Tranos & Nijkamp, 2015). Pajević & Shearmur (2017) refer to data sources on urban mobilities as, for example, social media (i.e., Twitter) or web-based service platforms (i.e., Über). Whereas the first group is widely mentioned as the Big Data source of continuing growth (Ahmadi et al., 2016) applied for different business purposes, the latter seems to be more specific for individuals' mobilities. Then, we can also refer to sources of data used particularly for public transport studies as GPS points and traces, smart card data, automated data (i.e., automated passenger counts—APC, automated fare control—AFC, automated vehicle location—AVL), or sensor data (Welch & Widita, 2019).

The important feature of the transport Big Data is that it is usually much finer at both spatial and temporal scale comparing with conventional data sources such as travel survey and census, which provides a new perspective to examine the relationship between locations and activities (Wan et al., 2018). For example, commuting patterns accessed through live Twitter feeds or Facebook postings could affect organizational responses, products and services, and their strategies (George et al., 2014). Appropriate use of these sources can lead to better informed decision-making particularly advantageous for firms' innovation processes. Altogether it can result in improvement of the adoption and market success of new products (Niebel et al., 2019). However, taking into account the character of described mobilities, it seems very promising for the process of design of new services for which commuting can be a characteristic distinguishing particular segments of consumers. It seems natural to think that commuting may affect spatial spending patterns as people can do their shopping near their workplace or along their commuting path. Additionally, households may become more familiar with shopping options next to the work-place locations of some of their members (Agarwal et al., 2017).

14.3 Methodology

At the beginning of the research process, a critical analysis of the state of the art has been implemented as the research method. Then the case study method was adopted as this research strategy allows understanding the dynamics present in single settings (Eisenhardt, 1989), which in the case of this study relates to results of service development stemming from application of Big Data on commuting. The case-study approach is perceived as important because it motivates the research (studying consumers mobility should, in theory, lead to better understanding of their needs connected with these phenomena, so better performance in product and service providing), inspires for looking better design of products and services as well as can be a valuable illustration in the context of making a conceptual contribution (Siggelkow, 2007).

The multi-case study method was applied as it enables broader exploration of the phenomena studied. Theoretical sampling was adopted as it allowed for presentation of success stories of companies using Big Data on commuting for development of their products and services. Data collection for the study includes gathering of archival as well as updated sources on selected case studies (reports, websites, media news, scientific publications, etc.). The detection time falls in August and September of 2019. Data analysis included examination of single cases at first and then comparisons across the cases.

14.4 Results

Internet-based multiple case studies referred for the purpose of this chapter are presented and shortly characterized in Table 14.1. Inspirations for some cases were found in the process of the review of the state of the art, even though the authors cited did not mention directly the business application of Big Data on commuting. Undoubtedly, it is not a full review of products and services as the research method applied does not aim at the complete and representative study. However, the table gathers examples of direct usage of Big Data on commuting for development of products and services.

Cases listed above include business to consumer orientations, for instance, carsharing or car producing companies but also business to business relations such as mobile app design or advertisers. It means that Big Data on commuting can be applied in both these configurations. What is more, Strava Metro represents undoubtedly also business to government (regional, urban, local) relations. In the literature, government to public actions based on usage of Big Data on commuting are widely commented but this lies beyond the scope of this study.

Taking into account the character of solutions described in the table, some of them are directly and closely connected with commuting itself. It seems naturally that knowledge on commuting patterns can help into a process of providing consumer with some support in organization of their daily routines (carsharing, car equipment, real estate business). Though, it should be noticed that there exist solutions which do not contribute actively to this sphere of life of consumers (i.e., pricing strategy of insurance companies) or commuter analytics and insights solution for advertising.

14.5 Discussion

Review of the selected cases proves that Big Data on commuting can support design of products and services which answer consumer needs better or help other

Table 14.1 Main Business Applications and Solutions Based on Big Data on Commuting

Business Applications	Solution Based on Big Data Use	Example/ Information Source
Carsharing companies	A tool helping to find carsharing partners who share both home and work postcode on a daily basis	LUCA—Telefónica's data unit, Spain/ company's blog
Car manufacturers and telematics companies	Adopting more smart innovations based on Big Data to provide access a vast wealth of information directly through vehicles about the driving world around	Raju (2015)/Digitalist Magazine by SAP
Real estate business	Search by drive time utility—GPS signals from nearly 100 million drivers to help new home buyers determine their typical drive times to and from work throughout various times of the day	Windermere Real Estate/company's blog, inspiration: Sonka (2014)
Mobile app design	Services for business based on Big Data on users logged in the app, i.e. more precise targeting of consumers, reaching new audience, etc.	Bike commuting: Strava Metro/ mobile app and website, inspiration: Sun (2017)
Advertisers, marketing companies	A recommendation engine that tailors information for advertisers so that advertising campaigns are able to strategically reach consumers across different transportation platforms	MOOVIN'— Southeast Asia's OOH commuter analytics and insights solution/ StarHub's website
Insurance sector	A Big Data application for mobile phones that tracks precisely clients' driving habits in order to more accurately assess a driver's risk. As a result, careful drivers pay less for their insurance while more risk-taking drivers pay more.	Example of Aviva/ Gray (2015), press report by Financial Times

Source: Own review.

companies to do it better. Simply writing, it can be useful for business to gain new consumers or maintain the present ones. These findings are in line with previous research according to which this source of information is useful for public management and for private business, even though little has been done so far to explore this topic from the perspective of private companies.

In this part of this chapter, it is necessary to point out that this study refers mainly to direct use of Big Data on commuting by the business sphere. There is a vast range of scientific research based on this topic and source of information which can have practical applications for doing business. Kreindler and Miyauchi (2019) prove that commuting flows constructed from cell phone transaction data predict the spatial distribution of wages and income in cities and conclude that generally Big Data also contain a wealth of information regarding individual choices. Athey et al. (2018) propose a structural model of individual travel choice based on mobile location data. Although it is not purely connected to commuting (for sure with individual mobilities), the authors try to answer basic questions about product design and product choice incorporating individual-level heterogeneity in preferences for product attributes and travel time into the model. Noteworthy example of incorporation of the commuting issue is the model describing restaurant consumption in NYC based on a dataset derived from mobile phone locations (Davis et al., 2017). The model assumes that when selecting a venue, individuals must take a decision on a way of traveling (public transit or a car) and whether to visit restaurant from home, work, or deviate from the commuting path. Results prove that consumers are less likely to visit venues more distant from their home and work locations as well as the commuting path. All mentioned studies can have practical implications in the process of decision making, for example, on localization of particular services. Certainly, this study can inspire companies offering any products or services addressed to commuters for using Big Data in the process of development of their offer. Moreover, it provides a strong point for business to business operations—Big Data on commuting can help to better address advertising activities.

However, unlike traditional statistical or administrational data, some sources of Big Data can be characterized by few documented mature and systematic procedures and methodologies to ensure its representativeness and reliability. Thus, Zhou et al. (2017) propose to use data from traditional sources to support verification and calibration. Possible sources are indicated, for example, by Bęręsewicz et al. (2018) and include the Urban Audit or analysis of commuters based on administrative registers or the Census of Population and Housing.

14.6 Conclusion

The findings presented above refer to the statement of the opportunity of using Big Data on commuting by the private sector. Case studies analyzed prove the importance of Big Data on commuting for the design of products and services targeted to commuters but not only. Providing more precise advertising and targeting of different communication activities seem to be promising areas of application of Big Data on commuting, even though this direction of use does not arise from needs of commuters. Then, the discussion referring to practical implications and wider background of business applications indicated by previous research allow to expect wider use of this data possible to implement in the future. It can be concluded that science to business transfer of analytical methods as well as interdisciplinary approach (merging, for example, business, economic, geography, and IT) can really facilitate the process of decision making regarding new products and services.

References

Agarwal, S., Jensen, J. B., & Monte, F. (2017). *The Geography of Consumption. NBER Working Papers 23616*, Cambridge, National Bureau of Economic Research, Inc.

Ahmadi, M., Dileepan, P., & Wheatley, K. K. (2016). A SWOT analysis of big data. *Journal of Education for Business, 91*(5), 289–294.

Athey, S., Blei, D., Donnelly, R., Ruiz, F., & Schmidt, T. (2018). Estimating heterogeneous consumer preferences for restaurants and travel time using mobile location data. *American Economic Association Papers and Proceedings, 108*, 64–67.

Beręsewicz, M., Lehtonen, R., Reis, F., Di Consiglio, L., & Karlberg, M. (2018). *An Overview of Methods for Treating Selectivity in Big Data Sources*. Publications Office of the European Union.

Davis, D. R., Dingel, J. I., Monras, J., & Morales, F. (2017). How Segregated is Urban Consumption? *NBER Working Papers 23822*, National Bureau of Economic Research, Inc.

Drejerska, N., & Chrzanowska, M. (2014). Commuting in the Warsaw suburban area from a spatial perspective - an example of empirical research. *Acta Universitatis Lodziensis. Folia Oeconomica, 6*(309), 87–96. Retrieved September 25, 2019, from https://www.czasopisma.uni.lodz.pl/foe/article/view/380.

Eisenhardt, K. M. (1989). Building theories from case study research. *Academy of Management Review, 14*(4), 532–550.

Filipczyk, B., Kania, K., Filipczyk, G., & Paliszkiewicz, J. (2019). Assessing data quality. Determining what data to trust and use. In B. H. Khan, J. R. Corbeil, M. E. Corbeil (Eds.), *Responsible Analytics and Data Mining in Education. Global Perspectives on Quality, Support, and Decision Making* (pp. 195–212). New York, Routledge Taylor & Francis Group,

Fujita, M., Krugman, P., & Venables, A. J. (1999). *The Spatial Economy. Cities, Regions, and International Trade*. Cambridge, MIT Press.

Fujita, M. (2012). Thünen and the new economic geography. *Regional Science and Urban Economics, 42*(6), 907–912.

George, G., Haas, M. R., & Pentland, A. (2014). Big data and management. *Academy of Management Journal, 57*(2), 321–326.

Gray, A. (2015, February 1). *Democratising Finance: Big Data Homes in on Insurance*. Financial Times. Retrieved September 27, 2019, from https://www.ft.com/content/0e19375c-a316-11e4-9c06-00144feab7de#slide0.

Kreindler, G. E., & Miyauchi, Y. (2019, February 21). *Measuring Commuting and Economic Activity Inside Cities with Cell Phone Records.* Retrieved September 27, 2019, from https://economics.mit.edu/files/14088.

Maciejewski, M. (2017). To do more, better, faster and more cheaply: using big data in public administration. *International Review of Administrative Sciences, 83*(1_suppl), 120–135.

Niebel, T., Rasel, F., & Viete, S. (2019). BIG data – BIG gains? Understanding the link between big data analytics and innovation. *Economics of Innovation and New Technology, 28*(3), 296–316.

Pajević, F., & Shearmur, R. G. (2017). Catch me if you can: Workplace mobility and big data. *Journal of Urban Technology, 24*(3), 99–115.

Raju, M. (2017). *Three Ways Smart Innovations Are Making Commutes Easier.* Digitalist Magazine by SAP, Retrieved September 25, 2019, from https://www.starhub.com/about-us/newsroom/2019/february/moove-media-taps-on-starhub-big-data-analytics.html.

Siggelkow, N. (2007). Persuasion with case studies. *Academy of Management Journal, 50*(1), 20–24.

Sonka, S. (2014). Big data and the Ag sector: More than lots of numbers. *International Food and Agribusiness Management Review, 17*(1), 1–20.

Sun, Y. (2017). Exploring potential of crowdsourced geographic information in studies of active travel and health: Strava data and cycling behaviour. In: *ISPRS Geospatial Week 2017,* Wuhan, China, 18–22 Sep 2017, 1357–1361.

Terulin, I. J., (2000). Theoretical and methodological framework. In I. J. Terulin, J.H. Post, (Eds.), *Employment Dynamics in Rural Europe* (pp. 17–38). Wallingford, CAB International.

Tranos, E., & Nijkamp, P. (2015). Mobile phone usage in complex urban systems: A space–time, aggregated human activity study. *Journal of Geographical Systems, 17,* 157–185.

Wan, L., Gao, S., Wu, C., Jin, Y., Mao, M., & Yang, L. (2017). Big data and urban system model - Substitutes or complements? A case study of modelling commuting patterns in Beijing. *Computers, Environment and Urban Systems, 68,* 64–77.

Welch, T. F., & Widita, A. (2019). Big data in public transportation: a review of sources and methods. *Transport Reviews, 39*(6), 795–818.

Zhou, J., Wang, M., & Long, Y. (2017). Big data for intrametropolitan human movement studies. *International Review for Spatial Planning and Sustainable Development, 5*(3), 100–115.

Chapter 15

How to Support Real-Time Quantitative Big Data by More Future-Orientated Qualitative Data for Understanding Everyday Innovative Businesses

Teppo Heimo, Sara Tilabi, and Josu Takala

University of Vaasa

Contents

15.1 Introduction

In today's world, we are generating data more than ever, i.e., data from social media, GPS signals, transaction records, digital images, scanners, sensors, etc. Innovation has played a significant role in producing all this data and it will play a dominant role in managing it. Big Data is an incentive factor for innovation. In more detail, when the size of the data becomes bigger than a certain limit, innovation process starts in order to store, organize, analyze, share, and use it in a meaningful way (Gobble, 2013). Not only Big Data is considered as a frontier for innovation, but also it promotes productivity and stimulates the competition considering its potential to create new business opportunities and revenues. It is estimated that Big Data would improve more than half of existing business and further billions of dollars of new business in the coming decades (Manyika, Chui, Brown, Bughin, Dobbs, Roxburgh, & Byers, 2011). For example, Alyass, Turcotte, and Meyre (2015) studied how Big Data supports personalized medicine, and Dasgupta (2013) investigated the role of Big Data in helping farmers to adopt climate changes or to identify issues with a racing car in Formula 1 competition. Besides, there are studies showing how Big Data could be monetized by implementing the right choice of business strategy (Najjar & Kettinger, 2013). To sum up, Big Data causes a revolution in the way we live, work, and think (Mayer-Schönberger & Cukier, 2013). We observed this transformation within the past few years through the successful implementation of technological innovations like Uber and WeChat (Yang, Huang, Li, Liu, & Hu, 2017).

As the application of Big Data is increasing, innovators are raising the questions associated with the challenges of Big Data to offer better quality services and products or to decrease the cost. As data is a great source of innovation, existing business is leveraging it to simplify the process, increasing efficiencies and to improve customer services. But innovation itself is a data-intensive activity, and organization, which considers it serious, produces a lot of data from ideas to lab test and documentation which could be analyzed and taken into account in further step of innovation process. In this regard, data generally and Big Data specifically have a major impact on driving and reshaping innovation process (Gobble, 2013). The prominent tool for the use of Big Data in companies is the Balanced Scorecard (BSC) (Vanani & Kheiri, 2018).

This research focuses on decision-making process regarding innovation and ultimately could facilitate innovation strategy. The results of this research show how the analytical model can quantitatively evaluate the state of companies' innovation strategy by using data derived from the company. Regarding the importance of data and its role in stimulating and reshaping innovation process, the results of this research work could have a significant practical implementation toward innovation strategy. The rest of this chapter is organized as follows: first theoretical background and research gap are presented. Then, the method section comes, and afterward empirical part is presented. And the final part is discussion and conclusion.

15.2 Theoretical Background

15.2.1 Innovation

Although the definition of innovation varies slightly in different existing scientific literature, there is agreement about its aim: creating tangible value by implementing sustainable solution to fulfill customer needs (Dziallas & Blind, 2019; Racherla, Huang, & Liu, 2016). The decision about innovation strategy is among the most fundamental strategic decision for every firm because of its inevitable role in helping the company to enter new markets, increase its share in the existing market, and sustain its competitive advantage (Gunday, Ulusoy, Kilic, & Alpkan, 2011). This emphasis on innovation is due to intensifying the competition in both the global and domestic markets generated by rapid changes in technology (Bower & Christensen, 1995). Market studies show that a company that innovates more is more capable to sustain its competitive position in global market (Cegarra-Navarro, Reverte, Gómez-Melero, & Wensley, 2016). Therefore, innovation constitutes a inseparable part of firm business strategies. There are different reasons behind that, for example, the need to offer new products or improved ones, the need to improve efficiencies and productivity, and the need to perform better in some critical market (Karlsson & Tavassoli, 2016). Innovation process could be classified into three different segments: front-end innovation (FEI), i.e., first and most important phase of innovation before the development and the commercialization process takes place, new product development (NPD) where the actual development of the innovation happens, and commercialization stage (Cegarra-Navarro et al., 2016; Mohan, Voss, & Jiménez, 2017).

Innovation strategy could be categorized into two main classes: open and closed innovation processes. Closed innovation is related to those companies that are mostly internally focused (Chesbrough, 2003a). In other words, in closed innovation model, company uses its own internal process in research and development (R&D) process (Chesbrough, 2003b). On the other hand, in open innovation (OI) model, the inflows and outflows of traditional closed innovation process change. This results in two different innovation models: inside-out and outside-in innovation models or inbound and outbound models, respectively (Bogers, Chesbrough, & Moedas, 2018). In outside-in OI strategy, company chooses to integrate external knowledge into its internal innovation process by different means like supplier integration or customer involvement (Ahn, Ju, Moon, Minshall, Probert, Sohn, & Mortara, 2016). Implementing inside-out innovation model helps the company to compensate its lack in internal resources and capabilities. On the other hand, in the inside-out model, company implements process to allow other companies to use its ideas and innovations in their business strategy and core operations (Gassmann & Enkel, 2004). There is another OI model which is coupled OI strategy in which the process of innovation from exploration, creation, and commercialization is done in cooperation with one or several external collaborators. In fact, this model is the integration of outside-in and inside-out models (Cheng & Huizingh, 2014).

15.3 Research Gap

Innovation strategy could be considered based on company's resources and capabilities. Since resources of the firm are valuable, rare, inimitable, and substitutable (VRIN), they are the target of in-sourcing and out-licensing in corporate-level strategic issues, e.g., mergers and acquisitions (M&A) and joint ventures. This provides an opportunity for firms to apply external knowledge which is embedded in their overall strategy (Brem, Nylund, & Hitchen, 2017). Studies show that technologically motivated M&As encourages innovation in general. In detail, innovation efficiency increases where the technologies are complementary between the merged entities while it decreases in case of substitution of technologies (Colombo & Garrone, 2006). This shows that OI strategy, i.e., using external source of knowledge for innovation is in line with M&As and supports innovation process ultimately (Brem et al., 2017). Previous studies investigate the OI impact from various perspectives, i.e., in terms of new units of analysis, small and medium enterprises (SMEs), non-profit organizations (NGOs), and different companies in low- and high-tech industry sector (Bogers et al., 2018). However, there is a need for studies that investigate the subject quantitatively. Therefore, this study is an attempt toward quantitative modeling of innovation process considering sustainable competitive advantages and tries to answer the following research questions:

1. How can Big Data help companies to maintain their competitive advantage in today's turbulence business environment?
2. What are the strengths that Big Data brings to the discourse on innovation analytics?
3. Can the state of innovation be quantitatively analyzed using data extracted from the company?

15.4 Method

15.4.1 Analytical Hierarchy Process

"The Analytic Hierarchy Process (AHP) method is a multi-attribute decision instrument that allows considering quantitative, qualitative measures and making tradeoffs" (Wind & Saaty, 1980; Pecchia, Bath, Pendleton, & Bracale, 2011).

This method is based on pairwise comparison and is conducted in two stages: first respondents are given two different criteria regarding the object and they should choose which of them is more important. In the second step, the respondents should weight the chosen criterion from 1 to 9. If the respondents choose one, it means both criteria are equal. The questionnaire for this study consisted of six pairwise questions of the four different main attributes. The main attributes are shown in Figure 15.1.

When calculating the AHP, inconsistency ratio (ICR) should be taken into consideration. ICR shows how logically respondents answered the questionnaire. As an example, if respondents answered A > B and B > C, then this statement should be A > C. If the respondents answered C > A, then its answer is not inconsistent. The ICR < 0.3 is acceptable in most of the studies, but ICR < 0.1 is preferred.

15.4.2 Innovation Strategy Index

Derived from manufacture strategy index (MSI), we define innovation strategy index (ISI). MSI is calculated by assigning the attribute in AHP questionnaire as a component of RAL model, i.e., quality, time, cost, and flexibility and transfers the results to Miles and Snow business strategy type (Daft, Murphy, & Willmott, 2010), i.e., prospector, analyzer, defender, and reactor. RAL is the abbreviation of Responsiveness, Agility, and Leanness and connects quality, time, cost, and flexibility as the main factors, which connects business performance to Miles and Snow typology. Once the share of quality, cost, flexibility, and time is calculated, the next step is to normalize the values. After normalization, a specific formula is used to calculate MSI indices (Ranta & Takala, 2007). We follow the same steps to calculate ISI (Figure 15.2).

	9	8	7	6	5	4	3	2	1	2	3	4	5	6	7	8	9	
Knowledge																		Technology
Knowledge																		Development
Knowledge																		Co-operation
Technology																		Development
Technology																		Co-operation
Development																		Co-operation

Figure 15.1 Pairwise comparison of the main criteria. (Own research based on Heimo, 2019.)

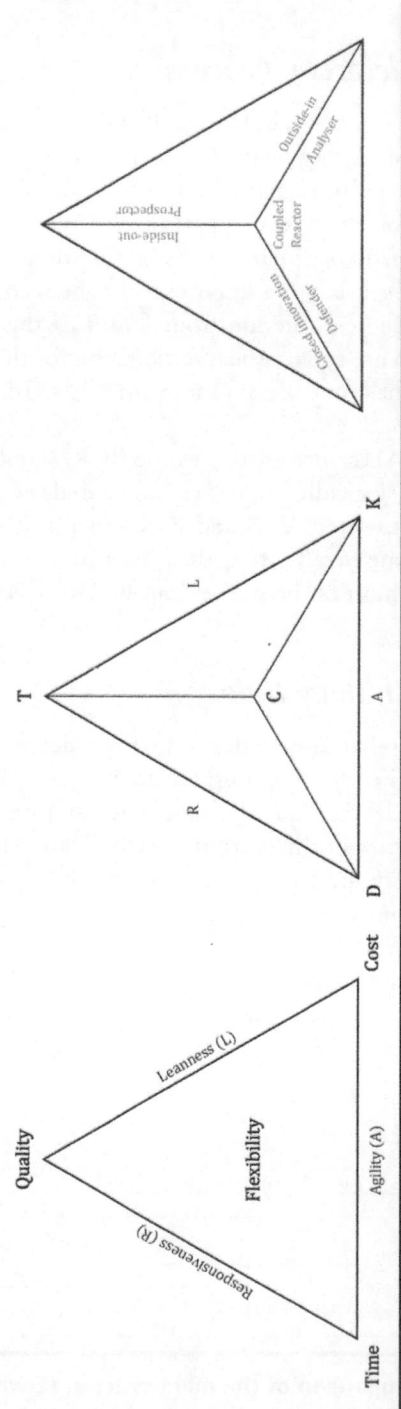

Figure 15.2 The demonstration RAL model, MSI, and ISI triangles. (Own research based on Ranta & Takala, 2007; Heimo, 2019.)

In order to calculate ISI, we use the information obtained from AHP questionnaire comparing technology (T), knowledge (K), development (D), and cooperation (C) factor. The ISI could be presented in the following equation:

$$ISI = f_{ISI}(T, K, D, C)$$

The next step is to normalize the component using the following formulas:

$$T' = \frac{T}{T + K + D}$$

$$K' = \frac{K}{T + K + D}$$

$$D' = \frac{D}{T + K + D}$$

$$C' = \frac{C}{T + K + D + C}$$

Having normalized the component ISI are calculated as follow:

$$InO = \emptyset - 1 - \left(1 - T\%^{\frac{1}{3}}\right)(1 - 0.9 \times D\%)(1 - 0.9 \times K\%) \times C\%^{1/3}$$

$$OuI = \gamma - 1 - 1(1 - C\%)$$

$$\times \left[ABS[(0.95 \times T\% - 0.285) \times (0.95 \times D\% - 0.285) \times (0.95 \times K\% - 0.285)]\right]^3$$

$$CI = \emptyset - 1 - \left(1 - K\%^{\frac{1}{3}}\right)(1 - 0.9 \times D\%)(1 - 0.9 \times T\%)C\%^{1/3}$$

$$CO = \frac{1}{2}(\text{Inside} - \text{out} + \text{close innovation})$$

In the equations above the InO stands for inside-out, OuI for outside-in, CI for closed innovation strategy, and CO for coupled strategy in innovation strategy.

15.4.3 Weak Market Test

Here, the weak market test (WMT) is used to validate the results of the study since it is the first attempt to quantitatively model the innovation strategy of the case companies with this model. Conducting WMT means to show the results of the study to a responsible person in the company and ask his/her opinion about the constructed model and obtained results.

15.5 Empirical Research

This research was done using AHP method to gather data, which was at later stage converted to information by ISI method. The research attributes for the AHP method was determined based on the four most important main criteria in terms of closed innovation and OI. The initial research of OI was used as a theoretical framework for this study. Furthermore, the method for ISI follows the method developed by Takala, Shylina, Forss, and Malmi (2013) for operations strategy environment, which has been validated and verified to work in several studies (Liu & Takala, 2009). In this study, the WMT was performed in a form of interviews with the case companies and used to validate the results obtained with the methods and models described earlier.

15.6 Sample and Analysis

The research consisted of two case companies operating in biotechnology and *in vitro* diagnostics (IVD) industries. The companies were SMEs and large multinational enterprise (LMNE), which has a subsidiary doing sales and marketing, R&D, and production operations in Finland. The answers were collected from individuals operating in the top management of these companies.

15.6.1 Case Company 1

Based on the ISI model, the past timeframe innovation strategy type of the case company 1 (CC1) were closed innovation and outside-in OI strategy type in the future timeframe as the individual values for different innovation types were highest in these strategy types and significantly above the average (AVG) values of other innovation strategies (Table 15.1). The order of the innovation strategy types for the past timeframe was closed innovation > coupled > inside-out > outside-in, and outside-in > inside-out > coupled > closed innovation for the future timeframe, respectively.

The standard deviation (SD) of the innovation strategy types was above 0.015, which were the predetermined threshold used in this study, and implies that there is sufficient variation between different innovation strategy types in the past timeframe. The coefficient of variation (CV-%) of 5.50% further supports this fact. In the future timeframe, the SD of the innovation strategy types was also significantly above 0.015, which also supports that there was sufficient variation between the innovation strategy types in the future timeframe as well. The CV-% in the case of

Table 15.1 Innovation Strategy Type Results of the Case Companies 1 and 2

	Case Company 1		Case Company 2	
	Past	*Future*	*Past*	*Future*
Inside-out	0.9293	0.9301	0.9411	0.9592
Outside-in	0.8473	0.9564	0.9010	0.8923
Closed innovation	0.9612	0.8955	0.9159	0.9324
Coupled	0.9453	0.9128	0.9285	0.9458
AVG	0.9208	0.9237	0.9216	0.9324
SD	0.0507	0.0260	0.0172	0.0289
CV (%)	5.50	2.81	1.86	3.10
Area	1.0804	1.1167	1.0978	1.1182
ICR	0.031	0.004	0.156	0.111

Source: Own research.

the future timeframe was 2.81%, which is lower compared to the past timeframe but still elevated to point out that there is one innovation strategy type that protrudes from the other innovation strategy types.

The ISI model results correlated with the priority weight results in both timeframes in the case of CC1. In the past timeframe, the highest values of the ISI and the priority weight models were the closed innovation strategy, and in the future timeframe, the highest values were in the outside-in OI strategy (Figure 15.3). The order of the innovation strategy models was the same in the ISI and priority weight models at both the past and the future timeframe. The total innovation potential based on the triangle area in the past timeframe was 1.0804 and 1.1167 in the future timeframe, respectively. From the ΔA, it is possible to determine that the total innovation potential is estimated to grow 3.35% from the past innovation experience to the future innovation expectation. In the following figures, the I represents inside-out OI strategy, the O represents outside-in OI strategy, and the C_i represents the closed innovation strategy.

According to the WMT, the empirical experience of the company's innovation strategy for the past timeframe has been closed innovation strategy supported by the fact that the innovation resources within the company have been largely assigned to its own R&D. Accordingly, the expectations for the future timeframe innovation strategy type of the company are outside-in OI strategy because of their ambition to seek in-organic growth from external technologies and innovations (Figure 15.4a). The company also incorporates inside-out innovation type in the

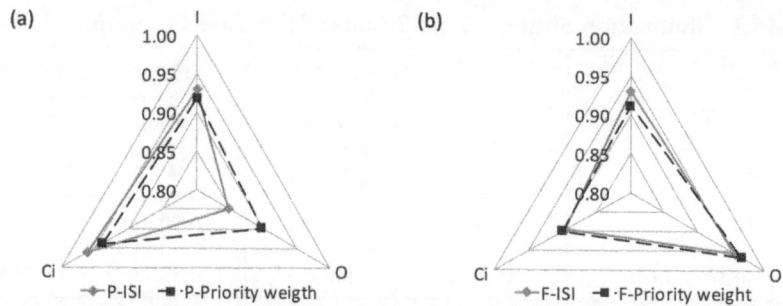

Figure 15.3 Innovation strategy index and priority weight comparison in CC1. RAL model (a) in the past timeframe and (b) in the future timeframe. (Own research.)

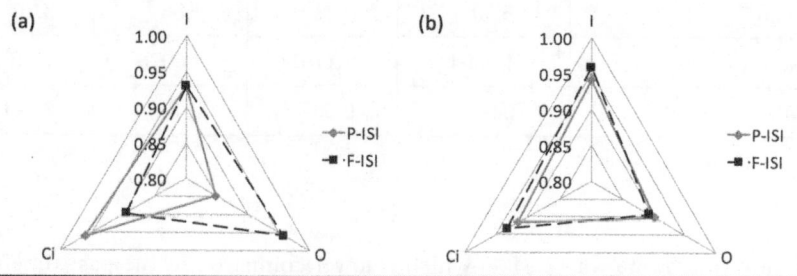

Figure 15.4 Innovation strategy index models. Past and the future timeframe innovation strategies in RAL model of (a) CC1 and (b) CC2. (Own research.)

past and the future timeframe as well. However, this innovation strategy type is not considered as important as the closed innovation strategy in the past timeframe nor the outside-in OI strategy in the future timeframe. Based on the WMT, the experience of the past and the expectations of the future are well in line with the past and the future timeframe ISI model results.

15.6.2 Case Company 2

The innovation strategy type based on the ISI model in the past timeframe was inside-out OI strategy determined by the individual values of the different strategy types. The ISI value for inside-out OI strategy was moderately above the AVG value of other innovation strategy types. Based on the values determined for the future timeframe, the innovation strategy type was inside-out OI strategy, respectively. The values for this strategy type were the highest and sufficiently above the AVG value of the other innovation strategy type values as well (Table 15.1). The order of the different innovation strategy types based on their individual values in the case of CC2 was entirely different compared to the CC1. In the CC2, the order of the innovation strategy types in the past timeframe was inside-out > coupled > closed innovation > outside-in, and for the future timeframe inside-out > coupled > closed innovation > outside-in, respectively.

The value for coupled OI strategy type appeared to be relatively high as well in the past timeframe scenario. The SD of all the innovation strategy value of 0.0172, which is marginally above the predetermined threshold used in this study, indicates that there is some variation between the innovation strategy types in the past timeframe. However, the CV-% of 1.86% supports the coupled OI strategy as it implies that the dispersion around the innovation strategy values is low. Correspondingly, in the future timeframe, the SD for the innovation strategy types was 0.0289, which is higher compared to the past timeframe scenario and significantly above the predetermined threshold of 0.015. This supports the higher variation between the innovation strategy types in comparison with the other OI strategy types obtained from the past timeframe. Furthermore, the CV-% in the future timeframe was 3.10%, which was also higher in comparison with the past timeframe scenario and, therefore, supports the inside-out OI strategy type for the future timeframe even further.

In the past timeframe, the ISI model results correlated moderately with priority weight values but did not correlate in the future timeframe (Figure 15.5). In the past timeframe, the highest value in the innovation strategy was in the inside-out OI strategy in both the ISI and the priority weight model. Correspondingly, in the future timeframe, the highest value of the innovation strategy types was in the inside-out OI strategy in the ISI model and outside-in OI strategy in the priority weight model respectively. According to the triangle area, the total innovation potential was 1.0978 in the past timeframe and 1.1182 in the future timeframe, respectively. As a result, the innovation potential is expected to grow 1.19% from the past innovation experience to the future innovation expectations.

Based on the WMT, the empirical experience of the company's innovation strategy has been controversial. Majority of the answers obtained through interviews demonstrate the coupled innovation strategy in both the past and the future timeframe scenarios (Figure 15.4b). Nonetheless, both closed innovation and inside-out

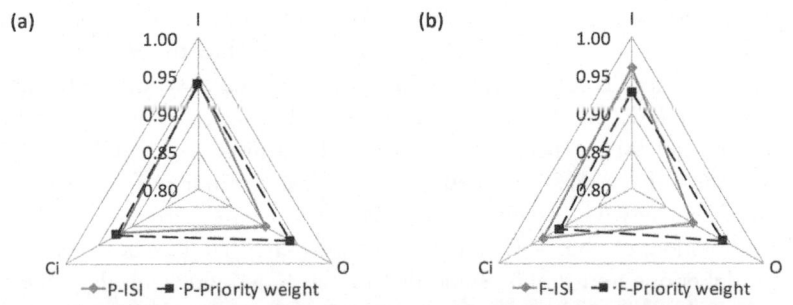

Figure 15.5   Innovation strategy index and priority weight comparison in CC2. RAL model (a) in the past timeframe and (b) in the future timeframe. (Own research.)

OI strategies were mentioned as well. The logical explanation for the coupled OI strategy is that the three inside-out, outside-in, and coupled OI strategies are all in place at the CC2. According to the company, its strategy includes acquiring other companies and external technologies. To conduct this, they have dedicated business development department and established channels to seek potential targets. The company also uses crowdsourcing to support their idea gathering process along with strategic co-operations and alliances with SMEs. In the past, they have also sold part of their operations which they see that do not fit into their future vision of the business. On the other hand, the company has a separate model of funding for the ideas that do not currently fit under any existing business development projects.

Because the CC2 operates on a relatively wide area of innovation environment, it is harder to determine the effective innovation strategy for the company using the ISI model. Anyway, according to the WMT results obtained by interviewing the person in top management of the Finnish subsidiary, the ISI model and the pattern of both the past and the future RAL model figures cannot be ignored either (Figure 15.4b). Based on this, it can be determined that the past experience and the future expectations of the company are in line with the innovation strategy derived from the past and the future timeframe ISI models.

15.7 Discussion

In this chapter, we demonstrated that the ISI model derived from MSI can be used for assessment of companies' innovation strategy, as both timeframe ISI models correlated in both case companies with the WMT obtained by interviewing the top management. However, the ICR has a significant impact on the reliability of the results. Although in this research the predetermined baseline of the ICR was set to 0.30, it was observed with the MSI model that the results were more credible when the ICR was below 0.1. This can be especially confirmed by the case of CC2, where the ICR was 0.156 in the past timeframe and 0.111 in the future timeframe, respectively. Based on the results, the outside-in and coupled OI strategy plays an important role in the case of companies' future scenarios, which has also been recognized in other studies concerning OI (Lichtenthaler, Hoegl & Muethel, 2011). According to Lichtenthaler et al. (2011), the inside-out OI strategy is very often impeded by "not-sold-here" syndrome by the companies, and therefore, the outside-in and coupled OI is favored. Although in knowledge-intensive industries, there is a demand for both in-licensing and out-licensing business models, the inside-out OI strategy still plays a minor role compared to the outside-in OI strategy (Gassmann & Enkel, 2004).

The limitation of the AHP method is, however, that has been experienced to be too laborious and cumbersome due to the ICR, which needs to be taken into account. In order to harness it in companies, it needs to be connected to the enterprise resource planning (ERP) systems or financial reporting system, e.g., income statement or balance sheet. This integration would deploy the Big Data of the company and provide the raw information to be used in the analytics of the company's innovation status. Only then the information generated with this model could also be used as part of BSCs in a companies' innovation management (Campos, Sharma, Jantunen, Baglee & Fumagalli, 2017). However, this integration needs to be implemented individually into separate companies, as the cost centers in the income statement vary significantly between different industries and business entities.

15.8 Conclusion

According to the results, the ISI model correlated with the past and future innovation strategy status and projections of the case companies (RQ3). Therefore, the proposed model will help companies to maintain their competitive advantage in global turbulent business environment (RQ1). However, the analysis of coupled OI strategy is problematic due to its nature, which includes both types of outside-in and inside-out OI strategies. Therefore, the determination of coupled OI strategy includes other factors as well in addition to the ISI values derived from the AHP questionnaire, such as the shape of the triangle which is influenced by the AVG values of all the innovation strategy values, SD, and CV-%. However, lower ICR increases the reliability of the ISI values significantly in the case of coupled OI strategy as well. The ICR values were below 0.30 in all cases of the case companies. This concludes that the answers derived from this study are reliable and support that the results can be used in the decision-making process (Takala et al., 2013).

The ΔA of the past experience to the future expectation gives valid information about the development of the total innovation potential of the company. However, the deeper function of this parameter was left out of scope of this study.

Although the AHP part of the method was experienced laborious to use when considering ICR, the value of the model in terms of managerial implications comes from the quantitative analysis of the current and future innovation strategy of the companies (RQ2). Despite this, in the future research, the proposed model should be validated and verified with other industries as well and not only with knowledge-intensive biotechnology and IVD industries. Additionally, more thorough connection to BSC should be investigated either through integration of the financial statements or ERP system of the company.

References

Ahn, J. M., Ju, Y., Moon, T. H., Minshall, T., Probert, D., Sohn, S. Y., & Mortara, L. (2016). Beyond absorptive capacity in open innovation process: The relationships between openness, capacities and firm performance. *Technology Analysis & Strategic Management, 28*(9), 1009–1028.

Alyass, A., Turcotte, M., & Meyre, D. (2015). From big data analysis to personalized medicine for all: Challenges and opportunities. *BMC Medical Genomics*, 8(33). doi:10.1186/s12920-015-0108-y.

Bogers, M., Chesbrough, H., & Moedas, C. (2018). Open innovation: Research, practices, and policies. *California Management Review, 60*(2), 5–16.

Bower, J., & Christensen, C. (1995). Disruptive technologies: Catching the wave. *Long Range Planning, 28*(2), 155.

Brem, A., Nylund, P. A., & Hitchen, E. L. (2017). Open innovation and intellectual property rights: How do SMEs benefit from patents, industrial designs, trademarks and copyrights? *Management Decision, 55*(6), 1285–1306.

Campos, J., Sharma, P., Jantunen, E., Baglee, D. & Fumagalli, L. (2017). Business performance measurements in asset management with the support of big data technologies. *Management Systems in Production Engineering, 25*(1), 143–149.

Cegarra-Navarro, J. G., Reverte, C., Gómez-Melero, E., & Wensley, A. K. P. (2016). Linking social and economic responsibilities with financial performance: The role of innovation. *European Management Journal, 34*(5), 530–539.

Cheng, C. C. J., & Huizingh, E. K. R. E. (2014). When is open innovation beneficial? The role of strategic orientation. *Journal of Product Innovation Management*, 31, 1235–1253. doi:10.1111/jpim.12148.

Chesbrough, H. (2003a). *Open Innovation – The New Imperative for Creating and Profiting from Technology* (pp. 30–53). Boston, MA: Harward Business School Press.

Chesbrough, H. W. (2003b). The era of open innovation. *MIT Sloan Management Review, 44*(3), 35–41.

Colombo, M. G., & Garrone, P. (2006). The impact of M&A on innovation: Empirical results. In: B. Cassiman & M. Colombo (Eds.), *Mergers and Acquisitions: The Innovation Impact* (1st ed., pp. 104–133). Cheltenham: Edward Elgar Publishing.

Daft, R. L., Murphy, J., & Willmott, H. (2010). Organization theory and design: Cengage learning. In: *Organization Theory and Design*, R. L. Daft. (Ed.) 10th Edition. Mason, OH: Cengage Learning.

Dasgupta. (2013). *Big Data: The Future is in Analytics*. https://www.geospatialworld.net/article/big-data-the-future-is-in-analytics/. (Accessed September 18 2019).

Dziallas, M., & Blind, K. (2019). Innovation indicators throughout the innovation process: An extensive literature analysis. *Technovation*, 80–81, 3–29. doi: 10.1016/j.technovation.2018.05.005.

Gassman, O. & Enkel, E. (2004). *Towards a Theory of Open Innovation: Three Core Process Archetypes*. R&D Management Conference. Lisbon: RADMA.

Gobble, M. M. (2013). Big data: The next big thing in innovation. *Research Technology Management, 56*(1), 64–66. doi:10.5437/08956308X5601005.

Gunday, G., Ulusoy, G., Kilic, K., & Alpkan, L. (2011). Effects of innovation types on firm performance. *International Journal of Production Economics, 133*(2), 662–676. doi: 10.1016/j.ijpe.2011.05.014.

Heimo, T. (2019). *Open Innovation in High-Technology Companies: Case Study of Biotechnology and Pharmaceutical Companies*. Vaasa: University of Vaasa.

Karlsson, C., & Tavassoli, S. (2016). Innovation strategies of firms: What strategies and why? *Journal of Technology Transfer, 41*(6), 1483–1506. doi:10.1007/s10961-015-9453-4.

Lichtenthaler, U., Hoegl, M. & Muethel, M. (2011). Is your company ready for open innovation? *MIT Sloan Management Review*, 53(1), 45–48.

Liu, Y., & Takala, J. (2009). Modelling and evaluation of operational competitiveness of manufacturing enterprises. *Kvalita Inovácia Prospeira*, 13(2), 1–19.

Manyika, J., Chui, M., Brown, B., Bughin, J., Dobbs, R., Roxburgh, C., & Byers, A. H. (2011). *Big Data: The Next Frontier for Innovation, Competition, and Productivity*. New York: McKinsey Global Institute. https://www.mckinsey.com/~/media/McKinsey/Business%20Functions/McKinsey%20Digital/Our%20Insights/Big%20data%20The%20next%20frontier%20for%20innovation/MGI_big_data_full_report.ashx/ (Accessed September 12, 2019).

Mayer-Schönberger, V., & Cukier, K. (2013). *Big Data: A Revolution That Will Transform How We Live, Work, and Think*. Boston, MA: Houghton Mifflin Harcourt.

Mohan, M., Voss, K. E., & Jiménez, F. R. (2017). Managerial disposition and front-end innovation success. *Journal of Business Research*, 70, 193–201. doi:10.1016/j.jbusres.2016.08.019.

Najjar, M. S., & Kettinger, W. J. (2013). Data monetization: Lessons from a retailer's journey. *MIS Quarterly Executive*, 12(4), 213–225.

Pecchia, L., Bath, P. A., Pendleton, N., & Bracale, M. (2011). Analytic hierarchy process (AHP) for examining healthcare professionals' assessments of risk factors: The relative importance of risk factors for falls in community-dwelling older people. *Methods of Information in Medicine*, 50(5), 435–444. doi:10.3414/ME10-01-0028.

Racherla, U. S., Huang, K. G., & Liu, K. (2016). Innovation and IPRs in China and India. In *China-EU Law Series* (Vol. 4). Singapore: Springer. doi:10.1007/978-981-10-0406-3.

Ranta, J. M., & Takala, J. (2007). A holistic method for finding out critical features of industry maintenance services. *International Journal of Services and Standards*, 3(3), 312–325. doi:10.1504/IJSS.2007.013752.

Takala, J., Shylina, D., Forss, T. & Malmi, J. (2013). Study on resource allocations for sustainable competitive advantage. *Management and Production Engineering Review*, 4(3), 65–75.

Vanani, I. R., & Kheiri, M. S. (2018). Big data and its role in facilitating the visualization of financial analytics. In R. Segall & J. Cook (Eds.), *Handbook of Research on Big Data Storage and Visualization Techniques* (1st ed., pp. 704–722). Hershey, PA: IGI Global.

Wind, Y. & Saaty, T. (1980). Marketing applications of the analytic hierarchy process. *Management science*, 26(7), 641–658.

Yang, C., Huang, Q., Li, Z., Liu, K., & Hu, F. (2017). Big data and cloud computing: Innovation opportunities and challenges. *International Journal of Digital Earth*, 10(1), 13–53. doi:10.1080/17538947.2016.1239771.

Index